Quantitative Studies

Quantitative Studies

RICHARD J. GADSDEN
BTech, MSc, PhD, FSS
Principal Lecturer
Sheffield City Polytechnic

ROGER W. QUINCEY
BSc, MSc, FIMA
Principal Lecturer
Sheffield City Polytechnic

ICSA Publishing · Cambridge

Published by ICSA Publishing Limited,
Fitzwilliam House, 32 Trumpington Street,
Cambridge CB2 1QY, England

First published 1989

British Library Cataloguing in Publication Data
Gadsden, Richard J.
    Quantitative studies.
    1. Accounting. Quantitative methods
    I. Title   II. Quincey, Roger W.
    657

    ISBN 0-902197-67-3

Designed by Geoff Green
Typeset by Vision Typesetting, Manchester
Printed in Great Britain by BPCC Wheatons Ltd, Exeter

Contents

Contents

Contents

Preface

An ability to deal with mathematical ideas and to summarise data in a meaningful way is becoming ever more important in all areas of business, especially accountancy. This book has been written with the aim of aiding the development of these skills, bringing together the basic mathematical and statistical ideas which are fundamental to study in accountancy, business and management courses.

The text is set out in 17 chapters. After an introduction to basic mathematical concepts, the reader is led through data collection and analysis, mathematical functions and the fitting of equations, time series and index numbers, aspects of financial mathematics, probability and probability distributions, and hypothesis testing; the text is completed with a detailed coverage of linear programming. There is also a glossary of terms at the end for easy reference.

The style adopted is to explain the various quantitative techniques and illustrate their use by worked examples. However, to appreciate fully the workings of these techniques, there is no substitute for practice. A companion book, *Quantitative Studies: a revision aid*, has been written which contains further worked examples and examples for the reader to attempt.

Although this book is aimed specifically at the Institute of Chartered Secretaries and Administrators' quantitative studies syllabus, it has also been written with the foundation examinations of the main accountancy bodies in mind. Hence, the text goes beyond the ICSA syllabus in covering the additional topics geometric mean, harmonic mean, binomial distribution, Poisson distribution, two-sample hypothesis tests and the simplex method of linear programming. We believe the inclusion of these topics gives a more comprehensive view of basic quantitative techniques.

Finally, we would like to express our appreciation and thanks to all those who have assisted us in the preparation of this book. Many colleagues at Sheffield City Polytechnic have given us helpful advice, but our main thanks is reserved for our partners, Pauline and Lyn, whose patience and support made the writing of this book possible.

R.J. Gadsden
R.W. Quincey

1

Some fundamental mathematical concepts

Introduction

This book aims to prepare the reader for the quantitative studies examination of the Institute of Chartered Secretaries and Administrators and a little beyond. It has also been written with the foundation courses of the main accountancy bodies in mind. Like all other books of this nature, we have to assume a basic numeracy in the reader. However, there are some basic concepts that, although they should be revision for most readers, are so fundamental to the understanding of the later topics that they will be covered first.

Sets and Venn diagrams

One of the most basic concepts in mathematics is that of the *set*. A *set* is any collection of items, together with a rule defining what links the items. A set can exist of anything, but usually sets of objects or numbers are considered. The items in a set are called *elements*.

For example, consider six sets defined as follows:

$A = \{$the set of all the customers of a company$\}$
$B = \{$the set of all delivery vehicles owned by a company$\}$
$C = \{$the set of the age range of the employees of a company$\}$
$D = \{$the set of all numbers between 16.2 and 65.4$\}$
$E = \{$the set of all integers between -2 and 7$\}$
$F = \{$the set of all even integers$\}$

A set could be defined that has no elements in it. For example $\{$the set of all of a company's employees aged over 100$\}$. Such a set is called *empty*. The empty set is usually denoted by $\emptyset$. At the other extreme, the set of all elements that could possibly be considered in the context of the problem is called the universal set. The universal set is usually denoted by I.

A useful way of illustrating sets is by using a *Venn diagram*. Here, the universal set is depicted by a rectangle and any set within it is depicted by a circle, as shown in Fig. 1.1.

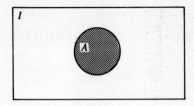

Fig. 1.1 A single set.

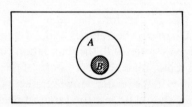

Fig. 1.2 A set with a subset.

A *subset* is a set that is contained entirely within another set. If B is a subset of A, then every element of B is also an element of A and we denote this by

$$B \subset A$$

For example, we could have

$A = \{\text{the set of all employees of a company}\}$
$B = \{\text{the set of all female employees of a company}\}$

This situation may be depicted as in Fig. 1.2.

The *complement* of a set A is the set of all elements in the universal set that do *not belong* to A. The complement of A is denoted by $\bar{A}$. Therefore, if

$A = \{\text{the set of all the employees of a company}\}$

then

$\bar{A} = \{\text{the set of all people who are not employees of the company}\}$

· This can be depicted as shown in Fig. 1.3.

The *union* of sets A and B is the set of all elements that belong to *either A or B*. It is denoted by $A \cup B$. For example, if

$A = \{\text{the set of all employees aged between 20 and 40}\}$

and

$B = \{\text{the set of all employees aged between 30 and 50}\}$

Fig. 1.3 Complement of a set.

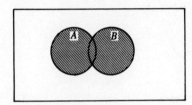

Fig. 1.4 Set union.

Then

$$A \cup B = \{\text{the set of all employees aged between 20 and 50}\}$$

or if

$$C = \{\text{numbers } x : 10 \leqslant x \leqslant 22\}$$

and

$$D = \{\text{numbers } x : 18 \leqslant x \leqslant 35\}$$

Then

$$C \cup D = \{\text{numbers } x : 10 \leqslant x \leqslant 35\}$$

This is depicted as Fig. 1.4.

The *intersection* of sets A and B is the set of all elements that exist in *both A and B*. It is denoted by $A \cap B$.

For example, if the sets are defined as before, then

$$A \cap B = \{\text{the set of all employees aged between 30 and 40}\}$$

and

$$C \cap D = \{\text{numbers } x : 18 \leqslant x \leqslant 22\}$$

This is depicted as Fig. 1.5.

If two sets A and B are such that

$$A \cap B = \varnothing$$

then they are described as *mutually exclusive*. This is shown in Fig. 1.6.

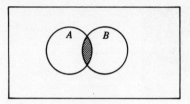

Fig. 1.5 Set intersection.

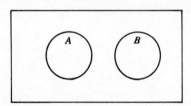

Fig. 1.6 Mutually exclusive sets.

Manipulation of equations

A number of rules apply to the manipulation of equations:

1. The same quantity can be added to each side of an equation; e.g. if

    $$x = 6$$

    then

    $$x + 4 = 6 + 4$$

    i.e.

    $$x + 4 = 10$$

    The quantity added could also be negative; e.g. if

    $$x = 6$$

    then

    $$x + (-2) = 6 + (-2)$$

    i.e.

    $$x + (-2) = 4$$

    In other words, *the same quantity can be subtracted from each side of an equation.*

i.e. if

$$x = 6$$

then

$$x - 2 = 6 - 2$$

or

$$x - 2 = 4$$

The quantity added could be *unknown*, so if

$$x = 6$$

then

$$x + y = 6 + y$$

or

$$x - z = 6 - z$$

This rule can be useful for gathering terms together to help solve equations; e.g.

$$2x = x + 10$$

To evaluate this the 'x' terms need to be on just one side of the equation. In other words, the 'x' term on the right-hand side must be eliminated. To do this a quantity must be added to each side of the equation to eliminate the 'x' term on the right-hand side, i.e. $(-x)$ must be added. Then

$$2x - x = \cancel{x} + 10 - \cancel{x}$$

and

$$2x - x = 10$$
$$x = 10$$

Similarly, if

$$-3x = 16 - 4x$$

Then to eliminate the x term from the right-hand side here $4x$ must be added to each side of the equation. Hence

$$-3x + 4x = 16 - \cancel{4x} + \cancel{4x}$$
$$-3x + 4x = 16$$
$$x = 16$$

Sometimes a number of different types of term must all be gathered together; e.g. if

$$3x - 5 = 2x - 11$$

Then the x terms must be eliminated from one side of the equation (e.g. the right-hand side) and the numbers eliminated from the other (the left-hand side). Note that it does not matter which side is chosen to concentrate each type of term on. Thus

$$3x - 5 - 2x = 2x - 11 - 2x$$
$$x - 5 = -11$$

Then

$$x - 5 + 5 = -11 + 5$$
$$x = -6$$

Note that this could all have been performed in one step.

$$3x - 5 = 2x - 11$$

Then

$$3x - \cancel{5} - 2x + \cancel{5} = \cancel{2x} - 11 - \cancel{2x} + 5$$

or

$$x = -6$$

Once the gathering together of terms has been completed it does not necessarily mean that the equation can be solved; e.g.

$$5x - 2y + 4 = 2x - y + 6$$

becomes

$$5x - 2y + 4 - 2x = \cancel{2x} - y + 6 - \cancel{2x}$$

or

$$3x - 2y + 4 = -y + 6$$

This is then

$$3x - 2y + 4 + y = -\cancel{y} + 6 + \cancel{y}$$

or

$$3x - y + 4 = 6$$

which becomes

$$3x - y + 4 - 4 = 6 - 4$$

i.e.

$$3x - y = 2$$

2. Both sides of an equation can be multiplied by the same quantity; e.g. if

$$x = 6$$

then

$$10(x) = 10(6)$$

or

$$10x = 60$$

or similarly if

$$x - 3y = 4$$

then

$$(-2)(x - 3y) = (-2)(4)$$

or

$$-2x + 6y = -8$$

The quantity does not need to be known; e.g. if

$$x = 6$$

then

$$a(x) = a(6)$$

or

$$ax = 6a$$

Since division by a can simply be viewed as multiplication by $1/a$, then it follows that both sides of an equation can be divided by the same quantity. Thus if

$$x = 6$$

then

$$\tfrac{1}{2}(x) = \tfrac{1}{2}(6)$$

$$\frac{x}{2} = 3$$

or if

$$7x = 42$$

then

$$\tfrac{1}{7}(7x) = \tfrac{1}{7}(42)$$

giving

$$x = 6$$

Note that this same rule can be applied to rearrange terms in more complex equations. For example if

$$xy = 3z - 4$$

and an expression is required for x. Then x can be isolated on the left-hand side of the equation by multiplying both sides of the equation by $1/y$,

i.e.

$$xy\frac{1}{y} = (3z - 4)\left(\frac{1}{y}\right)$$

$$x = \frac{3z - 4}{y}$$

Had the original expression been

$$5xy = 3z - 4$$

then each side would be multiplied by $1/5$ as well as by $1/y$ to obtain

$$5xy\left(\frac{1}{5}\right)\left(\frac{1}{y}\right) = (3z - 4)\left(\frac{1}{5}\right)\left(\frac{1}{y}\right)$$

$$x = \frac{3z - 4}{5y}$$

Likewise if

$$\frac{x}{2y} = \frac{10a}{b}$$

Then to isolate x on the left-hand side of the equation each side must be multiplied by $(2y)$, i.e.

$$\frac{x}{2y}(2y) = \frac{10a}{b}(2y)$$

or

$$x = \frac{20ay}{b}$$

Or if

$$\frac{5x}{3y} = \frac{a-b}{2c}$$

Firstly each side must be multiplied by $3y$

$$\frac{5x}{3y}(3y) = \frac{(a-b)}{2c}(3y)$$

$$5x = \frac{3(a-b)y}{2c}$$

and then multiply each side by $(1/5)$

$$5x\left(\frac{1}{5}\right) = \frac{3(a-b)y}{2c}\left(\frac{1}{5}\right)$$

$$x = \frac{3(a-b)y}{10c}$$

The most complicated form of rearrangement would be if

$$\frac{4y}{x} = \frac{3a}{b}$$

and it was required to rearrange for x.

First x is isolated on the left-hand side by multiplying each side by $1/4y$

$$\left(\frac{4y}{x}\right)\left(\frac{1}{4y}\right) = \left(\frac{3a}{b}\right)\left(\frac{1}{4y}\right)$$

$$\frac{1}{x} = \frac{3a}{4by}$$

Since we require x and not $(1/x)$, this can easily be found by turning the equation upside down; i.e.

$$x = \frac{4by}{3a}$$

Note that these techniques of rearrangement are often called *cross multiplication*. Note also that the first step in any rearrangement is to obtain an equation from which the variable in question can be isolated. Hence, if

$$\frac{y}{2x} - z = 4a - b$$

and it is required to rearrange for x, it is not possible as it stands to multiply each side by anything to isolate x and first z must be eliminated from the left-hand side:

$$\frac{y}{2x} - \cancel{z} + \cancel{z} = 4a - b + z$$

$$\frac{y}{2x} = 4a - b + z$$

Now

$$\left(\frac{\cancel{y}}{2x}\right)\left(\frac{1}{\cancel{y}}\right) = (4a - b + z)\left(\frac{1}{y}\right)$$

and

$$\frac{1}{2x} = \frac{4a - b + z}{y}$$

Then

$$\left(\frac{1}{\cancel{2}x}\right)(\cancel{2}) = \frac{(4a - b + z)}{y}(2)$$

and

$$\frac{1}{x} = \frac{2(4a - b + z)}{y}$$

So

$$x = \frac{y}{2(4a - b + z)}$$

3. Two or more equations can be added together; e.g. if

$$x = 6 \quad \text{and} \quad y = 2$$

then

$$x + y = 6 + 2$$

or

$$x + y = 8$$

Again, since $y = 2$ could first be multiplied on both sides by (-1) before adding to $x = 6$, we see that one equation can be subtracted from another; e.g.

$$x - y = 6 - 2$$

or

$$x - y = 4$$

Similarly, if

$$3x + y = 15 \qquad \text{and} \qquad x + y = 13$$

Then

$$3x + y + x + y = 15 + 13$$

or

$$4x + 2y = 28$$

Note that with these same two equations, had they been subtracted instead of added, the result would have been

$$3x + y - x - y = 15 - 13$$

or

$$2x = 2$$

which gives

$$x = 1$$

Since

$$x + y = 13 \qquad \text{and} \qquad x = 1$$

we obtain

$$(1) + y = 13$$
$$1 + y = 13$$
$$1 + y - 1 = 13 - 1$$
$$y = 12$$

In such cases where there are two equations in two unknowns (or three equations in three unknowns etc.) it is usually possible to find values for the unknowns satisfying each equation simultaneously. We are, therefore, considering the solution of simultaneous equations.

The solution of simultaneous equations

Notice that in the previous example

$$3x + y = 15 \qquad\qquad (1)$$
$$x + y = 13 \qquad\qquad (2)$$

(2) was subtracted from (1) to obtain a third equation from which one of the variables, y, had been eliminated:

$$2x = 2$$

This equation was then used to solve for x

$$x = 1$$

which in turn gave

$$y = 12$$

Had, instead, the two original equations been

$$3x + y = 15 \qquad\qquad (1)$$

and

$$x - y = 13 \qquad\qquad (2)$$

we would have *added* (1) and (2) to obtain a third equation from which y had been eliminated

$$3x + \cancel{y} + x - \cancel{y} = 15 + 13$$
$$4x = 28$$

or

$$x = 7$$

Then since

$$x - y = 13 \qquad \text{and} \qquad x = 7$$

then

$$7 - y = 13$$
$$\cancel{7} - y - \cancel{7} = 13 - 7$$
$$-y = 6$$

or

$$y = -6$$

So simultaneous solution is $x = 7$, $y = -6$.

This then gives the basis for solving two simultaneous equations. The permitted rules must be used for manipulating equations to obtain a third equation from which one of the variables has been eliminated; e.g.

$$3x + 2y = 11 \tag{1}$$
$$2x - y = 5 \tag{2}$$

This time y will be eliminated because it looks somewhat easier and to this effect equation (2) is manipulated to make the term in y the same (to within a '+' or '−') as in equation (1). To do this each side of (2) is multiplied by 2:

$$2(2x - y) = 2(5)$$

or

$$4x - 2y = 10 \tag{3}$$

To eliminate y we now add (1) and (3)

$$3x + 2y + 4x - 2y = 11 + 10$$
$$7x = 21$$
$$x = 3$$

Since

$$2x - y = 5 \quad \text{and} \quad x = 3$$
$$2(3) - y = 5$$
$$6 - y = 5$$
$$\cancel{6} - y - \cancel{6} = 5 - 6$$
$$-y = -1$$
$$y = 1$$

Hence the simultaneous solution is

$$x = 3 \quad \text{and} \quad y = 1$$

Note that it does not matter which variable is eliminated to solve the equations. As already stated we usually choose the one that appears easiest. However, in the previous example we could have begun by eliminating x.

$$3x + 2y = 11 \tag{1}$$
$$2x - y = 5 \tag{2}$$

This time we must manipulate both equations to make the 'x' term the same in each. We do this by multiplying both sides of (1) by 2 to obtain

$$2(3x + 2y) = 2(11)$$

i.e.

$$6x + 4y = 22 \tag{3}$$

And by multiplying both sides of (2) by 3 to obtain

$$3(2x - y) = 3(5)$$

i.e.

$$6x - 3y = 15 \qquad (4)$$

We now have

$$6x + 4y = 22 \qquad (3)$$

and

$$6x - 3y = 15 \qquad (4)$$

If we now subtract (4) from (3) we obtain

$$6x + 4y - (6x - 3y) = 22 - 15$$
$$\cancel{6x} + 4y - \cancel{6x} + 3y = 22 - 15$$

or

$$7y = 7$$

i.e.

$$y = 1$$

Then, since

$$2x - y = 5 \qquad (2)$$
$$2x - 1 = 5$$
$$2x - \cancel{1} + \cancel{1} = 5 + 1$$
$$2x = 6$$
$$x = 3$$

Hence the solution is again

$$x = 3 \qquad \text{and} \qquad y = 1$$

The same methods can be applied to simultaneous equations with more unknowns. An example of this will be shown in Chapter 8.

2

Data sources

Introduction

In the present technological age the need for numerical information is ever increasing. Microcomputers, minicomputers and personal computers are now commonplace in companies and these give managers at all levels ready and immediate access to details of their business. As well as internal company information there is a wealth of published information. This is produced by the Government and by a variety of other public and private organisations, covering all aspects of our life and environment.

To be able to use such information it is necessary to make use of statistical and mathematical techniques. This chapter starts by looking at the types of information that can be produced in a numerical form and their nature. Then it looks at the many official sources of information.

Primary sources

The term *data* is generally used to describe a collection of numerical information. Primary data is the term used to describe a set of data collected specifically to answer a particular question or series of questions. This data will come from a known source. How the data was collected and the degree of accuracy to which the measurements have been made will also be known. As yet this data has not been analysed but will be used to furnish answers for particular questions.

As an example, suppose a managing director wishes to know the optimum number of computer terminals to install within a company where the company's stock control and accounting systems are to be computerised. As an investigation would need to be carried out specifically to answer this problem, any results generated would constitute primary data. This primary data would then be used to make a decision regarding the optimum number of computer terminals.

Secondary data

Secondary data is the term used for data which is used other than for the purpose it was originally collected. It may be that the data has been collected to answer particular questions but is useful for answering another question or questions. If the production manager of a factory wishes to know how much overtime is presently being worked then this information can be obtained from the wages department. By checking the records used to calculate each employee's pay the amount of overtime worked can be extracted. In this case the information was originally collected to ensure correct wage payments but is now being used to answer the production manager's query and so is being used as secondary data.

In this example the data required was exactly the same as the data available. This is not always the case. Sometimes a set of data is available which is not exactly what is required but is close enough to be an adequate replacement. By using such data, time and/or expense can be saved. Suppose a marketing manager wishes to send details of a new product to every person aged 18 or over in a certain area. To do this precisely he would need to carry out a survey of the area to establish exactly who lived there and was 18 years of age and over. However, if the appropriate Register of Electors is used, he can obtain a list very close to what is required. There will be slight differences due to movements in and out of the area since the register was compiled. There will also be people who have not registered their vote. These differences, however, will be minimal and the list obtained should be more than adequate for the marketing manager's purpose. Remember that it is the purpose for which data is used rather than the data itself that determines whether it is primary or secondary data.

Internal and external data

In general, business data can be categorised in two ways, as internal or external data. Internal data is data that a company or organisation already holds, perhaps on a computer database, on filing cards or record sheets of some sort. External data is generally data obtained from published sources outside a company or organisation.

Internal data is normally regarded as being better since it is more likely to be directly related to a company and its needs. It is usually known exactly how the data was collected and what it represents. With external data the exact source and method of collection of the data may not be so clearly known.

Consider the following example. A production manager wishes to know the average time between breakdowns of a certain machine on the shop floor. The manager can refer to the machine manufacturer's handbook for reliability figures or can directly check how many times the particular machine has broken down in a certain time. The manufacturer's handbook provides information which is generally true for machines of this type. This constitutes external data. On the other hand direct observation of the particular machine supplies data which is directly relevant to this machine and so is more reliable. This constitutes internal data.

Internal data, then, is data collected within a company whereas external data is obtained from outside a company.

Variables

Any measurement which can vary from item to item or from person to person is called a *variable*. The following are examples of variables:

1. The time taken to fulfil an order.
2. The number of employees at a factory.
3. The number of faults in a length of a product.
4. The weight of a product.

Variables are classified into two types depending on the values that they can take:

1. Discrete variables. A discrete variable is a measurement which can take only certain values, usually whole numbers. The most common discrete variables are measurements which represent a count. The number of items produced in an hour on a machine, the number of employees in the accounts department of a company are both examples of discrete variables.
2. Continuous variables. A continuous variable is a measurement which can take any decimal or fractional value within a certain range (limited only by the accuracy to which a measurement can be made). Most measurements of physical characteristics are continuous variables. The length of a component, the time between machine breakdowns are examples of continuous variables.

Official sources of data

In the United Kingdom the Government, through the Central Statistical Office (CSO), publishes information on many aspects of business activity and of everyday life. There are two major reasons why this role is carried out. Firstly, in any organisation relevant information is required for planning and decision-making and the Government is no different in this respect. Secondly, the provision of such statistical information can assist individual companies to develop their own business strategies.

The data for Government statistical publications is usually generated by the separate governmental departments. The Central Statistical Office then acts as a focus for the publication and use of the data. In particular, the CSO has an overall remit for co-ordination, control and planning within Government statistical activities.

There are three main types of official statistical publication: guides to statistical sources, summary books of statistics and books of raw data. These are now dealt with separately (see also Bibliography for full details).

Guides to official sources of statistics

1. *Guide to Official Statistics.* This publication is a regularly produced and updated reference book, designed to provide a comprehensive description of all official statistical sources. It also contains references to some of the more important unofficial statistical sources. It does not contain any actual statistics since the aim of the guide is to inform users of statistics where to find the information they require. Some sixteen areas of interest are covered, ranging from population, through goods and services, to climate. There are nearly 1,000 subsections identifying and listing well over 2,000 sources. There is an easy-to-use index and bibliography also included.

2. *Statistical News.* This publication is designed to give an overview of current developments in UK official statistics. It contains descriptions of current activities within the area of official statistics, including details of any new publications. It also contains articles which deal with special items of interest concerning official statistics. This information is given under such headings as industrial statistics and health and social statistics.

3. *Guide to Public Sector Financial Information.* This publication describes the main statistics concerning the various aspects of public sector finance. Government finance and financing of local authorities, of the nationalised industries and of other public bodies are all covered. In addition, wider reference is made to certain international financial statistics. Sources for particular aspects are given and these are followed by a list of all relevant sources.

4. *Others.* Many supportive booklets and pamphlets are produced by the CSO and by individual government departments. A series of studies in official statistics has been published to give details of the compilation and analysis of particular statistical series and sets of data.

Occasionally research publications covering specific topics like

index numbers and unemployment are issued. Also publications aimed
at encouraging the use of government statistics appear from time to
time. These are all intended to make official statistics easier to
understand for the non-expert.

Summary publications of statistics

1. *Annual Abstract of Statistics.* This annual publication is the main
   source of general statistical information for the United Kingdom. It is
   published in the form of tables which cover nearly every aspect of our
   social and business environment. There are sections for climate;
   population; social services; education; justice and crime; defence;
   manufacturing and agricultural production; transport and communi-
   cations; retail distribution and miscellaneous services; external trade
   and balance of payments; national income and expenditure; personal
   income, expenditure and wealth; home finance; banking and insurance; and prices. In each table the abstract gives several years' past
   data.

2. *Monthly Digest of Statistics.* This monthly publication is a condensed
   form of the *Annual Abstract of Statistics.* Its tables cover nearly all the
   same topics, giving monthly and quarterly figures from the recent past.
   Further into the past annual figures are given.

   It is worth noting that there sometimes appear to be inconsistencies
   and differences between the *Monthly Digest* and the *Annual Abstract.*
   These occur because of the continual updating of figures which takes
   place. Always use the figures given in the most recent publication. Each
   year a supplement is produced. This contains definitions, explanatory
   notes and an index of sources for the various tables.

3. *Economic Trends.* This monthly publication contains all the major
   economic indicators. It makes use of charts and diagrams in addition to
   tables when illustrating these indicators. It is divided into three main
   sections. The first section gives the most up-to-date statistical information available that month and includes a calendar of the latest
   economic events. The second section gives figures for the key economic
   indicators over the last five years. The third section consists of a chart,
   covering twenty years, which shows the movements of four composite
   economic indicators. In addition to these sections, quarterly articles on
   the national accounts and on the balance of payments appear. There
   are also occasional articles detailing new developments in the field of
   economic statistics or commenting on specific topics within economic
   statistics. Notes, definitions and extended runs for the key indicators
   are given in an annual supplement.

4. *Social Trends.* This annual publication is designed to illustrate changing social circumstances in the United Kingdom. Divided into chapters, it draws together information from many other government publications. It gives statistical summaries on population, families, education, unemployment, finance, health, social services as well as many other areas of our lives.

5. *Regional Trends.* This annual publication gives annual statistics for the regions of the United Kingdom. These statistics are illustrated by a multitude of maps, charts and tables. Information on population, employment, education, crime and many other areas are included to show what changes are taking place in the regions.

6. *Financial Statistics.* This monthly publication gives monthly and quarterly records for the major financial and monetary statistics of the United Kingdom. It contains information from both private and public sectors. Areas covered include government income and expenditure, money supply, institutional investment, company finance as well as exchange and interest rates. Like *Economic Trends* there is an annual supplement containing explanatory notes and definitions.

Raw data source

1. *British Business.* This weekly publication from the Department of Industry contains a statistical section. In this section monthly and quarterly figures covering such topics as United Kingdom trade, external trade, production, transport and hire purchase are given along with information on the Census of Production.

2. *Employment Gazette.* This monthly publication from the Department of Employment gives detailed statistical summaries on employment, unemployment, vacancies, working practices, wages, retail prices, labour costs, output and stoppages. Some statistics are recorded over a period of years, others over a limited number of months.

3. *British Labour Statistics.* This annual publication summarises the major labour statistics over an extended period. It contains a great deal of information on how the figures have been collated and details of the records themselves.

4. *United Kingdom National Income and Expenditure.* Known as the 'Blue Book', this annual publication is the main source of the United Kingdom's national accounts statistics. It contains detailed estimates of Gross National Product (GNP), income and expenditure. To illustrate how the different sectors of the economy interrelate, the statistics are given by sector. The main sectors are as follows: people; public corporations; companies; central government; local government; and overseas trade. Statistics are recorded over a number of

years for each measurement and sector. Given the difficulties in defining what national accounts are or should be the Blue Book gives lengthy definitions and extensive notes explaining calculations, assumptions made, etc.

5. *United Kingdom Balance of Payments.* Known as the 'Pink Book', this annual publication records the present 'balance of current account' for the United Kingdom and how it was established from the various figures concerning trade between the United Kingdom and the rest of the world. As with the Blue Book statistical information is recorded over a number of years, illustrating trends and the performance of the United Kingdom in comparison to the rest of the world.

There are many other sources of data not mentioned here. A major recent new source of data is the European Economic Community (EEC). Various publications detail the operation and characteristics of the Community. All the major banks publish a business review (publication intervals vary from monthly to quarterly). Newspapers and journals publish financial data, most notable amongst these being the *Financial Times* and the *Economist*. There are several business research organisations which now publish their findings concerning business activity. Finally there are the market research organisations which, as well as carrying out particular studies or commissions, now publish regular surveys in the area of consumer goods.

Family expenditure survey

Every year a survey of expenditure is carried out based on approximately 11,000 households. Its original purpose was to assist in determining the weightings to be used in the calculation of the Retail Price Index (see Chapter 11 for a detailed discussion of the RPI). Whilst this is still one of its major functions, it is now of more general interest since it supplies information on the relationship between income and expenditure as well as any trends in this relationship. It also attempts to highlight the influence of tax and benefit policies.

This survey, called the *Family Expenditure Survey*, is carried out continuously throughout the year. Selected households are asked to complete a *Household Schedule* which details all items of household expenditure and an *Income Schedule* which details all income for all persons in the household aged 16 or above. This part of the survey is carried out by an interviewer. Then, each member of the household is asked to keep a daily *Diary Record Book* of all items of expenditure for 14 consecutive days.

There is no compulsion to take part in the survey but, in general, about two-thirds of households approached agree to take part, giving a sample of about 7,000 households.

The aggregated results from the survey are then published annually.

3

Sampling methods

Introduction

In order to make sensible decisions in business the decision maker needs relevant information. This information is often in the form of numbers. Whether it is required to know the number of employees at a factory or the average annual salary of those employed in a city, it is necessary to consider what methods can be used to obtain data which can then be used to answer such questions.

To obtain relevant information it is necessary to consider how much data it is necessary to collect or how much data collection can be afforded. Then consideration must be given to what techniques are appropriate or available to furnish this data. Finally methods must be chosen to actually collect the data.

Populations and samples

At the outset a clear distinction is needed between on the one hand the groups of people or items about which conclusions are to be drawn and on the other hand the individuals or items which are actually checked or investigated. The term *population* is used to describe the total group of people or items under investigation. The term *sample* is used to describe the individuals or items actually investigated. Hence a sample is a part of the population. Care should be taken with the word population since its statistical meaning is much more general than in everyday language. For instance, reference may be made to a population of desks in an office or bottles of bleach in a warehouse as well as to a population of adults living in Yorkshire.

Suppose a weights and measures inspector wishes to check whether the contents of packets of sugar in a warehouse meet their weight specification. If the inspector checks 500 packets chosen randomly from throughout the warehouse, the packets actually weighed and checked form the sample and every packet in the warehouse forms the population.

Censuses and surveys

Ideally information is collected from every member of a population. If such a collection is carried out it is called a *census*. Any results obtained from a census can be thought of as being both representative and reliable. The Government carries out three main censuses. Perhaps the one we are most familiar with is the Census of Population which is carried out every ten years. The aim of this census is to obtain a 'snapshot' of certain characteristics of the whole population of the United Kingdom at a certain time. The second census is the Census of Production which is presently carried out every five years by the Business Statistics Office. It aims to cover all firms in the United Kingdom but small firms need to make only a limited response. The census covers manufacturing industries, building industries, public utility production, mines, etc., but excludes areas such as agriculture, fisheries and the service industries. Data collected and collated includes employment, wages, stocks, plant and machinery investment, and finished goods. Because of expense this census is supplemented annually by a sample survey rather than being carried out as an annual census.

The final census is the Census of Distribution which is carried out every five years, again supplemented by an annual sample survey. This census covers nearly all retail outlets and certain wholesalers. Information on employment, types and numbers of goods sold constitutes most of the data collected.

Whilst a census is the ideal, in practice it can often be inconvenient or even impossible to investigate every member of a population. It may be too costly or too time-consuming, or members of the population may be inaccessible. Under these circumstances we need to carry out a *survey* on part of the population, a sample.

Choosing an appropriate sample is an important consideration since our aim in sampling is to reflect, as closely as possible, the population as a whole. The closer the correspondence the more reliable results from our sample should be. This means when we choose a sample it should be representative of the whole population. Many techniques of sampling are available and the one chosen in a particular case reflects how much time or money is available, how reliable the results need to be and what can be carried out in practice.

When any sample is taken, the results are an attempt to reflect the results that would have been obtained from the population as a whole. (These population values are often called 'true' values or 'parameters'.) Different choices of sample lead to differing results. This is called sampling error and is the variation that naturally occurs between sample results and the true value we are trying to find. Unfortunately the extent of this sampling error is never known because the true value, which is what is to be estimated, is unknown!!

It is possible, however, to determine the likely size of these errors. Obviously, the smaller they are, the better or more reliable the sample results should be. The size of errors indicates the *precision* of the sample results. The word precision is used to describe how consistent different sample results are with *each other*, so care is still needed. It is quite possible that the sampling method will lead to consistent under- or overestimation of the true value. This under- or overestimation is called *bias*. Hence, the results could have high precision yet be inaccurate due to the influence of a bias or systematic error. The accuracy of sample results is the crucial factor. This accuracy is best shown by the absolute error of a result and is defined as

$$\text{absolute error} = \text{sample result} - \text{true value}$$

Techniques for sampling

The aim in sampling is to choose a representative group of items or individuals from a population so that the results from the sample mirror the population as closely as possible. There are many different techniques which can be used to determine which items or individuals should be sampled. Some are general techniques which can be applied in almost any situation, others are techniques developed for specific purposes. The technique chosen depends on many factors, but the main considerations are as follows:

1. Cost.
2. Time available.
3. Population to be investigated.

Before carrying out a survey using sampling it is necessary to know what the population consists of. Ideally, there should be a list of members of the population to be investigated. Any list which represents the population is called a *sampling frame*. In practice, a sampling frame is rarely a complete list of a population. This does not matter as long as it is fairly close to a full list and does not omit important or specific parts of a population.

Example
1. A list of serial numbers could be used as a sampling frame for video recorders produced at a particular factory. This frame should be a complete list and so represent the whole population.

Table 3.1. Random digits

45782	95722	69808	51443	67519
19557	55394	98227	60919	81050
28097	74635	88525	74203	79296
27987	99780	22732	55266	56589
90258	63086	76967	64028	11232

2. An electoral register could be used as a sampling frame to represent all persons over 18 living in a certain area. This frame will not generally be a complete list since people will have moved in or out of the area since the register was compiled, some people will not be on the register, etc. However, those not on the register will generally constitute only a small proportion of the population required, making the register an adequate sampling frame.

Simple random sampling

A random sample is one in which every member of the population has an equal chance of being included in the sample. The purpose of this method is to avoid any bias being either inadvertently or purposely introduced into the results by the sampling. This sampling method requires a list or sampling frame for the population. Having obtained a list the investigator must choose entries from it in a random way. One possibility is to put all the entries into a hat or tombola and draw out entries until the sample is filled. This can be a time-consuming procedure and it is often easier to use random numbers.

Use of random numbers
Random-number tables consist of blocks of figures where each digit is a random choice from 0 to 9 inclusive. These are grouped together in blocks for convenience as in Table 3.1. These numbers can be combined as required, to form random numbers of any size. Suppose random numbers from 0 to 999 are required. If numbers are combined in three successive columns we obtain such numbers. This can be done for any figures we require.

Example
A company has 836 employees. As a bonus the company has offered free holidays to four employees. Every employee is to have an equal chance of being awarded the bonus.

To use random numbers we will need to take random digits in groups of three, number the employees from 1 to 836, then use the random-number tables to generate four employees' numbers.

Any point in the tables may be used as a starting point, and the table worked through in any chosen way. The only thing that must not be done is to choose a particular point because a required number is there!! Starting in the third block, using three columns together and working downwards, the random numbers are

698,
982,
885,
227,
769

This means the employee numbered 698 would be given the bonus holiday, the number 982 does not correspond to an employee so is ignored and similarly number 885. The employees numbered 227 and 769 also would be given the bonus holiday. Only three bonus holidays have been given up to now so some more random numbers must be generated. These are obtained by taking the next three columns, so the next random number is 085, i.e. the last holiday is given to the employee numbered 85.

As can be seen in this example we do not necessarily need to use all the possible random numbers. However, it is sensible to make as much use as possible of any random numbers generated.

Example
Twelve advertisements are to be viewed in a random order. If these are numbered 1–12 random digits could be taken in pairs and only random numbers 01–12 used, ignoring any others. This would allow the advertisements to be placed in random order. Alternatively, to make more efficient use of the random numbers they could be allocated as shown in Table 3.2, ignoring random numbers 00, 97, 98, 99. (This is not the only allocation possible; any allocation where the same number of random numbers represent each advertisement would be acceptable.)

A final point to note is that the random digits are 0–9 so when digits are combined the lowest random number will be 0 or 00 or a series of zeros. This means the random numbers generated will start at 0, yet the numbering starts from 1. To overcome this problem the value 0 is used for the topmost figure. Suppose it is required to make a random choice from 100 items. Pairing random digits gives 00–99. If the items are numbered 1–100 use

Table 3.2. Allocation of random numbers

Random number		Random number	
01–08	Advertisement 1	49–56	Advertisement 7
09–16	Advertisement 2	57–64	Advertisement 8
17–24	Advertisement 3	65–72	Advertisement 9
25–32	Advertisement 4	73–80	Advertisement 10
33–40	Advertisement 5	81–88	Advertisement 11
41–48	Advertisement 6	89–96	Advertisement 12

random numbers 01–99 in the normal way and use the random number 00 to represent item 100.

To take a simple random sample a sampling frame is needed to work from. Entries are chosen from this frame in a random way and this constitutes the simple random sample.

Example
If a managing director wished to visit a representative sample of a company's United Kingdom customers, then initially a list of all customers, a sampling frame, must be drawn up. A sample can then be determined using a random method for choosing customers from this frame.

It is worth noting that this sample will consist of customers perhaps widely spread throughout the country and customers of varying importance to the company.

Simple random sampling is usually accepted as the fairest way of drawing an unbiased or representative sample. It does, however, assume that all members of the population are of the same 'type'. This is often not the case. If people are sampled, for instance, it may be thought that males and females form two subgroups within the population. In simple random sampling no account is taken to ensure subgroups like these are suitably represented in our sample.

In wider terms, simple random sampling can prove expensive and time-consuming in sampling effort. As was mentioned in the example of visiting customers a random sample could lead to a great deal of travelling and expense for the managing director.

Stratified random sampling

Stratified random sampling is an extension of simple random sampling which allows for possible different groups within a population. Each different group is called a *stratum* and a simple random sample is taken from each stratum, these samples collectively forming the stratified random sample from the whole population. When stratified random sampling is used or is thought to be called for, the population to be investigated must first be considered. The following questions must be asked:

1. Are there different groups within the population?
2. Are these differences important to the investigation?

If the answer to both questions is 'yes', then stratified random sampling is necessary. Under those circumstances it is necessary to decide which strata are to be used and to which strata members of the population belong. This is called stratification of the population.

Example
A survey of persons aged 18 or over is to be carried out. For this survey it is thought the sex of the respondent might have an influence and that the marital status of the respondent is important. When the population is stratified four strata are formed:

1. Male, married.
2. Male, single.
3. Female, married.
4. Female, single.

To carry out a stratified random sample the population must be stratified. The relative size of the strata must then be known so that the sample reflects these sizes. The random sample taken in a stratum should, relative to the total sample size, be proportional to the size of the stratum within the population.

Example
A survey of 200 owners of video recorders is to be carried out. It has been decided that type of video recorder is important and that whether the video recorder is manual or remote controlled is important. If the percentage of owners in each stratum are as shown in Table 3.3, then the total sample of 200 owners would consist of the size random samples in each stratum shown in Table 3.4.

The steps, then, in stratified random sampling, are as follows:

1. Specify the strata in the population.
2. Determine the percentage of the population contained within each stratum.

Table 3.3. Strata of video ownership

Video type	Beta	VHS	Other	Total
Manual	18	29	5	52
Remote	12	31	5	48
Total	30	60	10	100

Table 3.4. Random sampling of video owners

Video type	Beta	VHS	Other	Total
Manual	36	58	10	104
Remote	24	62	10	96
Total	60	120	20	200

3. Split the overall sample into the strata percentages.
4. Take a simple random sample of appropriate size from each stratum.
5. Combine these simple random samples to form the stratified random sample.

Example

Consider again the managing director visiting customers. In order to obtain a representative sample the following characteristics of the customer may need to be taken into account:

1. Regular/non-regular customer.
2. Annual value of orders placed.
3. Types of product customer purchases.
4. Size of customer's company.

To take a stratified random sample, a sampling frame will again be required. However, in this case more detail will be required so that customers can be classified into strata reflecting these characteristics. With this detailed frame the percentages of customers in each stratum can be found and the appropriate sample sizes for each stratum determined.

Stratified random sampling is the most appropriate method to use when a population consists of differing groups and these groups need to be reflected within the sample. The sample will be unbiased (as long as our strata have been chosen sensibly) but will lead to the same problems of possible expense and time already mentioned for simple random sampling. There is a further source of cost in that the sampling frame may need to contain more detail than for simple random sampling. Finally, the stratification of the population can be made as simple or as complex as is thought appropriate. This is a subjective judgement and can itself introduce inaccuracies into our sampling if not carried out properly.

Multi-stage sampling

Multi-stage sampling is an attempt to overcome the problems which arise in simple and stratified random sampling where the population to be investigated is widely spread. In multi-stage sampling the aim is to choose a series of areas which collectively represent the characteristics of the population as a whole. Sampling is then concentrated within these areas rather than from the whole population. This method is fairly easy to employ when the population is homogeneous. Simply split the geographical area into regions, choose a number of the regions randomly and take a simple random sample within each of the chosen regions. This helps to centralise the sampling to be carried out.

It is not quite as easy when different groups within the population are to be reflected. At least three approaches can be used. First, the area as a whole can be divided into regions which individually reflect the population as a whole. A random choice of these regions is then made and simple random samples taken in each chosen region. The second approach is to ignore the whole area and just concentrate on any areas that individually reflect the population. These can then be randomly sampled. The third approach is to select a series of regions which together reflect the population but do not necessarily reflect the population when taken individually. This set of regions is then randomly sampled.

Example
Consider further the managing director visiting customers. In this case regions would be looked for which reflect the customer population. If it is found that customers in Brighton, Leicester, Wrexham, York and Edinburgh reflect the profile of the customer population, then random sampling could be concentrated in these regions alone.

The main advantage of multi-stage sampling is that sampling is concentrated within localised regions and so should be less expensive and time-consuming to carry out. It should be borne in mind, however, that the choice of representative regions is a subjective one which could introduce bias.

Cluster sampling

If multi-stage sampling is taken one or two steps further a situation is reached in which one or a small number of regions represent the population as a whole, and these regions are then subjected to complete or 100% sampling. This sampling is known as cluster sampling.

Example
The managing director visiting customers could visit all the company's customers in just one or two locations. Perhaps customers in Preston and Stoke are representative of customers as a whole. All those customers would be visited.

Like multi-stage sampling the sampling is concentrated and since 100% sampling is being carried out fewer regions will need to be sampled. This should further reduce costs of sampling. Another advantage is that there is no real reason to have a sampling frame. As long as a region or group of regions is thought to be representative, only information for these regions is required. Of course, there is an even larger subjective element with this sampling technique and here we have no random sampling element, so any bias introduced would have a significant effect on our results.

Multi-phase sampling

Multi-phase sampling is a specific method of sampling used when general and detailed information is required. A general survey is carried out on a sample chosen by one of the techniques already outlined. Then to obtain more detailed information a follow-up survey based on a random sample drawn from the original sample is carried out. A particular example of this type of sampling concerns the Census of Population. A follow-up survey of approximately 10% of the population has been carried out in the past to determine more detailed information on social trends.

Example
For the managing director visiting customers, the first visit could be used to ascertain general trends in customer needs. A follow-up visit could then be used to obtain customers' reactions to specific planning initiatives.

The main advantage of this method is that a reasonable amount of general information can be obtained quickly and relatively inexpensively. Further detailed information can then be accumulated on a rather smaller scale. As with other techniques problems can arise because of the relatively small sample at the second stage. The smaller the sample size the greater the possibility of the sample being unrepresentative in some way even if it is drawn randomly.

Quota sampling

Quota sampling is a method often associated with market research studies and more especially with those carried out by interviewers. The method involves an interviewer being given a number of persons to interview (their quota). Often this quota is in the form of a stratified quota. A simple example might be to interview 10 males and 12 females. This sampling technique relies very heavily on the competence and reliability of the interviewer (discussed later in this chapter). If carried out properly there are no problems of filling the required sample size, it is inexpensive to carry out and can be completed quickly. It must, however, be borne in mind that the sample taken is non-random and there are very real dangers associated with selection bias. Further, the interviewers may introduce their own bias.

Systematic sampling

Systematic sampling is a method sometimes used instead of simple random sampling. To save the effort of determining the members of a random sample every nth entry in the sampling frame is chosen as a member of the sample. If our sample is to be 10% of the population then every tenth entry of the sampling frame is chosen. To try and introduce a random element into the choice of sample, the first entry to be selected is chosen randomly, then every nth entry after that is used. This does not make it a random sample.

Example
The managing director visiting 2% of the company's customers would choose every 50th entry on the customer list. The first entry (from 1 to 50 inclusive) would be chosen randomly.

Care needs to be taken in using systematic sampling since unintended bias can be introduced. In a household survey, if the houses chosen all have odd numbers this usually means they are on the same side of the street. If one side of the street has executive detached dwellings and the other side terraced dwellings the sample will not be representative of the overall population.

This technique is very popular for carrying out quality control checks since in this instance it reflects the passage of time and can indicate trends. More generally, it can be used where no sampling frame exists but where the items to be sampled are physically present or will be physically present. Its other advantages and disadvantages are similar to those for simple random sampling.

Panels

A panel is a group of people who agree to keep records of their life over a period of time. Depending on the purpose of the panel, this may involve very detailed recording of expenditure (e.g. the Household Survey) or may be specific to some aspect of life (e.g. recording all journeys made, their distance and method of transport used). Whilst the members of a panel are nominally chosen at random, there are only certain people who are willing to commit themselves to such a survey. This can cause its own bias. Also, as time passes by, members of the sample can find their own lives and way of life changed because they are on a panel. This then influences the results obtained from the panel.

Application of sampling techniques

So far we have concentrated on describing what each sampling technique involves, what its advantages and disadvantages are and where or how it might be used. We now look at how some of the techniques would be used to choose a sample from a small-scale population and what the constitution of these samples would be.

Example
Determin PLC owns a small manufacturing unit on a modern industrial estate. The unit is self-contained consisting of three sections, production, sales and accounts. Each section consists of a manager and associated staff. Total staff in production numbers fifteen, in sales numbers ten and in accounts numbers five. A full list of staff is given in Table 3.5 with details of name, age, section and position. Determin PLC wish to determine the views of this unit concerning flexible working hours. They have decided to take a sample to obtain representative views.
1. Simple random sample. Using random numbers digits must be taken in pairs to represent the thirty employees. Each employee can be allocated three random numbers, thus leaving ten unallocated. Let random numbers

Table 3.5. Details of employees of Determin PLC manufacturing unit

Name	Age	Section	Position
1. Allinson, Kay	20	Accounts	Accounts clerk
2. Auden, Roger	18	Production	Machine operator
3. Barnes, Anne	22	Sales	Salesperson
4. Brown, Paul	50	Production	Machine operator
5. Brown, Susan	19	Sales	Sales clerk
6. Coles, Eric	19	Production	Machine operator
7. Davies, Sarah	17	Production	Trainee
8. Denton, Stephen	18	Sales	Sales clerk
9. Durrell, Peter	42	Sales	Salesperson
10. Ford, Richard	20	Accounts	Accounts clerk
11. French, Diana	53	Production	Machine operator
12. Galloway, Marion	24	Production	Machine operator
13. Kingsley, Raymond	47	Production	Machine operator
14. Mardell, Ann	36	Sales	Sales manager
15. Meade, Graham	31	Accounts	Accounts clerk
16. Ossar, James	18	Production	Machine operator
17. Pallin, David	29	Sales	Salesperson
18. Peters, Pauline	17	Accounts	Accounts clerk
19. Quick, Robin	55	Production	Production manager
20. Race, William	20	Production	Machine operator
21. Roberts, Graham	29	Sales	Salesperson
22. Smith, David	16	Production	Trainee
23. Smith, Mary	26	Sales	Salesperson
24. Smith, Wendy	23	Production	Machine operator
25. Thorne, Maurice	49	Production	Maintenance engineer
26. Tindall, Ian	32	Production	Machine operator
27. Ventry, Paul	18	Production	Machine operator
28. West, Julia	25	Sales	Sales clerk
29. Wood, Linda	32	Sales	Salesperson
30. Wright, Kevin	52	Accounts	Accounts manager

01, 31, 61   represent employee 1
02, 32, 62   represent employee 2

and so on to

30, 60, 90   represent employee 30

with random numbers 00, 91–99 unallocated.

From the random numbers in Table 3.1, starting at the third column of the first block, second row, we have random numbers 55, 09, 98, 25, 29, 75, 79, 86, etc. To take a sample of five employees, those chosen would be as shown in Table 3.6. So Maurice Thorne, Peter Durrell, Linda Wood, Graham Meade and David Pallin form the sample.

Table 3.6. Random sampling of employees

RN	Employee	Name	Department
55	25	Maurice Thorne	Production
09	9	Peter Durrell	Sales
98		Unallocated	
25		Already chosen	
29	29	Linda Wood	Sales
75	15	Graham Meade	Accounts
77	17	David Pallin	Sales

Table 3.7. Random sampling of employees separated by sex

RN	Employee	Name	Sex
92		Unallocated	
65	5	Susan Brown	F
12	12	Marion Galloway	F
19	19	Robin Quick	M
50	20	William Race	M
96		Unallocated	
89	29	Linda Wood	F
32	2	Roger Auden	M

2. Stratified random sample. In the simple random sample just chosen there is only one female employee. If it is thought likely that male and female employees may have differing views on flexible working it is essential to ensure that male and female employees are suitably represented in our sample. There are 18 male and 12 female members of staff so our sample of five persons would need to contain 3 males and 2 females. This can be achieved by renumbering the male employees from 1–18 and using the method used in simple random sampling to obtain a sample of three males. Repeat the process for female employees numbering them from 1–12 and drawing a sample of two females. Combining these two samples gives the stratified sample required.

   An alternative method is to use the employee numbers as they are (i.e. 1–30) but work towards the number of male and female employees required. To illustrate, starting in Table 3.1 at column 2 of block 5, row 3 gives Table 3.7.

   Once the first two female employees have been chosen all further female employees chosen must be ignored. Hence, Linda Wood is not a member of the sample, which consists of those listed in Table 3.8.

Table 3.8. The sample determined

Male	Female
Roger Auden	Susan Brown
Robin Quick	Marion Galloway
William Race	

Table 3.9. Distribution of staff by department and sex

	Male	Female	Total
Production	11	4	15
Sales	4	6	10
Accounts	3	2	5
Total	18	12	30

Other characteristics may be considered relevant to views on flexible working hours. If it is thought that departments may differ in view then our stratified sample should take this into account. With fifteen production staff, ten sales staff and five accounts staff the proportions in the sample would need to be 3 : 2 : 1 so a minimum sample size of six would be required.

Both characteristics, sex and department, can be taken into account. The numbers in each are given in Table 3.9.

In practice, these could only be reflected fairly by taking a 100% sample. Notice that the more characteristics we wish to reflect the larger the minimum sample size required. This is generally the case so care needs to be taken when deciding which characteristics are important and should be reflected in the sample.

3. Systematic sample. To take a sample of five employees we require every sixth employee. If we choose the first (from employees 1–6) randomly, then take every sixth employee, this gives us a systematic sample. Using Table 3.1, column 5 of block 2, row 3, we obtain the random digit 5 so our first choice is employee 5, then 11, 17, 23 and 29. This gives:

Susan BROWN
Diana FRENCH
David PALLIN
Mary SMITH
Linda WOOD

Just as with taking a simple random sample there is no guarantee of a balance in our sample and here there are four female and one male employees. Remember this is only a problem if we believe the sex of the employee will have a definite effect on their view of flexible working hours.

4. Others. A cluster sample could be taken if we thought one department or part of a department was representative of the unit. All members of this department or part of a department would be sampled.

   A quota sample of five employees could be taken by an interviewer stationed at the entrance to the unit and choosing the first five employees to arrive or employees meeting a specified quota.

Conducting a survey

If it has been decided that a survey is required to obtain the information needed, then there is a series of steps which usually needs to be carried out. These can be listed as

1. Define the objectives of the survey
   Before doing anything else it must be decided why the survey is being carried out, what information is required from it and who the information is for. Without carrying out this step it is very easy to miss important factors and include irrelevant ones.

2. Specify the target population
   Decide precisely what type of items or people the survey is to cover. It is all too easy to be vague at this stage and find the survey is made unnecessarily complex as a result. Consider a simple question where it is required to find average weekly earnings in the United Kingdom. What is the target population here? Is it only people in employment who should be included? Is it all people of working age? Is it all people resident in the United Kingdom? These questions must be resolved so that the target population can be properly defined.

3. Choose a sampling technique
   Having decided on the objectives of the survey and the target population the sampling technique to be used must be chosen. The choice will inevitably be influenced by
   (a) how much money is available to carry out the survey
   (b) how quickly the results are required
   (c) the reliability required of the results
   If general impressions are required a quota sample will usually be quite satisfactory but if more detail is required then a method based on random sampling is really required.

4. Design the questionnaire (if necessary). With the objectives of the survey specified it is possible to decide whether the information required can be obtained by direct measurement or whether a questionnaire needs to be used. If the information required can be physically measured or counted, then this measuring can be carried out by ourselves or the person carrying out the survey. This method yields accurate results but can prove expensive and time-consuming. Of course there are only certain measurements which can be obtained directly such as weight, length, volume etc. Opinions cannot be obtained in this way, they need to be determined by asking appropriate questions. Care must be taken to use questions which give the information required and this is discussed further in the next section.
5. Carry out a pilot survey. A pilot survey is an initial survey carried out on a small sample. Its purpose is to check that the design of the survey is satisfactory and that it is giving the type of information required. It is most unusual for a survey design to be faultless and this gives the designer the chance to modify the design prior to the main survey. Wherever possible, a pilot survey should be carried out before the main survey.
6. Carry out the main survey. This is the major part of the work to be carried out. It is the collection of the information required, using the methods chosen, after any modifications indicated by the pilot survey.
7. Analyse and report the results. Once the main survey has been completed, the results must be collated. These results can then be analysed to see what they reveal. Any survey is only as good as the way its results are reported. A clear presentation of the information collected and the conclusions that can be drawn from this information are essential to complete a satisfactory survey.

Questionnaire design

In designing a series of questions, a questionnaire, one aim is to encourage people to answer the questions and to give correct or truthful replies. Although this appears to be a simple process there are numerous pitfalls and many considerations must be borne in mind if a questionnaire is to be successful.

Starting with the questionnaire itself, it should be presented in such a way that the person answering it, the respondent, finds it interesting to complete. It should look attractive and easy to complete. If the questionnaire is being administered by an interviewer there should be some explanation of the purpose of the survey (without influencing the respondent) but this should be kept to a minimum to avoid losing the respondent's interest. Alternatively, if the respondents themselves are to fill

in the questionnaire it should appear easy to work through. The number of
questions asked should be kept to a minimum. This means avoiding
questions which are not relevant to the survey. If the age of the respondent
is not to be used in the analysis of the survey there is no point in including a
question asking the respondent's age!

Any questions asked should be kept as short as possible, consistent with
obtaining the information required. There is no point in asking

> 'If you were walking down the street and saw a shop on fire, would you
> know how to put the fire out if there was a foam-based fire extinguisher
> available?'

when you could obtain the same information from

> 'Do you know how to use a foam-based fire extinguisher?'

It is also advisable to avoid technical terms wherever possible and to use as
simple a form of words in questions to avoid misunderstandings. A question
like

> 'Do you feel newsreaders form a fairly homogeneous group of people?'

might well be replaced by

> 'Do you feel newsreaders are similar types of people?'

A common mistake made in designing questions is to form questions which
are ambiguous. You can be sure that if there is a 'wrong' way of interpreting
a question someone will interpret it that way. The question

> 'Where do you work?'

might lead to answers such as 'Doncaster' or 'at home' or 'O.B. Chemicals'
or 'in an insurance office'. Make it clear what sort of answer you require,
perhaps by giving a choice of possible answers.

Another problem to avoid is that of leading questions, questions which
suggest a particular answer. A question such as

> 'You believe Sudzo is a good washing powder don't you?'

suggests the answer required is 'Yes'. Some people will answer 'Yes' because
that is what is suggested, others will answer 'No' to be contrary, the
difficulty is that the question is not necessarily obtaining the respondent's
own view. A better way of asking the same question might be

> 'Is Sudzo a good washing powder?'

The use of emotive language can lead to differing reactions from
respondents. Recent studies in the United Kingdom have shown different
responses to the following two questions

'Should get-rich-quick entrepreneurs be encouraged to develop inner cities?'

'Should the private sector be encouraged to develop inner cities?'

which is hardly surprising!!

The use of personal questions should be restricted to where personal reactions are required. A final point about the questions themselves. The more relevant the questions are to the respondent the more likely the respondent is to complete the questionnaire. When asking questions there are generally two types of answer that can be expected. The first is an open-ended reply, the second is the choice from a list of possible answers. Examples of open-ended questions are

'What sports do you play?'

'What would you take into account when buying a car?'

'What is your view of privatisation of the nationalised industries?'

Examples of questions with a choice of answers are

'Are you married?'   Yes/No

'What supermarket do you shop at?'

Shop	Yes	No
Sainsbury		
Tesco		
Gateway		
Asda		
Other		
None		

'Indicate your strength of agreement with the following statements:'

	Strongly agree	Agree	Neutral	Disagree	Strongly disagree
British industry is inefficient					
British industry requires modernisation					
British industry is quality conscious					

The analysis of a questionnaire can often be simplified quite dramatically by giving the respondents a set of possible answers. Care must be taken to ensure all reasonable answers are catered for in the list and as a safeguard the equivalent of 'Other' should be included wherever applicable.

The next consideration is how the survey will take place. There are at least three possible options now in regular use

1. Postal questionnaires.
2. Personal interviews (face-to-face).
3. Telephone interviews.

The choice of option may well lead to modifications in the questions asked. If an interviewer is being used some clarification of questions can be given verbally (provided this does not influence the response). This is not possible with a postal questionnaire so even more care must be taken to ensure the clarity of questions asked.

Once the questions have been decided, a pilot study is conducted which, it is hoped, will indicate any shortcomings and allow a suitably modified questionnaire to be used for the main study.

In conclusion, then, a questionnaire should

1. be as short as possible;
2. contain short questions wherever possible;
3. contain simple questions wherever possible;
4. avoid ambiguous questions;
5. avoid leading questions;
6. avoid emotive language;
7. ask relevant questions;
8. use a specified choice of answers wherever possible;
9. look interesting and simple to answer.

Postal questionnaires

This method of carrying out a survey involves sending the respondent a questionnaire which he or she fills in and then returns for collation and analysis. This method has always been thought of as the cheapest survey method since it does not use direct labour to obtain the data, direct labour being considered an expensive resource. Instead, the main cost is postage. This method has the further advantages of ease and convenience especially if the sample chosen is widely spread geographically.

These advantages have to be set against certain problems which can arise. Firstly the response rate (percentage of questionnaires returned) is generally low. A 30–40% response rate would be considered good.

Compulsion cannot be used on the sample members to respond except by the Government and this compulsion is used only for the Census of Population and the Business Censuses. There are certain things which can be tried to encourage people to return completed questionnaires. A necessary start is a pre-paid reply envelope or equivalent. Survey organisations are now also using inducements of free gifts, vouchers etc. More practical problems can arise with this method of data collection. The respondent may fail to understand certain questions or may not answer certain questions. A further potential problem is that only people with strong views will respond to the questionnaire, leading to a polarisation of views expressed and resulting in an unrepresentative sample of replies.

Finally, if this method is being used for the views of commercial organisations care must be taken to address the questionnaire so that it reaches the appropriate person who can supply the required answers.

Interviewing

There are two types of interviewing commonly in use, personal and telephone. Both require an interviewer to ask the questions in the questionnaire. If the results of the questionnaire are to be reliable, then the interviewer must have certain qualities. He or she must be honest, able to record responses accurately, have an interest in and basic knowledge of the subject of the questionnaire, be adaptable, have an even temperament and should be able to put respondents at their ease. There is a natural inclination for respondents to see the questionnaire as a sort of examination and the interviewer needs to be able to allay any apprehensions the respondent may have.

In carrying out the questionnaire the interviewer must not cause any bias in the responses obtained. This means avoiding hints at certain answers, avoiding the rephrasing of questions or inaccuracies in recording responses. The interviewer may face many problems when administering a questionnaire and should be well trained in how to deal with these problems. Common problems are the following.

1.   The respondent fails to fully answer a question.
2.   The respondent fails to give any answer to a question.
3.   The respondent gives an obviously inaccurate response.
4.   The respondent gives an irrelevant response.
5.   The respondent asks the opinion of the interviewer.

Usually these can be dealt with by repeating the question.

There are then the problems of recording responses. An interviewer may well receive a vague answer which is translated either by the interviewer's view of what the type of respondent should have answered or is translated so that it is consistent with responses already received. These can both lead to the introduction of bias and the interviewer should attempt to get the respondent to clarify their response.

Finally, the interviewer should never give the impression that he or she is trying to rush the respondent.

1. *Personal interviews.* In personal interviews the interviewer asks questions face-to-face with the respondent. This face-to-face interview may be in a public place (often called a street interview and based on a quota sample), at the respondent's home or place of work. This method of data collection can be fairly expensive especially if a large sample is required. It is, however, a quick and reliable way of obtaining data. There can be problems when a person refuses to take part in the survey especially when the survey is not based on a quota sample. This affects home and place-of-work surveys much more than street surveys.

    Normally a reasonably sized survey requires a team of interviewers. These interviewers require training and special emphasis needs to be placed on the need for the interviewers to act consistently to avoid differences between interviewers being passed on into the survey results. For home and place-of-work interviews appointments need to be made.

    This method of carrying out a survey is usually regarded as the most effective. The more the interviewers are aware of the aims of the survey, the more they are in a position to ensure the data collection progresses smoothly.

2. *Telephone interviews.* For telephone interviews the interviewer telephones the possible respondent. Being unsolicited this can lead to problems with those telephoned and the interviewer needs to be able to either deal with abuse or quickly persuade a person to take part in the survey. This method has a certain notoriety, having been used extensively as a sales medium, especially for insurance, double glazing and more recently security products. Nonetheless, purely as a survey method it has certain advantages. If carried out at off-peak telephone rates it can be cheaper than a postal questionnaire, especially since the response rate tends to be higher. Results can be collected very quickly, perhaps even keyed directly into a computer database.

    There is, however, one potential drawback to this method. Not everyone has a telephone, so the population for which the results are required must be reflected by the population of people who do have telephones, otherwise an unrepresentative sample will be taken.

4

Presentation of data

Introduction

The survey methods discussed in Chapter 3 are designed to produce data, often in the form of numbers. This data is known as raw data, and is likely to consist of a mass of numbers which, as they stand, do not make very much sense or tell the user anything useful. To make this data more manageable data presentation and data summary methods are used, designed to draw out any characteristics the data might exhibit.

Tabulation of data

The starting point is often a list or array of numbers. This generally gives very little useful information. The smallest and largest values can be isolated but how the values are distributed between these limits is difficult to discern. The figures in Table 4.1 give the number of orders received by a company on 45 successive working days.

Some study of the table reveals that the lowest figure is 2 and the largest is 12. To progress further it is necessary to find a way of summarising the data. For data like this a *frequency table*, also known as a frequency distribution, can be formed. Count up how many times a value occurs. This is its *frequency*. Then list all the values with their respective frequencies in the form of a table. When drawing up a table like this remember to indicate any units used and give the table a title. For the data on orders in Table 4.1 the frequency distribution is given in Table 4.2. (Remember that the total of the frequencies is the initial number of figures. This should always be checked when constructing a frequency table.) As can be seen, this gives much more of an idea of what the data represents. It can be seen here that the categories 6 or 7 orders a day are very common.

A close look at the table shows that it is rather sparse of information at each end. The use of *open-ended* intervals tidies up the table without losing any important information. In this example open-ended intervals 'under 5' and 'over 10', could be used, giving Table 4.3. These open-ended intervals

Table 4.1. Number of orders
received by a company on 45
successive days

8, 6, 7, 9, 6, 8, 7, 5, 6,
6, 7, 2, 8, 7, 6, 10, 7, 7,
6, 8, 7, 6, 9, 7, 6, 6, 7,
7, 7, 7, 6, 8, 9, 12, 7, 8,
9, 5, 7, 8, 7, 6, 8, 9, 6.

Table 4.2. Frequency of orders received on 45 successive
days

Number of orders	Number of days (frequency)
2	1
3	0
4	0
5	2
6	12
7	15
8	8
9	5
10	1
11	0
12	1
	—
	45

Table 4.3. Frequency of orders received on 45 successive
days

Number of orders	Number of days (frequency)
Under 5	1
5	2
6	12
7	15
8	8
9	5
10	1
Over 10	1
	—
	45

Table 4.4. Numbers of customers
entering a shop on 25 successive
days

97, 64, 141, 76, 104,
194, 83, 36, 182, 67,
84, 120, 58, 151, 138,
77, 218, 129, 164, 80,
112, 91, 126, 58, 73.

Table 4.5. Frequency table for numbers of customers on
25 successive days

Number of customers	Number of days (frequency)
0–49	1
50–99	12
100–149	7
150–199	4
200–249	1

should be used only for the occasional extreme value, otherwise the table
could give a misleading impression.

This example has dealt with a discrete variable over a limited range and
so the data could easily be drawn up into a discrete frequency table. When
the data is more widely spread a straightforward table like this is unhelpful
and it is necessary to use groups or intervals of values rather than individual
values. In Table 4.4 the numbers of people entering a shop on 25 successive
days are recorded. The smallest figure is 36 and the largest 218. Listing all
the values from 36 to 218 inclusive and then counting how often each
occurred would be pointless, since if a value occurs at all it is once (except
for 58 which occurs twice). The vast majority of such a list would have
frequency zero. To obtain a more manageable and useful table figures can
be grouped into groups or classes. The frequency then represents how many
figures occurred within the interval. For this data a possible interval
frequency table is given in Table 4.5.

It can be seen that between 50 and 99 customers in a day is common and
that there are few days when fewer than 50 customers use the shop.
Similarly, there are few days when 150 or more customers use the shop.

Choice of class intervals

There are many guidelines laid down for the choice of how many intervals to use and how wide these intervals should be. These can be summarised as:

1. Use a minimum of five and maximum of twelve intervals. This guideline is put forward, since if there are fewer than five intervals there are very few frequencies to compare. Similarly, if more than twelve intervals are used it is very difficult to view the table as a whole. The actual number of intervals used depends on the number of figures summarised into the table. The more raw data we start with the more intervals we can use.
2. The mid-point of an interval should be the average of values counted in that interval. This is to assist in the calculations carried out later.

These are only guidelines and should be treated as such. In practice, (2) is very difficult to achieve and is often ignored. In (1) it is sometimes impossible to limit the number of intervals to twelve. If this is the case use the number that the problem demands.

Once the number of intervals has been decided the limits of the intervals need to be chosen. A crude method is to find the smallest value in the raw data and subtract it from the largest value, so giving the range of the data. Finally this range is divided into equal intervals.

The weakness with this approach is that the intervals obtained can look rather odd and unhelpful from the point of view of interpretation. Intervals like 2.74-8.47, 8.48-14.21 etc. do not generally reflect meaningful values. A different approach advocated is to use common sense. People naturally think in units or multiples of 10 such as hundreds and thousands. Where there is no obvious choice for the intervals, widths of 10 or based on 10 should be used.

A further consideration is that certain values are of special importance. Wherever possible the table intervals should be designed to take account of this. A frequency table showing people's taxable income should be drawn up so that the figures where different tax rates apply are used as limits of intervals. The table can then be used directly to see how many people fall into each tax band.

In all the examples so far each interval within a table has had the same width. It is not necessary to insist on equal interval widths but it does make the table simpler to handle. However, there are cases where unequal interval widths need to be used. A common example is where the variable being recorded is age. Table 4.6 shows the age distribution in a company.

A final point is worth making about the choice of limits, especially for discrete variables. When selecting the limits try to make them as convenient

Table 4.6. Age distribution of employees at a company

Age (last birthday)	Number of employees
Under 18	6
18–20	37
21–29	29
30–39	16
40–49	13
50–64	9
	110

as possible. For example, intervals 100 units wide could be written in any of the following ways:

1.	256–355	2.	201–300	3.	200–299
	356–455		301–400		300–399
	456–555		401–500		400–499
	etc.		etc.		etc.

The last example is by far the easiest if it is necessary to count through a list of data since it is necessary to concentrate only on all 'two hundreds', all 'three hundreds' which is not the case with the first two examples.

The approach for choosing intervals for continuous variables is similar but care must be taken to avoid ambiguities arising. Consider the two examples below:

1.	£	2.	£
	5,000–6,000		5,000 but less than 6,000
	6,000–7,000		6,000 but less than 7,000
	7,000–8,000		7,000 but less than 8,000

In the first example a value of £6,000 would fit into the first two intervals. This choice of intervals is unsatisfactory because it causes ambiguity. In the second example no such ambiguity arises and intervals like these should be used.

Suppose that the volumes of 25 bleach bottles have been recorded as in Table 4.7 and it is required to summarise these figures into a frequency table. As the total frequency is low the number of intervals used in the frequency table should be small. Here, a frequency table for these data is as shown in Table 4.8.

Table 4.7. Volumes for 25 bleach bottles (ml)

992.9, 1,011.9, 1,007.4, 990.3, 986.2,
1,009.6, 1,000.4, 995.5, 1,014.4, 1,002.1,
1,013.6, 983.7, 1,005.0, 1,001.7, 998.4,
1,023.8, 1,009.3, 998.1, 1,008.6, 1,017.8,
1,003.6, 994.2, 1,006.9, 981.4, 1,004.5.

Table 4.8. Frequency table for volumes of bleach bottles (ml)

Volume	Number of bottles
980 but less than 990	3
990 but less than 1,000	6
1,000 but less than 1,010	11
1,010 but less than 1,020	4
1,020 but less than 1,030	1
	25

Histograms

A histogram is the diagram usually used to represent a frequency table. It consists of a series of vertical columns representing the frequencies and a horizontal scale for the measurement. For the bleach-bottle volumes example a histogram is shown in Fig. 4.1.

If the table illustrated has unequal intervals then care must be taken in drawing the histogram. In a histogram the *area* of a column represents frequency so that the picture gives a fair representation. For the example in Table 4.9 the histogram is shown in Fig. 4.2. This diagram uses a width of 30 seconds as standard so with the double-width intervals of '60 but less than 120 seconds', '120 but less than 180 seconds', the frequency is halved to obtain the height of the column. Similarly, with the interval '180 but less than 300 seconds' the width is 4 times as wide so the frequency is divided by 4 to obtain the column height.

If there is an open-ended interval to be illustrated in a histogram it is conventional to draw the open-ended interval with the same width as its adjacent interval. This does not imply that this is the true width of the open-ended interval; it is just a convenient method of illustration. On the scale of the histogram it should be clearly stated that the column represents an open-ended interval to avoid any confusion. The data in Table 4.10 is

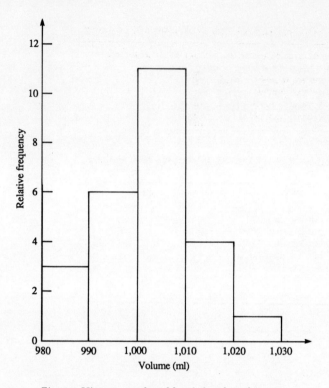

Fig. 4.1 Histogram of 25 bleach bottle volumes.

illustrated in Fig. 4.3. The interval next to the open-ended interval is a double-width interval. This means the column height for the open-ended interval is half of the interval frequency, i.e. 1.

Frequency polygons

An alternative illustration for a frequency table is a frequency polygon. The relative frequency for an interval is plotted at the mid-point for that interval. These points are then joined by straight lines. For the example in Table 4.8, the frequency polygon, superimposed on the histogram, is shown in Fig. 4.4.

A frequency polygon is designed to emphasise the shape of the data. At the ends the polygon can be joined to the horizontal axis at points which

Table 4.9. Frequency table for times to serve 75 customers

Time to serve customer (s)	Number of customers
0 but less than 30	5
30 but less than 60	27
60 but less than 120	18
120 but less than 180	15
180 but less than 300	10
	75

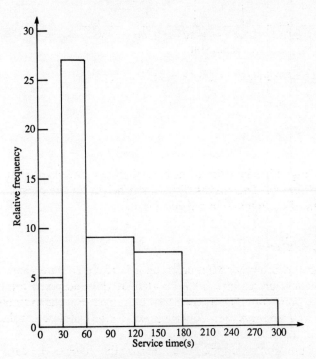

Fig. 4.2 Histogram of times to serve 75 customers.

Table 4.10. Frequency table of 160 weights

Weight of packet (g)	Number of packets
200 but less than 225	4
225 but less than 250	28
250 but less than 275	74
275 but less than 300	40
300 but less than 350	12
350 or over	2
	160

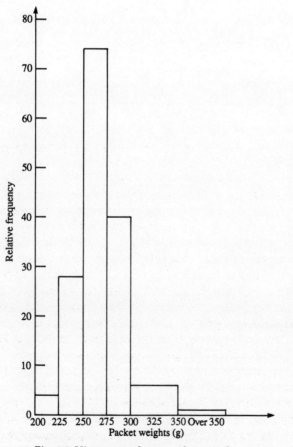

Fig. 4.3 Histogram of 160 packet weights.

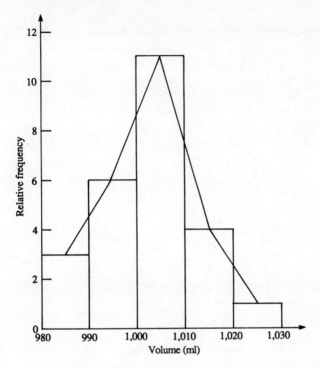

Fig. 4.4 Histogram and frequency polygon for the volume of 25 bleach
      bottles.

would correspond to mid-points of similar intervals if these were added at
each end of the diagram. For the example in Table 4.10 this extension of the
diagram is shown by dotted lines in Fig. 4.5.

   If we wish to make comparisons between two frequency tables, one
histogram or frequency polygon can be drawn on the same diagram as the
other. Using frequency polygons usually gives a clearer picture.

   To compare the weekly sales figures of two salespersons, as given in
Table 4.11, two frequency polygons can be drawn on the same diagram, as
shown in Fig. 4.6.

   This type of comparison can be made directly only if total frequency is the
same for each distribution. When the totals are different, the individual
frequencies must be converted into proportions or percentages of total
frequency before drawing the picture. This ensures the pictures have
comparable scales.

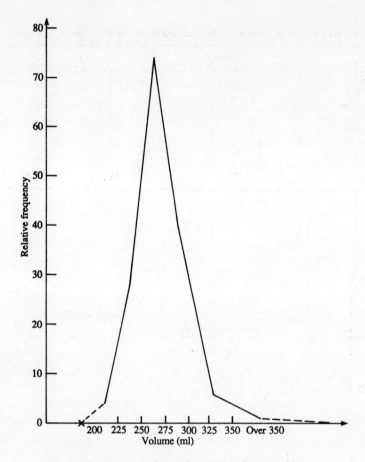

Fig. 4.5 Frequency polygon for 160 packet weights.

Cumulative frequency curves

A common question which arises when dealing with frequency data is 'How many are less than . . .'. This type of question can be answered by calculating a cumulative frequency distribution and by drawing a cumulative frequency curve. A cumulative frequency distribution is a running total of frequencies calculated for a frequency table. For Table 4.10 the cumulative frequency distribution is given in Table 4.12.

The last cumulative frequency figure should always equal the total frequency. To illustrate a cumulative frequency distribution, a cumulative frequency curve or ogive can be drawn by plotting the cumulative

Table 4.11. Frequency table of weekly sales achieved by two salespersons

Sales (£)	Salesperson A (number of weeks)	Salesperson B (number of weeks)
Under 1,000	1	0
1,000 but less than 2,000	17	4
2,000 but less than 3,000	24	14
3,000 but less than 4,000	6	25
4,000 but less than 5,000	0	4
5,000 or over	0	1
	48	48

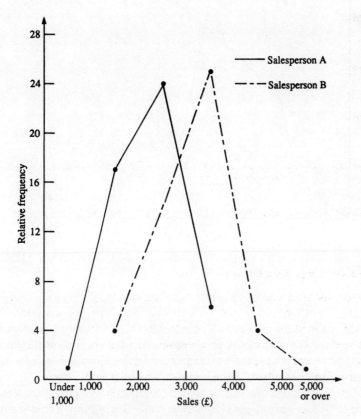

Fig. 4.6 Frequency polygon for sales of two salespersons.

Table 4.12. Cumulative frequency distribution for times to serve 75 customers

Time to serve customer (s)	Number of customers	Cumulative frequency
0 but less than 30	5	5
30 but less than 60	27	32 (5+27)
60 but less than 120	18	50 (32+18)
120 but less than 180	15	65 (50+15)
180 but less than 300	10	75 (65+10)
	75	

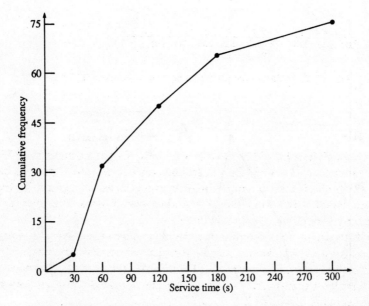

Fig. 4.7 Cumulative frequency curve for times to serve 75 customers.

frequencies against the *top limit* of the interval (i.e. plot 5 against 30, plot 32 against 60 etc.). The cumulative frequency curve for Table 4.12 is shown in Fig. 4.7. The points are joined by straight lines and if there are open-ended intervals, these are treated in the same way as for histograms.

Strictly speaking this diagram is called a 'less than' cumulative frequency curve or 'less than' ogive since it is used to read off how many are less than some quantity. For the packet weights in Table 4.10, to find how many

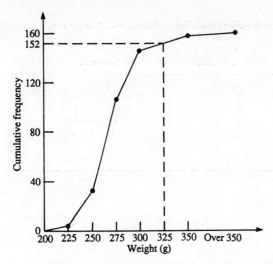

Fig. 4.8 Cumulative frequency curve for weights of 160 packets.

packets weigh less than 325 g draw a cumulative frequency curve as in Fig. 4.8. Reading across from 325 g the graph gives a figure of 152 packets less than 325 g. This is only an approximation as it is based on a graph. To find the exact number the original data would need to be used. The approximations are generally perfectly adequate.

An alternative to a cumulative frequency curve is the cumulative percentage curve. This is used to indicate what percentage of figures are less than a certain value. For the data in Table 4.10, if the percentage of packets less than 260 g is required, a cumulative percentage distribution can be calculated as in Table 4.13.

The corresponding cumulative percentage curve is shown in Fig. 4.9, and reading across from 260 g, the graph gives approximately 39% weighing less than 260 g.

Following the same idea, a 'greater than' cumulative frequency curve can be drawn. The cumulative frequencies already calculated for a 'less than' cumulative frequency curve are subtracted, in turn, from total frequency. These resulting figures are 'greater than' frequencies and are plotted against the *top limit* of the interval. A 'greater than' frequency curve for Table 4.12 is calculated as in Table 4.14 and illustrated in Fig. 4.10. For this curve the number of customers taking longer than 90 seconds to be served can be read off as 34 customers.

Table 4.13. Cumulative percentage table for weights of 160 packets

Weight (g)	Frequency	Cumulative frequency	Cumulative percentage
200 but less than 225	4	4	2.50
225 but less than 250	28	32	20.00
250 but less than 275	74	106	66.25
275 but less than 300	40	146	91.25
300 but less than 350	12	158	98.75
350 or over	2	160	100.00
	160		

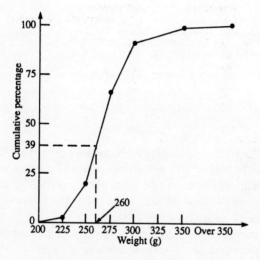

Fig. 4.9 Cumulative percentage curve for weights of 160 packets.

Lorenz curves

A cumulative frequency curve shows how frequency of a measurement accumulates as that measurement increases. A Lorenz curve shows how the cumulative totals for one measurement compare to the cumulative totals of another measurement. This graph is then used to see to what degree the two distributions are similar. If the two distributions are exactly equal, then a 45° line is obtained. This is drawn as the start of a Lorenz curve for comparison purposes. The cumulative totals of one measurement are then plotted against the cumulative totals for the other, these points being joined to form the Lorenz curve.

In Table 4.15 the firms in an industrial sector are categorised by size

Table 4.14. 'Greater than' frequencies for 75 times to serve customers

Time to serve customer (s)	Frequency	Greater than cumulative frequencies
0 but less than 30	5	70
30 but less than 60	27	43
60 but less than 120	18	25
120 but less than 180	15	10
180 but less than 300	10	0
	75	

Table 4.15. Firms from an industrial sector by size and net output

Number of employees	Number of firms	Net output (% of industrial sector output)
Under 50	3	1
50 but less than 100	60	9
100 but less than 200	45	20
200 but less than 300	24	28
300 but less than 500	15	33
500 or over	3	9
	150	100

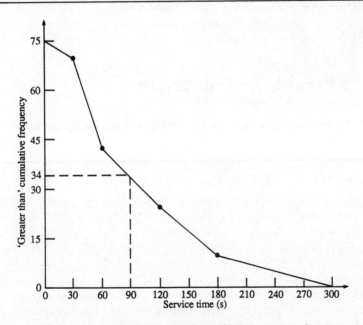

Fig. 4.10 'Greater than' cumulative frequency curve for times to serve 75 customers.

60   Presentation of data

Table 4.16. Cumulative percentages of firm size and net output

Number of employees	Percentage of firms	Cumulative percentages	Net output (%)	Cumulative percentages
Under 50	2	2	1	1
50 but less than 100	40	42	9	10
100 but less than 200	30	72	20	30
200 but less than 300	16	88	28	58
300 but less than 500	10	98	33	91
500 or over	2	100	9	100
	100		100	

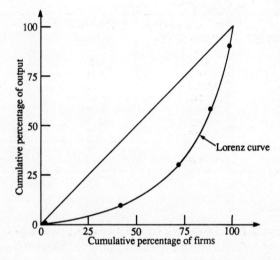

Fig. 4.11 Lorenz curve for distribution of size of firm and net output.

(number of employees) and the percentage of net output for the sector produced by that size of firm. To draw a Lorenz curve, cumulative totals (in percentages) must be calculated as in Table 4.16. The corresponding Lorenz curve is shown in Fig. 4.11. This curve does not follow the 45° line so shows there is no close similarity between the distributions. The further away from the 45° line the curve is, the greater the inequality in the distributions.

Sometimes the measurements to be accumulated are not given specifically. Suppose the personal wealth of persons in part of a city is given in Table 4.17. Before these figures can be used to compare the distribution of *total* personal wealth with the distribution of number of persons, the total personal wealth for each interval must be found. As these figures are not given they are calculated as

Table 4.17. Distribution of personal wealth in a UK city

Personal wealth (£)	Number of people
Under 5,000	153
5,000 but less than 10,000	441
10,000 but less than 20,000	670
20,000 but less than 30,000	462
30,000 but less than 50,000	196
50,000 but less than 100,000	76
100,000 but less than 200,000	2
	2,000

Table 4.18. Calculations for percentage of total wealth

Interval mid-point (£'000s)	Frequency	Personal wealth for interval (£'000s)	Percentage of personal wealth
2.5	153	382.5	0.98
7.5	441	3,307.5	8.45
15.0	670	10,050.0	25.67
25.0	462	11,550.0	29.52
40.0	196	7,840.0	20.04
75.0	76	5,700.0	14.57
150.0	2	300.0	0.77
	2,000	39,130.0	100.00

interval total = mid-point of interval × interval frequency

The mid-point of an interval is found by averaging the two end-point values for the interval. In Table 4.17, the end points are £100,000 and £200,000, so the mid-point of this interval is

$$\frac{100,000 + 200,000}{2} = £150,000$$

The remaining mid-points are calculated in a similar way.

For the figures in Table 4.17 these calculations give those shown in Table 4.18. The cumulative frequencies are then given in Table 4.19 and the corresponding Lorenz curve is shown in Fig. 4.12. This curve is well below the equality line and illustrates that personal wealth is not equally distributed but that instead, a few people own a substantial amount of total personal wealth. This curve can then be used to ascertain what percentage of total personal wealth is owned by the least wealthy quarter of persons. Reading across from 25% on the horizontal axis, a figure of approximately 8% is obtained.

Similarly, if the percentage of most wealthy people owning 20% of

Table 4.19. Cumulative percentages of persons and personal wealth

Interval mid-point (£'000s)	Cumulative % persons	Cumulative % personal wealth
2.5	7.65	0.98
7.5	29.70	9.43
15.0	63.20	35.10
25.0	86.30	64.62
40.0	96.10	84.66
75.0	99.90	99.23
150.0	100.00	100.00

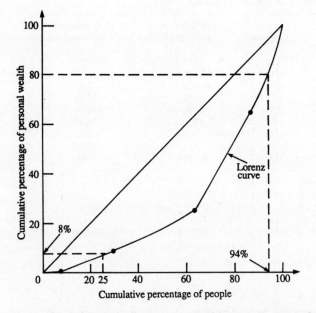

Fig. 4.12 Lorenz curve of the distribution of personal wealth.

personal wealth is required, look up 80% on the vertical axis (20% above it) and read off 94% on the horizontal axis. This indicates that the most wealthy 6% of people own 20% of personal wealth.

Bar charts

So far the diagrams have been used to illustrate frequencies for a numerical measurement. Not every measurement recorded is a number. When a measurement is not a number a bar chart can be used to illustrate data.

Table 4.20. Colour of 80 new cars purchased

Colour	Number of cars
White	13
Red	25
Blue	11
Green	10
Yellow	7
Black	14
	80

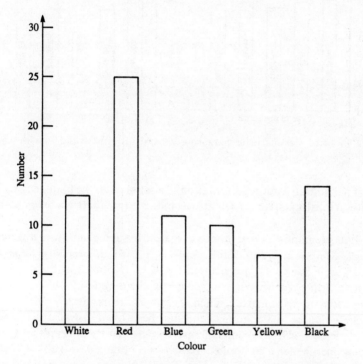

Fig. 4.13 Bar chart for the colour of 80 new cars purchased.

1. Simple bar charts. A car salesroom has recorded the colour of new cars purchased and the figures are given in Table 4.20. To illustrate these data a simple bar chart as shown in Fig. 4.13 can be drawn.

    When drawn the bar chart must have equal columns with equal widths evenly spaced. There is no reason why the columns have to be vertical. The diagram could be turned on its side and the columns drawn horizontally.

Table 4.21. Demand figures for five
margarines at a chain store in a week

Margarine	Demand (kg)
Sunhour	400
Vitafull	390
Butterlike	370
Tastesame	390
Rightflav	380

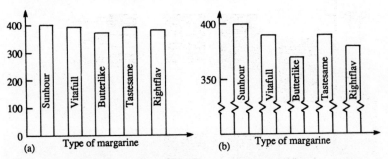

Fig. 4.14 Bar charts for margarine demand: (a) without and (b) with scale
breaks.

To maintain a fair representation of a set of data, the frequency scale
should ideally start at zero or at least indicate that there is a break in the
scale.

If the demands for five brands of margarine at a chain store during a
week are as given in Table 4.21, then two different versions of
acceptable bar charts are given in Fig. 4.14. (Notice how the break in
the vertical scale is clearly indicated on the diagram.)

2. Component bar charts. When a bar chart is drawn the totals
    represented by the columns can often be broken down into various
    components. If the columns themselves are split up to represent these
    components then a component bar chart is obtained. In Table 4.22 the
    production figures for three factories making compact disc players
    have been recorded over three consecutive months.

    A component bar chart can be drawn by first drawing a simple bar
    chart based on total production. The columns can then be subdivided
    to illustrate figures for each factory as in Fig. 4.15. From this chart it is
    possible to compare total figures and any trends in the components of
    that total. Care has to be taken, though, since the more components
    that are used the more difficult it is to identify what is happening to
    each individual component.

Table 4.22. Compact disc player production at three factories over three months

	May	June	July
Preston	12,000	15,000	15,000
Derby	7,000	8,000	9,000
Crawley	8,000	7,000	6,000

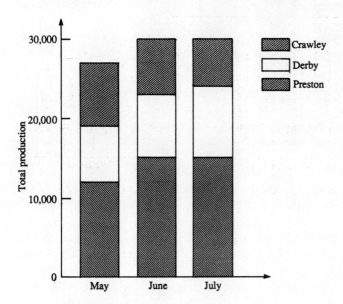

Fig. 4.15 Component bar chart for compact disc player production.

It is important to include a key, otherwise the chart will be meaningless. Here, different shading methods have been used but different colours could have been used instead.

3. Percentage component bar chart. If interest centres on proportions of a total in a component bar chart rather than on the figures themselves a percentage bar chart can be drawn. The scale used is percentage and the percentage of the total for each component is illustrated.

For the compact disc player production figures in Table 4.22, a percentage bar chart is shown in Fig. 4.16. This chart highlights the percentage breakdown of a total but does not give any indication of how that total may vary. This particular chart illustrates very clearly the decreasing percentage of total production provided by the Crawley factory. This is not as clear in the ordinary component bar chart.

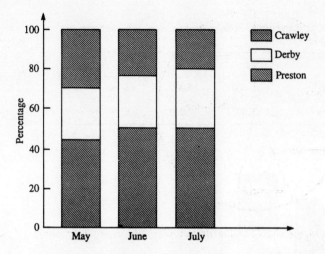

Fig. 4.16 Percentage component bar chart for compact disc player production.

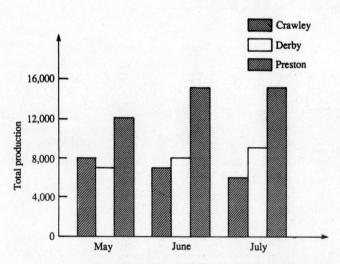

Fig. 4.17 Compound bar chart for compact disc player production.

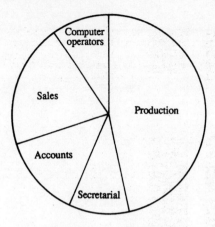

Fig. 4.18 Pie chart for distribution of employees by function.

4. Compound bar chart. The component bar chart illustrates how totals are split but is not particularly helpful for comparing one component against another. If this is the aim, then a compound bar chart can be used. For the data on compact disc player production, a compound bar chart is shown in Fig. 4.17. Here comparisons of performance for an individual component can be made, components can be compared against each other but the one detail missing is any real idea of total figures.

Pie charts

A pie chart is an alternative diagram to bar charts. It is especially useful where there are several divisions which make the bar charts impractical. In a pie chart a circle is divided in proportion to the components which make up the total.

If a company has 60 employees, 28 of whom are production staff, 6 are secretarial staff, 8 are accounts staff, 12 are sales staff, and 6 are computer operators, then these data can be illustrated by the pie chart in Fig. 4.18.

As a circle consists of 360°, the angle for the 'production' segment is

$$\frac{28}{60} \times 360 = 168°$$

and the angles for the remaining segments are calculated as shown in Table 4.23.

Table 4.23. Calculations for sector angles

Section	Number of employees	Angle of sector
Production	28	$\dfrac{28}{60} \times 360 = 168°$
Secretarial	6	$\dfrac{6}{60} \times 360 = 36°$
Accounts	8	$\dfrac{8}{60} \times 360 = 48°$
Sales	12	$\dfrac{12}{60} \times 360 = 72°$
Computer	6	$\dfrac{6}{60} \times 360 = 36°$

Table 4.24. Output figures for six factories in 1977 and 1987

Factory	1977	1987
Bristol	8,000	20,000
Carlisle	12,000	60,000
Morpeth	20,000	60,000
Norwich	10,000	50,000
Worthing	12,000	40,000
Yeovil	18,000	90,000
	80,000	320,000

A pie chart can be drawn using shadings or colours and then a key included, just as for bar charts.

To compare more than one total split into components, a series of pie charts can be drawn side by side. If the only concern is the proportional splits of totals, then the pie charts can be drawn the same size. If, however, an indication of differences in the total are also required, the area of the circle should be used to represent the total. This means that the radii of the circles should be proportional to the *square root* of the total.

Output figures from six factories have been recorded in 1977 and 1987 and are given in Table 4.24. As the totals are in the ratio 1 : 4, the areas of the circles should be in this ratio. In turn, this means the radii should be in the ratio 1 : 2.

These are shown in Fig. 4.19.

Table 4.25. Soft drink sales for one day at a shop

Soft drink	Number of litres
Lemonade	50
Orangeade	35
Cola	42
Mineral water	83
Cherryade	28

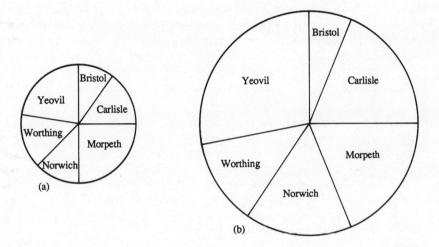

Fig. *4.19* Pie charts for distribution of production in (a) 1977 and (b) 1987.

Pictograms

A rather different type of illustration which can be used for frequencies or quantities is one where the diagram itself consists of pictures of what is being represented. A picture is chosen that can be easily seen to represent the quantities being illustrated. Any diagram of this type is called a pictogram.

The sales of different soft drinks at a shop on a particular day are recorded in Table 4.25. A possible pictogram is shown in Fig. 4.20. Here a particular sized picture is used to represent 10 litres. An alternative approach is to use the area of the picture to represent the size of the measurement.

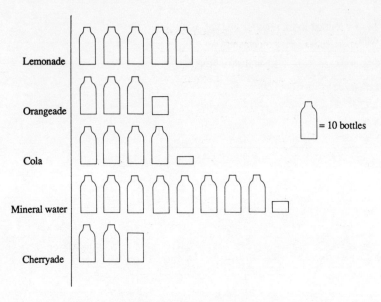

Fig. 4.20 Pictogram of soft drink sales.

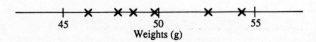

Fig. 4.21 Line graph of steel strip weights.

These pictures can sometimes be difficult to draw, especially if the symbol is complicated and a fraction of a unit has to be represented. They can, however, make a very effective visual impression.

Graphs

The simplest graph is a line graph where a single variable is illustrated by plotting its values on a single axis. This type of graph gives an indication of the spread of a set of data.

A line graph for the following weights of steel strips (in grams)

46.3, 47.9, 52.6, 48.7, 54.3, 49.8

is given in Fig. 4.21.

When two variables measured on the same item are to be illustrated, a *scatter diagram* or *scatter graph* is used. To illustrate the data on number of employees and annual turnover figures for ten companies given in Table 4.26 the scatter diagram is shown in Fig. 4.22.

Table 4.26. Numbers of employees and annual
turnover figures for ten companies

Company	Number of employees	Turnover (£'00,000s)
1	55	6.9
2	127	18.2
3	85	9.7
4	193	56.2
5	77	9.5
6	102	17.6
7	149	37.0
8	160	35.3
9	95	18.6
10	73	8.5

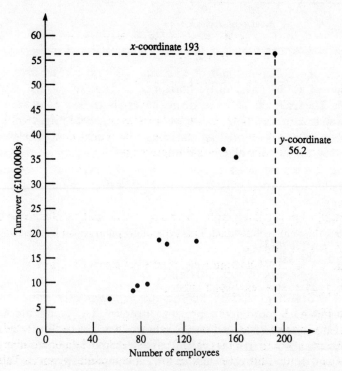

Fig. 4.22 Scatter diagram of turnover against number of employees.

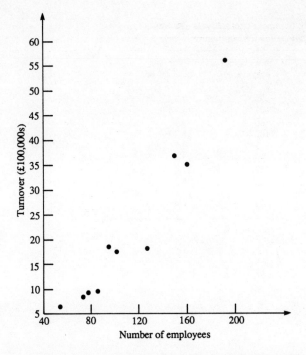

Fig. 4.23 Scatter diagram of turnover against number of employees.

Two axes, one horizontal and one vertical, are drawn. The axes are usually denoted as the x-axis for the horizontal axis and the y-axis for the vertical axis. The scales on these axes do not have to be the same and are not in this example. Although both axes start at zero (called the origin) in this illustration, they can be started at any value on the scales. If there were negative values for the variables (not appropriate for this example), the axes would need to be extended backwards for the horizontal axis and downwards for the vertical axis. Notice that the scatter diagram includes the following:

1. A title.
2. Names for the axes.
3. Scales on the axes.
4. Units for the scales (if appropriate).

Each point is drawn so that its x-coordinate represents the number of employees and its y-coordinate represents turnover. The points are not joined up as this would have no meaning in this example.

To emphasise any patterns that might be present in the data, the scatter diagram can be drawn with the scales starting at values different to zero, as in Fig. 4.23.

Table 4.27. Company annual sales figures

Year	Sales (£ millions)
1981	3.6
1982	2.9
1983	5.7
1984	6.3
1985	6.2
1986	5.8
1987	5.5

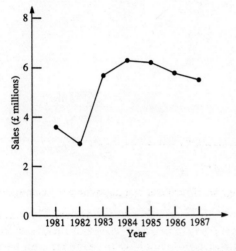

Fig. 4.24 Time series plot of annual sales figures.

When the data to be illustrated is a measurement recorded against time, this is called a *time series* and the graph of a time series is called a *time series plot* (or occasionally a *historigram*). Suppose a company records its sales figures as in Table 4.27. Then a time series of the data is given in Fig. 4.24. In this case the points are joined together since in this type of example the points show how a measurement develops or progresses. By joining the points an indication of trend can be highlighted.

As with bar charts, time series plots can be used to illustrate not only total figures but how those total figures are composed from different parts. For the output figures in Table 4.28, a *strata time series plot* can be drawn to show the division of total output between factories. Figure 4.25 illustrates the data.

This strata time series plot shows how a total is split up. If a comparison of the individual factories is required, then a *multiple time series plot* can be drawn as in Fig. 4.26.

Table 4.28. Quarterly output figures for television stands by factory

Factory	Jan/ Mar	Apr/ Jun	Jul/ Sep	Oct/ Dec	Jan/ Mar	Apr/ Jun	Jul/ Sep	Oct/ Dec
Aberdeen	1,160	1,320	1,580	1,730	1,880	1,980	2,210	2,460
Crewe	1,560	1,530	1,550	1,500	1,520	1,570	1,550	1,540
Dartford	1,920	1,860	1,850	1,830	1,750	1,730	1,660	1,620
Total	4,640	4,710	4,980	5,060	5,150	5,280	5,420	5,620

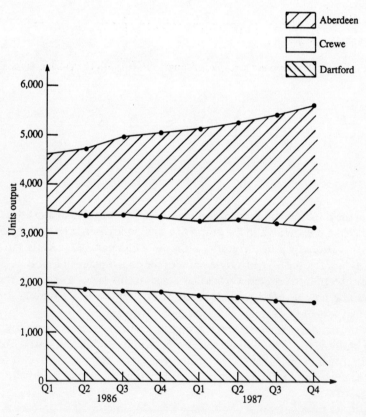

Fig. 4.25 Strata time series plot for quarterly output of television stands.

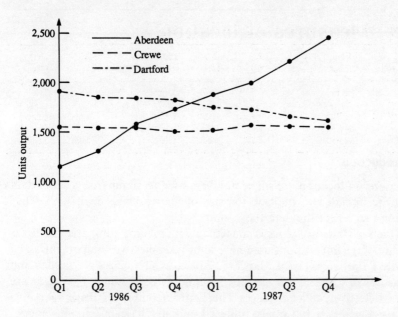

Fig. 4.26 Multiple series plot of quarterly output of television stands.

5

Measures of location

Introduction

Measures of location are single numbers used to summarise a set of data and are intended to indicate the size of figures being dealt with. They attempt to reflect the data they summarise.

Much of statistical work is concerned with making comparisons. So far certain of the illustrations used have allowed subjective comparisons to be made. To progress further, however, objective summaries are needed and measures of location are the most commonly used summaries. They are often collectively called averages. There are different types of average; some are used generally but others are used only in particular circumstances.

The arithmetic mean

The arithmetic mean is the most commonly used measure of location. It is the simple average of a set of data, calculated by adding all the data and then dividing by the number of figures the data set consists of. The arithmetic mean is denoted by $\bar{x}$ and is calculated using the formula

$$\bar{x} = \frac{\sum_{i=1}^{n} x_i}{n}$$

x_i is used to denote each individual figure in the data set so x_1 represents the first data figure, x_2 represents the second data figure and in general x_i represents the ith data figure, and so on, with x_n representing the last figure in the data set. The symbol n is used to represent the number of figures in the data set. The summation sign Σ means 'add up', so $\sum_{i=1}^{n} x_i$ means add up x-values from x_1 to x_n inclusive.

A car salesroom has recorded the number of cars sold on seven successive days as follows:

3, 8, 4, 5, 2, 1, 5

Table 5.1. Frequency of number of
employees absent through illness

Number of employees absent	Number of days
0	17
1	26
2	3
3	2
4	1
5	1

The arithmetic mean of these figures is given by

$$\bar{x} = \frac{3+8+4+5+2+1+5}{7}$$

$$= \frac{28}{7}$$

$$= 4$$

(Here $x_1 = 3$, $x_2 = 8$, $x_3 = 4$, $x_4 = 5$, $x_5 = 2$, $x_6 = 1$, $x_7 = 5$ and $n = 7$)

For any list of figures the formula above is used to find the arithmetic mean. It is called the *ungrouped data* formula for the mean.

As seen in Chapter 4, data is often presented in the form of frequency tables. If a discrete frequency table is presented for the number of employees absent through illness per day as given in Table 5.1, then the arithmetic mean is calculated using the *grouped frequency formula*:

$$\bar{x} = \frac{\sum_{i=1}^{n} f_i x_i}{\sum_{i=1}^{n} f_i}$$

where f_i is the frequency for the value x_i. The calculations to find the arithmetic mean for the data in Table 5.1 can be set out as in Table 5.2, giving

$$\bar{x} = \frac{\sum_{i=1}^{n} f_i x_i}{\sum_{i=1}^{n} f_i}$$

$$= \frac{47}{50}$$

$$= 0.94$$

Table 5.2

Number of employees absent	Number of days f	fx
0	17	0
1	26	26
2	3	6
3	2	6
4	1	4
5	1	5
	50	47

Table 5.3. Interval frequency table for volumes of shampoo bottles

Volume (ml)	Number of bottles
240 but less than 245	6
245 but less than 250	21
250 but less than 255	174
255 but less than 260	47
260 but less than 265	2
	250

Here, the mean number of employees absent on a day is 0.94. Obviously, on any one day the number absent cannot be 0.94, it is not an integer, but it tells the firm, *on average*, what number of employees will be absent.

The final type of presentation of data which may be used is a class interval frequency table. In Table 5.3 the figures for volume of shampoo bottles are given.

The grouped frequency formula for the arithmetic mean is used. The frequencies f_i are given by the table but specific x-values are not given, only intervals. Each interval is replaced by its mid-point, so the x_i are the interval mid-points. The arithmetic mean for the data in Table 5.3 is then calculated as follows (see Table 5.4):

$$\bar{x} = \frac{63,215.0}{250}$$

$$= 252.86 \text{ ml}$$

There are two situations where care must be taken when calculating the arithmetic mean with grouped data. Firstly, if the intervals are for discrete

Table 5.4 Interval frequency table for volumes of shampoo bottles

Interval mid-point (x)	Frequency (f)	fx
242.5	6	1,455.0
247.5	21	5,197.5
252.5	174	43,935.0
257.5	47	12,012.5
262.5	2	525.0
	250	63,215.0

Table 5.5. Number of machine breakdowns

Number of breakdowns	Mid-point
0–4	2
5–9	7
10–14	12
15–19	17
20–24	22

Table 5.6. Intervals of age last birthday

Age (at last birthday)	Mid-points
20–29	25
30–39	35
40–49	45
50–59	55
60–69	65

data the mid-point of an interval must be found logically. If a count of the number of machine breakdowns per week is made and the intervals in Table 5.5 used, then the mid-points are as given in the second column, i.e. the average of the two end-points. However, with some measurements, e.g. age, extra care must be taken. Looking at the data in Table 5.6, then the mid-points are as given. This is because, if the '20–29' interval is considered, anyone who has reached their 20th birthday but has yet to reach their 30th birthday would be counted in this interval. Hence, the limits of the interval are actually '20 but less than 30', and the mid-point is the average of these two limits, i.e. 25.

Table 5.7. Widths for 120 components

Width of component (cm)	Number of components
2.00 but less than 2.10	2
2.10 but less than 2.20	13
2.20 but less than 2.30	22
2.30 but less than 2.40	63
2.40 but less than 2.50	18
2.50 or over	2
	120

The second situation is when open-ended intervals are used in the table. When drawing these intervals in histograms they were treated as having the same width as their adjacent interval. This is exactly how they are treated for calculating the arithmetic mean.

For the data on widths of components given in Table 5.7 the calculations are based on the usual mid-points. The mid-point of the open-ended interval is found by treating it as having width equal to its adjacent interval '2.40 but less than 2.50', i.e. as having a width of 0.1 cm.

$$\bar{x} = \frac{279.00}{120}$$

$$= 2.325 \, \text{cm}$$

Sometimes, if the numbers we are dealing with are large, the calculations can become rather messy, especially if no calculator is available. The arithmetic mean can be calculated by the following alternative method. Start by subtracting a suitable number from each data value. This is denoted by A and is usually the smallest x-value. For the data in Table 5.3, this would be the first mid-point 242.5. Next, divide each new value by the class interval C. In this case we divide by 5 to obtain values denoted by d. The mean is then found by using the formula

$$\bar{x} = A + C \left(\frac{\sum_{i=1}^{n} f_i d_i}{\sum_{i=1}^{n} f_i} \right)$$

This leads to the calculation shown in Table 5.8, giving

$$x = 242.5 + 5 \left(\frac{518}{250} \right)$$

$$= 242.5 + 10.36$$
$$= 252.86 \, \text{g}$$

Table 5.8

Mid-points (x)	x − A	$d = \frac{1}{5}(x-A)$	f	fd
242.5	0	0	6	0
247.5	5	1	21	21
252.5	10	2	174	348
257.5	15	3	47	141
262.5	20	4	2	8
			250	518

Table 5.9

Time taken (days)	Number of orders
0 but less than 10	7
10 but less than 20	22
20 but less than 40	15
40 but less than 60	9
60 but less than 100	7
	60

Table 5.10

Mid-points	x − 5	$d = \frac{1}{5}(x-5)$	f	fd
5	0	0	7	0
15	10	2	22	44
30	25	5	15	75
50	45	9	9	81
80	75	15	7	85
			60	285

the result obtained previously. When using this method care must be taken to calculate the 'd' values correctly. If unequal class intervals are used in the original table then simply writing 'd' values of 0, 1, 2 . . . will lead to the wrong answer. Suppose we wish to find the mean time to fulfil an order based on the data in Table 5.9.

The calculations would give the figures shown in Table 5.10, so that

$$x = 5 + 5\left(\frac{285}{60}\right)$$

$$= 5 + 23.75$$
$$= 28.75 \text{ days}$$

This method can be used for calculating the mean for any set of data but is most commonly used for class-interval data where the values are large.

The median

The median is literally the middle figure once the data set has been put in numerical order. This gives an indication of the centre of the data set and is especially useful when extreme values are recorded as 'greater than . . .' or 'less than . . .' rather than specific values. For the data in Table 5.1, the figures in numerical order are

1, 2, 3, 4, 5, 5, 8
         ↑
middle figure

and we can see 4 is the middle figure. This tells us 4 cars is the median value. If there are n figures, the median is the $[(n+1)/2]$th figure in numerical order. Here there are 7 figures so the median is the $[(7+1)/2]$th $=4$th in order.

If there are an even number of figures such as these numbers of complaints received at a shop on 8 working days

0, 4, 1, 3, 2, 6, 0, 4

then putting the figures in order gives

0, 0, 1, 2, 3, 4, 4, 6
         ↑
middle figure

and the median is the $(8+1)/2=4.5$th in order. This is halfway between the fourth and fifth figures in order, so the median is

$$\frac{2+3}{2}=2.5$$

Considering next the grouped frequency table for discrete data given in Table 5.2, the median is still the middle figure, i.e. the $[(n+1)/2]$th figure once the figures are in order. In a frequency table the figures are automatically in order, so if the figures were listed in order we would obtain

$$\underbrace{0, 0, \ldots, 0,}_{17 \text{ times}} \underbrace{1, 1, \ldots, 1,}_{26 \text{ times}} 2, 2, 2, 3, 3, 4, 5$$

The median is then the $[(n+1)/2]=25.5$th value. This is halfway between the 25th and 26th values, both of which are 1. Hence, the median is 1 employee absent. A simpler way is to calculate cumulative frequencies and the value for which cumulative frequency first reaches or exceeds $[(n+1)/2]$ is the median (see Table 5.11).

Table 5.11

Number of employees absent	Number of days	Cumulative frequency
0	17	17
1	26	43 ←Median
2	3	46
3	2	48
4	1	49
5	1	50

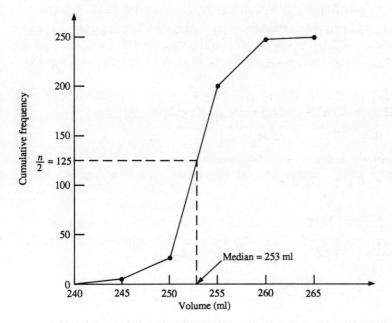

Fig. 5.1 Cumulative frequency curve for shampoo bottle volumes.

When grouped data is in the form of an interval frequency table, then two methods can be employed to find the median, one graphical and one calculation. The graphical method starts with a cumulative frequency curve being drawn (as detailed in Chapter 4). Figure 5.1 shows the cumulative frequency curve for the data in Table 5.3.

The median is found as the value corresponding to a cumulative frequency of $n/2$. (Here the accuracy of using $(n+1)/2$ is unnecessary since the measurement being investigated is continuous.) From the graph the median is approximately 253 ml.

If more accuracy is required, a calculation method can be used. Firstly, a

Table 5.12

Volume (ml)	Number of bottles	Cumulative frequency
240 but less than 245	6	6
245 but less than 250	21	27
250 but less than 255	174	201
255 but less than 260	47	248
260 but less than 265	2	250

cumulative frequency table is drawn up. The interval for which cumulative frequency first reaches or exceeds $n/2$ is then found. This interval contains the median and is known as the *median interval*. For the data in Table 5.3 the median interval is '250 but less than 255 ml' since cumulative frequency first exceeds 125 in this interval (see Table 5.12).

To find the median within the interval the following formula is used:

$$M = L_1 + (L_2 - L_1)\frac{(n/2 - \Sigma f_1)}{(\Sigma f_2 - \Sigma f_1)}$$

where M is the median, L_1 is the lower limit of the median interval, L_2 is the upper limit of the median interval, Σf_1 is the cumulative frequency total below the median interval, Σf_2 is the cumulative frequency total up to and including the median interval, and n is the total frequency.

For the bottle volume data in Table 5.3 the median is found using

$$L_1 = 250, \ L_2 = 255, \ n = 250, \ \Sigma f_1 = 27, \ \Sigma f_2 = 201$$

The median is

$$M = 250 + 5\frac{(125 - 27)}{(201 - 27)}$$

$$= 250 + 5\frac{(98)}{(174)}$$

$$= 252.82 \text{ ml}$$

The mode

The mode is the least commonly used of the main measures of location. It is the value which occurs with the highest frequency, making it the most typical value. For the data of new cars sold in Table 4.1 the figures were as follows:

1, 2, 3, 4, 5, 5, 8

Table 5.13

Number of employees absent	Number of days
0	17
1	26 ←Mode
2	3
3	2
4	1
5	1

The figure '5' occurs twice, whereas all the other figures only occur once, making 5 the mode.

The mode can be difficult to determine since it can be ambiguous. Suppose the data collected is

$$1, 2, 2, 2, 4, 6, 8, 8, 9, 11, 11, 11, 13$$

then the figures '2' and '11' both occur three times (more often than any other values) but which is the mode? In this case the mode cannot be determined uniquely.

When discrete data is given in the form of a grouped frequency table, the mode is found as the discrete value having the highest frequency. For the data concerning number of employees absent given in Table 5.1 the mode is 1 employee absent since this has the highest frequency of 26 (see Table 5.13).

When grouped data in the form of interval frequency data is given, then two methods, one graphical, the other calculation, are available. To find the mode using a graphical method a histogram of the data is drawn. The column which is highest indicates the *modal interval*, the interval which contains the mode. For the bottle volume data of Table 5.3 the modal interval is '250 but less than 255 ml'. The mode is found by joining the top corners of the highest column diagonally to the corner where the adjacent columns meet this modal column as shown in Fig. 5.2. Where these two lines cross indicates the mode as approximately 253 ml.

To find the mode by calculation, the formula used is

$$Mo = L_{Mo} + w_{Mo}\left[\frac{c_1}{c_1 + c_2}\right]$$

where Mo is the mode, L_{Mo} is the lower limit of the modal interval, w_{Mo} is the width of the modal interval, c_1 is the difference in column height between the modal interval and its preceding interval and c_2 is the difference in *column* height between the modal interval and its following interval.

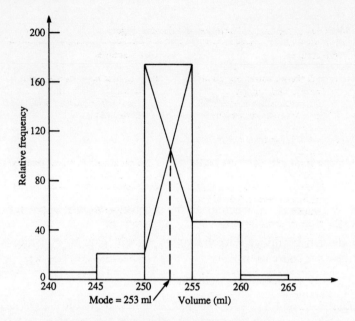

Fig. 5.2 Histogram of shampoo bottle volumes.

For the bottle volume data of Table 4.3

$$L_{Mo} = 250, \ w_{Mo} = 5, \ c_1 = 174 - 21 = 153, \ c_2 = 174 - 47 = 127$$

so the mode is found as

$$Mo = 250 + 5 \left[\frac{153}{153 + 127} \right]$$
$$= 250 + 2.73$$
$$= 252.73 \ ml$$

Comparison between mean, median and mode

The three measures of location have the advantages and disadvantages shown in Table 5.14. (For a more detailed discussion of skewness see Chapter 6.)

The mean is the measure of location most widely used. It is especially appropriate for data where the distribution is fairly symmetrical. It is widely used for measures of weight, length and volume.

The median is used in place of the mean when there is a noticeably skewed distribution, where there are a significant number of extreme values or where there are values in open-ended intervals. In reliability trials the

Table 5.14. Measures of location: advantages and disadvantages

	Advantages	Disadvantages
Mean	1. It is the measurement common sense would suggest. 2. It is representative of all the data since all are used in its calculation. 3. It can be written simply as a formula	1. It cannot cope with extreme values very well. 2. It is not particularly useful for skewed data.
Median	1. It represents the centre of the data. 2. It can be used where extreme values or open-ended values are present. 3. It can be used for skewed data.	1. It cannot easily be represented by a formula. 2. It only uses the central data values. 3. It cannot be developed further in statistics.
Mode	1. It represents the most popular or common value. 2. It is easy to understand. 3. It can be used where extreme values or open-ended values are present.	1. It may not exist. 2. It may not give a unique value. 3. It does not use all the data. 4. It cannot be developed further in statistics.

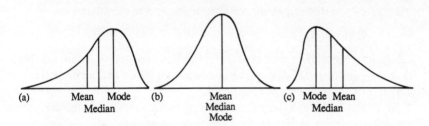

(a)   Mean   Mode   (b)   Mean   (c) Mode Mean
          Median   Median   Median
                                 Mode

Fig. 5.3 (a) left or negative skew; (b) symmetrical distribution; (c) right or positive skew.

median is sometimes used for lifetime averages since in the trials some of the data values can be 'still working at x hours'.

The mode is only rarely used and then only when the most frequent value is called for. The major place where the mode is quoted is in wage distributions, indicating the wage earned by the largest number of people.

For different shapes of data distribution these measures occur in certain orders. If the mean is smallest, median is next and the mode largest, then the distribution will be *left* or *negative* skew. If all three measures are approximately the same the distribution is fairly symmetrical. If the mode is the smallest value, the median is next and the mean is largest, then the distribution has *right* or *positive* skew. These are illustrated in Fig. 5.3.

As well as these measures of location there are other measures which are used in specific situations.

Table 5.15. Yearly sales figures for a company

Year	Sales (units)	Proportional growth	Percentage of previous year	Percentage growth
1983	100	—	—	—
1984	120	$\frac{120}{100} = 1.2000$	120.00	20.00
1985	160	$\frac{160}{120} = 1.3333$	133.33	33.33
1986	150	$\frac{150}{160} = 0.9375$	93.75	−6.25
1987	165	$\frac{165}{150} = 1.1000$	110.00	10.00

The geometric mean

If the average proportional growth rate over a number of time periods is required, then the measure of average is the *geometric mean*. It gives the average of a series of proportional changes and is calculated as

$$GM = \sqrt[n]{(x_1 x_2 x_3 \ldots x_n)}$$

i.e. the nth root of the product of the individual proportional changes. Note that the proportional changes must always be either proportions (i.e. 0.7, 1.3 etc.) or the percentage equivalent.

In Table 5.15 the sales of a company (with associated annual yearly growth rates) are given. To find the average growth rate, the geometric mean must be calculated.

Using the annual growth rates

$$\begin{aligned} GM &= \sqrt[4]{[(1.2)\,(1.3333)\,(0.9375)\,(1.1)]} \\ &= \sqrt[4]{(1.659)} \\ &= 1.1334 \end{aligned}$$

an average annual growth rate of 0.1334 or 13.34%. The geometric mean indicates that an annual rate of growth of 13.34%, sustained over 4 years, would lead to the latest sales figure.

The harmonic mean

The harmonic mean is an even more specialised measure of average. It is used to average rates and is mainly used for speeds and efficiency/productivity measures. The harmonic mean is calculated as

$$HM = \cfrac{1}{\cfrac{1}{n} \sum_{i=1}^{n} \cfrac{1}{x_i}}$$

and is the reciprocal of the mean of reciprocal values. Suppose a firm has spent £1,250 on machine parts at £1 each and £1,250 on machine parts at £1.25 each, then to establish the average price per part it is incorrect to take the average of the two unit prices.

In fact, 1,250 parts were purchased at the first price and a further 1,000 parts were purchased at the second price. The total price was £2,500 and, as 2,250 parts were purchased, their average price is

$$£\frac{2,500}{2,250} = £1.1111$$

Using the harmonic mean, this result is obtained directly as

$$HM = \cfrac{1}{\frac{1}{2}\left(\cfrac{1}{1.00} + \cfrac{1}{1.25}\right)} = \frac{1}{0.9}$$

$$= £1.1111 \text{ as expected.}$$

6

Measures of dispersion

Introduction

So far we have used measures of location as a summary of a set of data. To use this single value for comparing different distributions can lead to oversights since we are not using all the information available. In Fig. 6.1 histograms for two distributions are given.

Both sets of data have the same mean yet their distribution characteristics are rather different. The first set of data is much more closely grouped than the second set. Measures of dispersion are used to indicate the degree of spread or variation in a set of data and as such are usually linked with a particular location measure. The two measures together usually form an adequate summary of a set of data.

Standard deviation (and variance)

The most commonly used measure of dispersion is the standard deviation. It is usually calculated as the measure of dispersion for the arithmetic mean. Standard deviation is denoted by s and is calculated using the formula

$$s = \sqrt{\left[\frac{1}{n} \sum_{i=1}^{n} (x_i - \bar{x})^2\right]}$$

To calculate s, the deviations from the mean are first squared then added. This total is then divided by n and finally, a square root is taken so that the result obtained has the same units as the original data. If the square root is not taken, then the measure is called *variance*. Variance equals the square of standard deviation.

For the data of new car sales in Table 5.1 the standard deviation is calculated as shown in Table 6.1, giving $\bar{x} = 4$

$$s = \sqrt{\left[\frac{1}{7}(32)\right]}$$
$$= \sqrt{4.5714}$$
$$= 2.14$$

Table 6.1

x	$x - \bar{x}$	$(x - \bar{x})^2$
3	−1	1
8	4	16
4	0	0
5	1	1
2	−2	4
1	−3	9
5	1	1
28	0	32

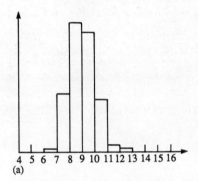 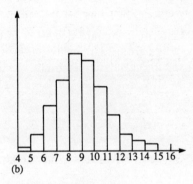

(a)   (b)

Fig. 6.1 Histograms of two distributions with equal means.

As an alternative method of calculation the formula

$$s = \sqrt{\frac{\sum_{i=1}^{n} x_i^2}{n} - x^2}$$

may be used but when using this formula the exact mean must be substituted and not just a rounded figure. The one major advantage of using this formula is the calculations can be done in two columns rather than three (see Table 6.2).

Table 6.2 leads to $\bar{x} = 4$

$$s = \sqrt{\left(\frac{144}{7} - 4^2\right)}$$

$$= \sqrt{(20.5714 - 16)}$$
$$= \sqrt{4.5714}$$
$$= 2.14 \text{ (as before)}$$

Table 6.2

x	x^2
3	9
8	64
4	16
5	25
2	4
1	1
5	25
28	144

Hence, the standard deviation of the number of cars sold is 2.14 cars.

For a grouped frequency table of discrete data the formulae which can be used for calculating standard deviation are

$$s = \sqrt{\left(\frac{\sum\limits_{i=1}^{n} f_i x_i^2}{\sum\limits_{i=1}^{n} f_i} - \frac{(\sum\limits_{i=1}^{n} f_i x_i)^2}{(\sum\limits_{i=1}^{n} f_i)^2} \right)}$$

or

$$s = \sqrt{\left(\frac{1}{\sum\limits_{i=1}^{n} f_i} \sum\limits_{i=1}^{n} f_i (x_i - \bar{x})^2 \right)}$$

The second of these *grouped frequency formulae* is generally easier to apply and is used to find the standard deviation for the data on numbers of employees absent, given in Table 5.3 (see Table 6.3):

$$\bar{x} = 0.94$$

$$s = \sqrt{\left(\frac{97}{50} - \frac{47^2}{50^2} \right)}$$

$$= \sqrt{(1.94 - 0.8836)}$$
$$= \sqrt{(1.0564)}$$
$$= 1.028$$

Hence, the standard deviation is 1.028 employees absent.

When the data is a class interval frequency table, the mid-points of the intervals are used as the x-values in the grouped frequency formulae for

Table 6.3

Number of employees absent (x)	Days (f)	fx	fx^2
0	17	0	0
1	26	26	26
2	3	6	12
3	2	6	18
4	1	4	16
5	1	5	25
	50	47	97

Table 6.4

Volume (ml)	Mid-point	Number (f)	fx	fx^2
240 but less than 245	242.5	6	1,455.0	352,837.50
245 but less than 250	247.5	21	5,197.5	1,286,381.25
250 but less than 255	252.5	174	43,935.0	11,093,587.50
255 but less than 260	257.5	47	12,102.5	3,116,393.75
260 but less than 265	262.5	2	525.0	137,812.50
		250	63,215.0	15,987,012.50

standard deviation. Open-ended intervals are treated in the same way as when calculating the arithmetic mean.

For the bottle volume data in Table 5.3 the standard deviation is laid out as in Table 6.4, which leads to

$$\bar{x} = 252.86$$

$$s = \sqrt{\left[\frac{15,987,012.50}{250} - \left(\frac{63,215.0}{250} \right)^2 \right]}$$

$$= \sqrt{(63,948.05 - 63,938.18)}$$
$$= \sqrt{9.8704}$$
$$= 3.142$$

so the standard deviation of bottle volume is 3.142 ml.

As can be seen in this example the numbers generated by the calculations rapidly become large and unmanageable. As with the arithmetic mean, there is an alternative method for calculating standard deviation. The approach is similar. Start by subtracting a suitable value from all data values. Denoted by A, this is again usually chosen as the smallest x-value. Repeating the calculations for the bottle volumes in Table 5.3, subtract

94   Measures of dispersion

Table 6.5

Mid-point (x)	x − A	$d=\frac{1}{5}(x-A)$	f	fd	fd²
242.5	0	0	6	0	0
247.5	5	1	21	21	21
252.5	10	2	174	348	696
257.5	15	3	47	141	423
262.5	20	4	2	8	32
			250	518	1,172

242.5 from all the mid-points (see Table 6.5). Next, divide by the class interval, C, to obtain d-values. The standard deviation is then found using the formula

$$s=C\sqrt{\left[\frac{\sum_{i=1}^{n} f_i d_i^2}{\sum_{i=1}^{n} f_i}-\left(\frac{\sum_{i=1}^{n} f_i d_i}{\sum_{i=1}^{n} f_i}\right)^2\right]}$$

which gives

$$s=5\sqrt{\left[\frac{1172}{250}-\left(\frac{518}{250}\right)^2\right]}$$

$$=5\sqrt{(4.688-4.2932)}$$
$$=5\sqrt{0.3948}$$
$$=5(0.62834)$$
$$=3.142$$

the same result as previously. It is especially noticeable in the calculation of standard deviation how much more manageable the figures are, an important fact if you have not got a calculator.

Quartile deviation

The quartile deviation is a measure of dispersion used with the median. The range covered by the middle half of the data distribution (called the inter-quartile range) is found; this is then halved to obtain the quartile deviation.

The quartile deviation shows how far away from the median the 25% and 75% points of the data distribution are, on average.

Before looking in detail at the quartile deviation it is necessary to see how to calculate *percentiles*. A percentile is the data value which corresponds to

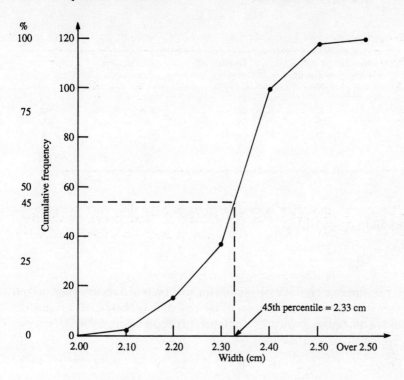

Fig. 6.2 Cumulative frequency curve for widths of 120 components.

a specified cumulative percentage. The 12 percentile is the value which corresponds to a cumulative percentage of 12% and similarly for any other percentage. Special names are used for some percentiles:

The 10, 20, 30, . . . percentiles are known as *deciles*.
  The 25 percentile is known as the *first quartile* (Q1).
  The 75 percentile is known as the *third quartile* (Q3).
  The 50 percentile is the *median*.

To find the percentiles a percentage cumulative frequency curve is drawn and the figures are read off for the appropriate percentage.

For the component width data in Table 5.6, the percentage cumulative frequency curve in Fig. 6.2 is obtained.

To find the 45th percentile, look up 45% on the cumulative frequency scale, read across to the curve and read off the corresponding value on the other scale. Here, the value is approximately 2.33 cm.

Table 6.6

Number of employees absent	Number of days	Cumulative frequency
0	17	17
1	26	43
2	3	46
3	2	48
4	1	49
5	1	50

The quartile deviation is calculated as half the difference between the third and first quartiles

$$QD = \frac{Q3 - Q1}{2}$$

This measurement is not easily found for small sets of data since the $(n/4)$th and $(3n/4)$th data values (in order) must be found. In these cases the median would be quoted on its own. The numbers of people employed at 20 factories on an industrial estate are:

33, 40, 15, 21, 36, 21, 18, 7, 48, 22, 33, 12, 19, 26, 17, 38, 27, 21, 30, 15

The quartile deviation is calculated as follows. To start, the data must be arranged in numerical order:

7, 12, 15, 15, 17, 18, 19, 21, 21, 21, 22, 26, 27, 30, 33, 33, 36, 38, 40, 48
            ↑   ↑
           Q1   Q3

There are twenty figures so the first quartile is the 5th figure in order.

$$Q1 = 17$$

The third quartile is the 15th value in order

$$Q3 = 33$$

The quartile deviation is then calculated as

$$QD = \frac{33 - 17}{2}$$

$$= 8 \text{ employees}$$

If the data is given as a discrete grouped frequency table then the quartile deviation is calculated after the cumulative frequencies have been found.

For the data on number of employees absent given in Table 5.2, the quartile deviation is found from the cumulative distribution shown in Table 6.6. The first quartile is given by the value for which cumulative frequency first equals or exceeds $n/4$, so for this example it is when 12.5 is reached. This total is first reached in the interval 'No employees absent' so

$$Q1 = 0$$

The third quartile is the value for which the cumulative frequency first equals or exceeds $3n/4$, so here it is when 37.5 is reached. This total is first reached in the interval '1 employee absent', so

$$Q3 = 1$$

Hence, the quartile deviation is

$$QD = \frac{1-0}{2}$$

$$= 0.5 \text{ employees}$$

When the data is in the form of a class interval frequency table the quartile deviation can be found by either a graphical or a calculation method. To use the graphical method, a cumulative frequency curve must be drawn. For the bottle volume data in Table 5.3 the cumulative frequency curve is given in Fig. 6.3. From the graph, the first quartile (corresponding to a cumulative frequency of 62.5) is approximately 251 ml. The third quartile (corresponding to a cumulative frequency of 187.5) is approximately 254.5 ml.

The quartile deviation is the

$$QD = \frac{254.5 - 251}{2}$$

$$= \frac{3.5}{2}$$

$$= 1.75 \text{ ml}$$

To calculate the quartile deviation, the first and third quartile must be calculated in much the same way that the median was calculated. As a first step, the interval which contains the first quartile must be found. This is the interval for which cumulative frequency first equals or exceeds $n/4$. The first quartile is then calculated using the formula

$$Q1 = L_{Q1} + (L_{Q1+1} - L_{Q1})\left[\frac{(n/4) - \Sigma f_{Q1-1}}{f_{Q1}}\right]$$

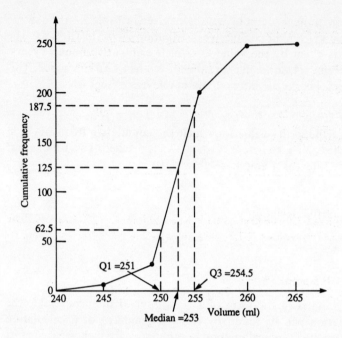

Fig. 6.3 Cumulative frequency curve for volumes of 250 shampoo bottles.

where L_{Q1} is the lower limit of the interval containing the first quartile, L_{Q1+1} is the upper limit of the interval containing the first quartile, Σf_{Q1-1} is the cumulative frequency up to the interval before the one containing the first quartile and f_{Q1} is the frequency for the interval containing the first quartile.

Similarly, to find the third quartile, the interval which contains it must be determined. This is the interval for which cumulative frequency first equals or exceeds $3n/4$. The third quartile is then found using the formula

$$Q3 = L_{Q3} + (L_{Q3+1} - L_{Q3})\left[\frac{(3n/4) - \Sigma f_{Q3-1}}{f_{Q3}}\right]$$

where L_{Q3} is the lower limit of the interval containing the third quartile, L_{Q3+1} is the upper limit of the interval containing the third quartile, Σf_{Q3-1} is the cumulative frequency for the interval before the one containing the third quartile and f_{Q3} is the frequency for the interval containing the third quartile.

To calculate the quartile deviation for the bottle volumes in Table 5.3, we first need a cumulative frequency column in the frequency table as given in Table 6.7.

Table 6.7. Cumulative frequency for volumes of 250 shampoo bottles

Volume (ml)	Frequency f	Cumulative frequency
240 but less than 245	6	6
245 but less than 250	21	27
250 but less than 255	174	201
255 but less than 260	47	248
260 but less than 265	2	250
	250	

Since $n/4$ equals 62.5, the first quartile is in the interval '250 but less than 255 ml'. Also, as $3n/4$ equals 187.5, the third quartile is also in this interval. Hence

$$L_{Q1} = 250, \ L_{Q1+1} = 255, \ \Sigma f_{Q1-1} = 27, \ f_{Q1} = 174$$
$$L_{Q3} = 250, \ L_{Q3+1} = 255, \ \Sigma f_{Q3-1} = 27, \ f_{Q3} = 174$$

and

$$Q1 = 250 + (255 - 250)\left[\frac{(62.5 - 27)}{174}\right]$$

$$= 251.020 \, \text{ml}$$

$$Q3 = 250 + (255 - 250)\left[\frac{(187.5 - 27)}{174}\right]$$

$$= 254.612 \, \text{ml}$$

The quartile deviation is then

$$QD = \frac{254.612 - 251.020}{2}$$

$$= 1.796 \, \text{ml}$$

The range

The range is the least commonly used measure of dispersion. It is simply the difference between the largest and smallest figure in the data. For the data of new cars sold in Table 5.1, the smallest figure is 1, the largest figure is 7, so the range is

$$R = 7 - 1 = 6 \, \text{cars}$$

Table 6.8. Family car ownership

Number of cars owned by family	Number of families
0	173
1	932
2	206
3	19
4	0

For a discrete grouped frequency table the same procedure can be used. For the data of employees absent in Table 5.2 the smallest figure is 0, the largest figure is 5, so the range is

$$R = 5 - 0 = 5 \text{ employees absent}$$

Care must be taken with the car ownership data in Table 6.8 since one of the end classes has a frequency of zero, i.e. there are no values of that size. The smallest value is 0, the largest value is 3 so the range is

$$R = 3 - 0 = 3 \text{ cars}$$

For class interval data the range cannot be found exactly. The best that can be done is to find the lower limit of the first interval and use it as the smallest value. Then find the upper limit of the last interval and use this as the largest value. If there is an open-ended interval then the range cannot be found.

For the bottle volume data of Table 5.3 the lower limit of the first interval is 240 ml and the upper limit of the last interval is 265 ml, so the range is

$$R = 265 - 240 = 25 \text{ ml.}$$

Comparison of standard deviation, quartile deviation and range

These measures of dispersion have the advantages and disadvantages shown in Table 6.9.

These measures of dispersion are rarely quoted on their own. Standard deviation is quoted with the mean and so is the most commonly used. The quartile deviation is quoted with the median and can be particularly helpful if the data is skewed. The range, although rarely used, is to be found in statistical quality control work where a simple measure of dispersion is required. In these circumstances it is used with the mean, so replacing the standard deviation. All measures of dispersion get larger as the data becomes more widely spread.

Table 6.9. Measures of dispersion: advantages and disadvantages

	Advantages	Disadvantages
Standard deviation	1. It measures spread about the mean, making it a natural partner for the mean. 2. It is representative of all the data since all values are used in its calculation. 3. It is important in further statistical work.	1. It cannot cope with extreme or open-ended values very well. 2. It is not particularly useful for skewed data. 3. The answer is difficult to visualise.
Quartile deviation	1. It is the natural partner to the median. 2. It is easy to visualise as indicating approximately 50% of values are within a quartile deviation either side of the median.	1. It is rather awkward to calculate. 2. It may not be representative if there are few values.
Range	1. It is very simple to calculate. 2. It is easy to visualise.	1. It is easily influenced by extreme values. 2. There is no natural measure of location as a partner.

The coefficient of variation

Standard deviation is an absolute measure of dispersion and has the same units as the original data. When making comparisons a more appropriate method might be to consider relative variation, independent of units. The coefficient of variation is the ratio of the standard deviation and mean, given as a percentage, and so is unit-free.

$$CV = \left(\frac{s}{\bar{x}} \times 100 \right)\%$$

Suppose a company makes two components, each being produced on a different machine. The first component is made on machine 1 and the lengths of the components have

$$\bar{x} = 2.50 \, \text{cm}, \qquad s_1 = 0.30 \, \text{cm}$$

The second component is made on machine 2 and the lengths of these components have

$$\bar{x}_2 = 20.00 \, \text{cm}, \qquad s_2 = 1.25 \, \text{cm}$$

If the standard deviations are compared then the variation or spread of values caused by machine 2 is much greater. However, the components produced on this machine are themselves much larger. By calculating the coefficient of variation for each length a fairer comparison can be made.

$$\text{Component 1} \qquad \text{CV} = \frac{0.30}{2.50} \times 100 = 12\%$$

$$\text{Component 2} \qquad \text{CV} = \frac{0.25}{20.00} \times 100 = 6.25\%$$

so, relatively, machine 2 causes less variability.

This measure is especially useful where different units are used and just converting from one set of units to the other is not entirely satisfactory for making comparisons. If the variation in consumer spending in Japan and the United Kingdom are to be compared, then the standard deviation figure, in yen, for Japan could be converted into sterling. This, however, does not take account of relative wealth in Japan and the United Kingdom. By calculating the coefficient of variation such effects are removed.

If the median and quartile deviation have been found, then there are two similar coefficients which can be calculated. The *quartile coefficient of dispersion* is the ratio of the quartile deviation and the median, quoted as a percentage. It is analogous to the coefficient of variation:

$$\text{QCD} = \frac{\text{quartile deviation}}{\text{median}} \times 100\%$$

$$= \frac{Q3 - Q1}{2M} \times 100\%$$

An alternative measure is the *coefficient of quartile deviation* which is the difference between the third and first quartiles, divided by their sum, this ratio being given as a percentage.

$$\text{CQD} = \frac{Q3 - Q1}{Q1 + Q3} \times 100\%$$

Although it looks quite different from the previous measure, the sum of the first and third quartiles is similar to twice the median. This leads to similar values being obtained from the quartile coefficient of dispersion and the coefficient of quartile deviation.

Skewness

Skewness measures to what extent a distribution is non-symmetrical. A distribution is said to have *left* or *negative skew* if the distribution has a long tail of values to the left. Similarly, if the tail of values is to the right side of the distribution it is called *right* or *positive skew*. To identify whether a

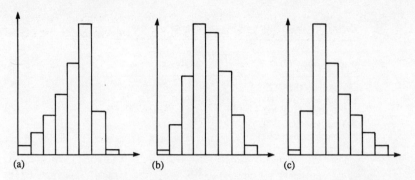

Fig. 6.4 Histograms of (a) left skew, (b) symmetrical and (c) right skew
distributions.

distribution is skewed a histogram is usually drawn and in Fig. 6.4 examples
of left skew, symmetrical and right skew distributions are given.

Many measures of skewness can be used. The most common is the
Pearson coefficient of skewness, calculated as

$$\text{Pearson's coefficient of skewness} = \frac{3(\text{mean} - \text{median})}{\text{standard deviation}}$$

$$\text{PCS} = \frac{3(\bar{x} - M)}{s}$$

This coefficient can take any value from -3 to $+3$. If the coefficient is
negative then the data has a left skew distribution, if the coefficient is zero
there is no skewness (a symmetrical distribution) and if the coefficient is
positive then the data has a right skew distribution. Any coefficient smaller
than -1 or larger than $+1$ indicates a high degree of skewness.

For the income data in Table 6.10 the calculations for the coefficient of
skewness are given in Table 6.11.

$$\bar{x} = \frac{17,600}{100} = £176$$

$$M = 160 + 40\left[\frac{50 - 45}{29}\right]$$

$$= 166.90$$

$$s = \sqrt{\left(\frac{3,288,000}{100} - (176)^2\right)}$$

$$= \sqrt{(32,880 - 30,976)}$$
$$= \sqrt{1,904}$$
$$= £43.63$$

Table 6.10. Distribution of weekly salaries

Weekly salary (£)	Number of employees
80 but less than 120	3
120 but less than 160	42
160 but less than 200	29
200 but less than 240	16
240 but less than 280	8
280 or over	2
	100

Table 6.11. Calculations for skewness of weekly salary data

Weekly salary (£) mid-point x	Number of employees (f)	fx	fx^2	Cumulative frequency
100	3	300	30,000	3
140	42	5,880	823,200	45
180	29	5,220	939,600	74
220	16	3,520	774,400	90
260	8	2,080	540,800	98
300	2	600	180,000	100
	100	17,600	3,288,000	

The Pearson coefficient of skewness is then

$$PCS = \frac{3(176 - 166.90)}{43.63}$$

$$= 0.626$$

a positive value indicating a degree of right skew in the data distribution.

A second measure of skewness sometimes used is the quartile coefficient of skewness. It is calculated using the formula

$$QCS = \frac{Q3 + Q1 - 2M}{Q3 - Q1}$$

For the income data the quartiles are

$$Q1 = 120 + 40\left[\frac{(25 - 3)}{42}\right]$$

$$= 140.95$$

$$Q3 = 200 + 40\left[\frac{(75-74)}{16}\right]$$

$$= £202.50$$

The quartile coefficient of skewness is then calculated as

$$QCS = \frac{202.50 + 140.95 - 2(166.90)}{202.50 - 140.95}$$

$$= \frac{9.65}{61.55}$$

$$= 0.156$$

7

Linear functions and equations

Introduction

The most basic concept in mathematics is that of the *variable*, i.e. a quantity that changes its (numerical) value. Production costs, quantities sold, selling prices, stock levels, manpower employed are all examples of variables from the business environment.

Obviously rules exist, or theories are put forward, that express relationships between variables. In other words, relationships exist that determine how changes in one variable can cause changes in a second variable. Examples of this are how total production costs increase as the quantity made increases, or how the quantity sold increases as the price charged decreases. These relationships are called *functions* and if we know, or believe, that a variable y changes as a result of a second variable x changing then we say that

y is a function of x

and write this mathematically as

$y = f(x)$

Naturally, much deeper analysis can be achieved only if the actual functional relationship is known. A particularly common type of functional relationship is called the *linear function*.

Linear functions

The properties of the linear function will be described with reference to the example of the total production costs as a function of quantity made.

Firstly, a number of costs are independent of the quantity made. In fact, assuming that the plant would still exist, these costs would still be incurred if no production occurred at all. These costs are called *fixed costs* and may include such things as heating and lighting of the buildings, rates, administration, and the cost of purchasing the plant.

Table 7.1. Tabulation for $T = 10,000 + 1.5q$

				q			
	0	5,000	10,000	15,000	20,000	25,000	30,000
T	10,000	17,500	25,000	32,500	40,000	47,500	55,000

In contrast to these costs, there are others that do depend upon the quantity made. These include the cost of the materials used, the manpower required, and the electricity used to run the plant. These costs are called *variable costs*, and if they are averaged out to give the variable cost of making one unit of product, then the *total cost* can be evaluated.

For example, if the fixed costs of running the plant, producing a certain product, for a year are £10,000 and the variable cost of producing one unit is £1.50, then the total cost of producing 5,000 units is

$$10,000 + (5,000 \times 1.50) = 10,000 + 7,500 = £17,500$$

and the total cost of producing 20,000 units is

$$10,000 + (20,000 \times 1.50) = 10,000 + 30,000 = £40,000$$

In general, if the fixed cost of the process is c and the variable unit cost is m, then the total cost T of producing a batch of q units is

$$T = c + mq$$

This is a typical *linear equation*.

In the above example, $c = 10,000$ and $m = 1.5$ and so

$$T = 10,000 + 1.5q$$

If a graph of this equation were to be drawn, plotting the values of q, the quantity made, along the horizontal axis and the values of T, the total cost, along the vertical axis, the figures shown in Table 7.1 would be obtained, giving Fig. 7.1.

It is seen that all the points lie on a *straight line* and this is why the relationship is called *linear*.

It is possible to determine the form of the linear equation from just two points on it.

Suppose, for example, we have a situation in which we are told that

1. Total cost $= £1,200$ when $q = 300$.
2. Total cost $= £2,000$ when $q = 700$.

Then we have

$$1,200 = c + 300m \tag{1}$$

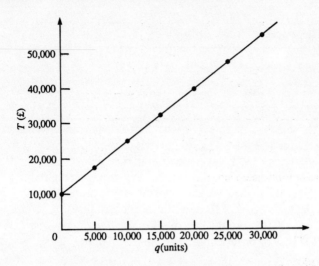

Fig. 7.1 Graph of $T = 10,000 + 1.5q$.

and

$$2,000 = c + 700m \qquad (2)$$

From (1)

$$c = 1,200 - 300m$$

and from (2)

$$c = 2,000 - 700m$$

Then

$$1,200 - 300m = 2,000 - 700m$$

or

$$700m - 300m = 2,000 - 1,200$$

that is

$$400m = 800$$

which gives

$$m = 2$$

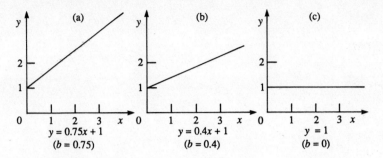

Fig. 7.2 Lines with differing slopes.

Then, substituting in (1)

$$1{,}200 = c + (300 \times 2)$$
$$1{,}200 = c + 600$$
$$c = 1{,}200 - 600$$

that is

$$c = 600$$

Then the equation is now

$$T = 600 + 2q$$

i.e. the fixed cost is £600 and the unit variable cost is £2.

Intercept and gradient

In general terms, where

$$y = a + bx$$

then a is called the *intercept*. It is the point where the line crosses the vertical axis and is the value of y when $x = 0$.

In Fig. 7.2 note that each line has the same intercept, i.e. the same value of a (= 1).

The only visual difference between the three lines, is that they each slope differently. Mathematically the difference is that they each have different values of b. Hence b is the measure of the slope of the line and is called the *gradient of the line*.

For the line

$$y = a + bx$$

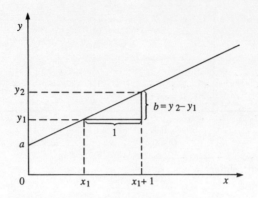

Fig. 7.3 Intercept and slope.

suppose

$$y = y_1 \text{ when } x = x_1$$

and

$$y = y_2 \text{ when } x = (x_1 + 1)$$

This is, if x increases from x_1 by 1, then the new value of y is y_2. Then

$$y_1 = a + bx_1 \tag{1}$$

and

$$y_2 = a + b(x_1 + 1)$$

or

$$y_2 = a + bx_1 + b \tag{2}$$

From (1) we see that

$$a = y_1 - bx_1$$

and from (2) that

$$a = y_2 - bx_1 - b$$

Hence

$$y_1 - bx_1 = y_2 - bx_1 - b$$

or

$$bx_1 + b - bx_1 = y_2 - y_1$$

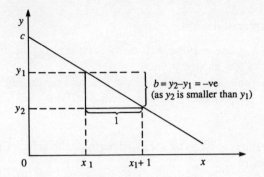

Fig. 7.4 Negative slope.

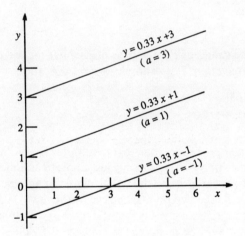

Fig. 7.5 Lines with differing intercepts.

i.e.

$$b = y_2 - y_1$$

Hence, *the gradient of the line is the amount y increases for an increase in x of 1* (see Fig. 7.3).

Note that if a line slopes *downwards*, then y decreases as x *increases* and the gradient of the line is *negative* (see Fig. 7.4).

Finally, if a number of lines have different intercepts but the same gradient then the lines are *parallel*. A negative intercept implies that the line crosses the y-axis below the origin. (See Fig. 7.5.)

Interpolation and extrapolation

It has been shown how a line may be well defined, either graphically or mathematically, from as few as two points.

For example, it has already been seen that the line passing through the points $T = 1,200$ when $q = 300$ and $T = 2,000$ when $q = 700$ is

$$T = 600 + 2q$$

Either the equation or the graph can be used to determine the value of T for various different values of q.

If it is required to determine the value of T for a value of q *between the two given points* this is called *interpolation*. For example, if $q = 450$, then

$$\begin{aligned} T &= 600 + (2 \times 450) \\ &= 600 + 900 \\ &= 1,500 \end{aligned}$$

If we wish to determine the values of T for a value of q *outside the two given points*, this is called *extrapolation*. For example, if $q = 1,000$, then

$$\begin{aligned} T &= 600 + (2 \times 1,000) \\ &= 600 + 2,000 \\ &= 2,600 \end{aligned}$$

Interpolation is a much safer procedure than extrapolation. Given that the relationship exists at the two points it is probably justifiable to assume that it exists between them. However, it is much less justifiable to assume that the relationship exists outside the two points, and the further away a point is from either of them the more unlikely it is that it does. For example, the production cost equation would be meaningless for negative values of q, and if $q = 2,000,000$ we would probably require a much larger plant, where the fixed costs would then be much bigger. It is useful, whenever possible, to give the range over which the relationship exists: for example, the equation above could be presented as

$$T = 600 + 2q \qquad (0 \leqslant q \leqslant 1,200)$$

Simultaneous equations

Often two (or more) graphs are drawn on the same axes and it is required to find where they intersect. (This has been discussed briefly in Chapter 1.) Naturally, in such a case the variables in the equations of each graph must be the same. For example, if the two graphs are of the equations

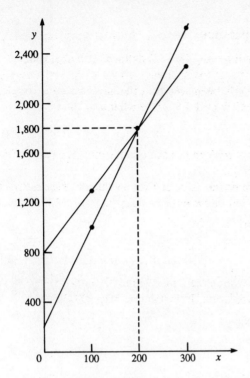

Fig. 7.6 Intercepting lines: a particular case.

$$y = 5x + 800$$

and

$$y = 8x + 200$$

they can be drawn as shown in Fig. 7.6.

The graphs show that the intersection occurs when $x = 200$ and $y = 1,800$ on each line.

In general terms, therefore, the problem is to find the value of x such that

$$y = a_1 + b_1 x$$

and

$$y = a_2 + b_2 x$$

give the same value of y. That is, the same value of x in each equation *simultaneously* gives the same value of y in each equation, and this situation is known as *simultaneous equations*.

To find the value of x:

$$y = a_1 + b_1 x$$

and

$$y = a_2 + b_2 x$$

Hence

$$a_1 + b_1 x = a_2 + b_2 x$$

or

$$b_1 x - b_2 x = a_2 - a_1$$
$$(b_1 - b_2)x = a_2 - a_1$$

$$x = \frac{a_2 - a_1}{b_1 - b_2}$$

Note that, if $b_1 = b_2$, x and y cannot be found, as one would be dividing by $b_1 - b_2 = 0$. This is consistent with what has been found earlier in the chapter (under 'Intercept and gradient'). If $b_1 = b_2$, then the lines are parallel and so there is no point of intersection.

The common value of y is given by

$$y = \frac{b_1(a_2 - a_1)}{b_1 - b_2} + a_1$$

$$= \frac{b_1(a_2 - a_1) + a_1(b_1 - b_2)}{b_1 - b_2)}$$

$$= \frac{b_1 a_2 - b_1 a_1 + b_1 a_1 - b_2 a_1}{b_1 - b_2}$$

$$= \frac{b_1 a_2 - b_2 a_1}{b_1 - b_2}$$

The example considered earlier could have been solved in the same way. If

$$y = 5x + 800$$

and

$$y = 8x + 200$$

Then

$$8x + 200 = 5x + 800$$
$$8x - 5x = 800 - 200$$
$$3x = 600$$
$$x = 200$$

and

$$y = (5 \times 200) + 800$$
$$= 1,000 + 800$$
$$= 1,800$$

An example will now be considered from the general business area of the application of simultaneous equations.

Break-even point

It has already been established that the total cost equation of a production process takes the form

$$T = mq + c$$

Suppose each unit of product is sold at a price p. Then the total revenue R is given by

$$R = pq$$

It is required to know where the production process *breaks even*, i.e. where the total cost equals the total revenue,

$$R = T$$

or

$$pq = mq + c$$

i.e.

$$pq - mq = c$$
$$(p - m)q = c$$

$$q = \frac{c}{p - m}$$

This is shown in Fig. 7.7.

The significance of a break-even point is that if less than this quantity is produced a loss is incurred, but if more than this quantity is produced a profit is obtained.

For a numerical example, in addition to the total cost equation obtained earlier,

$$T = 2q + 600$$

there is a revenue equation

$$R = 6q$$

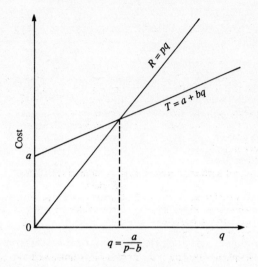

Fig. 7.7 Intercepting lines: a more general case.

i.e. a price of £6 is charged for each unit of product.

Then the break-even point is given by

$$R = T$$

i.e.

$$6q = 2q + 600$$

or

$$6q - 2q = 600$$
$$4q = 600$$
$$q = 150$$

Therefore, if less than 150 units are made then a loss is incurred, but if more than 150 units are made then a profit is produced (see Fig. 7.8).

Another consideration could be to determine the production quantity that produces a required level of profit. Hence, if we have as before

$$T = mq + c$$

and

$$R = pq$$

but now require a profit P from the production, then the revenue must do more than just break even and, in fact, produce a surplus of P. That is

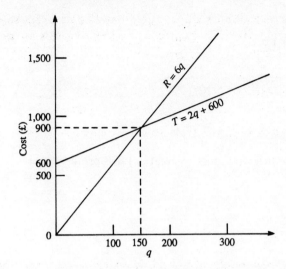

Fig. 7.8 Intercepting lines: a particular case.

$$R = T + P$$

Then

$$pq = mq + c + P$$

i.e.

$$pq - mq = c + P$$

or

$$(p - m)q = c + P$$

Giving

$$q = \frac{c + P}{p - m}$$

In our numerical example, where

$$T = 2q + 600$$

and

$$R = 6q$$

if we required a profit of £1,000 then

$$R = T + 1,000$$

We must, therefore, have

$$6q = 2q + 600 + 1,000$$

i.e.

$$4q = 1,600$$

or

$$q = 400$$

Therefore, we must produce 400 units to create £1,000 profit.

8

Quadratic functions and equations

Quadratic functions

Obviously not all relationships can be represented by linear functions or straight lines. If a continuous relationship exists that cannot be shown graphically by a straight line, then it is shown by a *curve* and the relationship is said to be a *non-linear function*. Just one non-linear function will be investigated here, the *quadratic function*.

A quadratic function depicting the relationship between y and x is, in general terms, given by

$$y = ax^2 + bx + c$$

If it is certain that a quadratic relationship exists, then three points are required to determine the values of a, b, and c.

For example, suppose it is known

1. $y = 5$ when $x = 1$
2. $y = 10$ when $x = 2$
3. $y = 19$ when $x = 3$

Then to find a, b, and c we must solve three simultaneous linear equations.

$$5 = a + b + c \tag{1}$$

$$10 = 4a + 2b + c \tag{2}$$

$$19 = 9a + 3b + c \tag{3}$$

Subtracting (1) from (2) gives

$$5 = 3a + b \tag{4}$$

and, subtracting (2) from (3) gives

$$9 = 5a + b \tag{5}$$

Next, subtract (4) from (5) to get

$$4 = 2a$$

or

$$a = 2$$

Then, from (4)

$$5 = 6 + b$$
$$b = 5 - 6$$

or

$$b = -1$$

Then finally, from (1)

$$5 = 2 - 1 + c$$
$$5 = 1 + c$$
$$c = 5 - 1$$

or

$$c = 4$$

Therefore, the relationship is

$$y = 2x^2 - x + 4$$

Notice, as in the linear form, that c gives the *intercept* on the vertical axis, i.e. the value of y when x is zero.

The graph of a quadratic relationship has the forms given in Fig. 8.1 for different signs of the values of a, b, and c. Note that in each case we show $c > 0$.

Notice that the curve has a *turning point*; either a *minimum point* as in (a) and (b) or a *maximum point* as in (c) and (d). The turning point is found when

$$x = -\frac{b}{2a}$$

and has the value

$$y = c - \frac{b^2}{4a}$$

although proof of this is beyond the scope of this book.

If $b = 0$, then the curve has the form shown in Fig. 8.2, with the turning point occurring when $x = 0$ giving a function value of $y = c$.

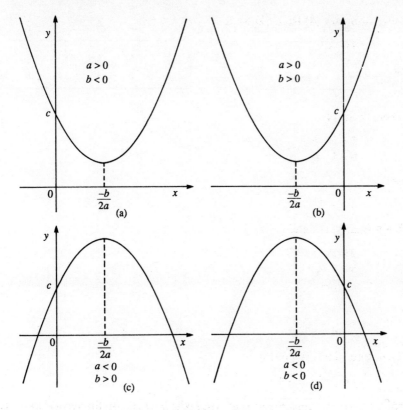

Fig. 8.1 Four forms of quadratic graph.

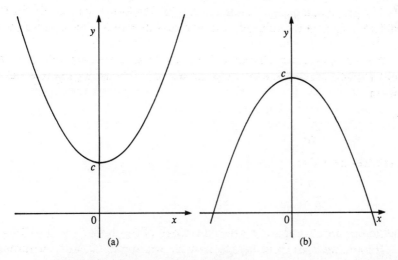

Fig. 8.2 Quadratic graphs with $b = 0$.

Table 8.1. Tabulation for $y = 2x^2 - x + 4$

x	-1	$-\frac{1}{2}$	0	$\frac{1}{2}$	1	$\frac{3}{2}$	2
$2x^2$	2	$\frac{1}{2}$	0	$\frac{1}{2}$	2	$\frac{9}{2}$	8
$y = 2x^2 - x + 4$	7	5	4	4	5	7	10

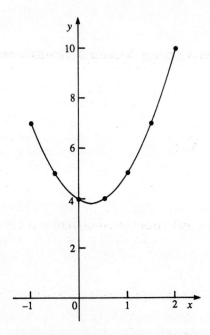

Fig. 8.3 Graph of $y = 2x^2 - x - 4$.

Considering the quadratic relationship described earlier

$$y = 2x^2 - x + 4$$

where $a = 2$, $b = -1$, $c = 4$. Then, since $a > 0$, $b < 0$, $c > 0$, the shape of the curve is as shown in Fig. 8.1(a). The minimum point is at

$$x = -\frac{(-1)}{(2)(2)} = \tfrac{1}{4}$$

where

$$y = 4 - \frac{(-1)^2}{(4)(2)}$$

$$= 4 - \tfrac{1}{8} = 3\tfrac{7}{8}$$

This can be confirmed by plotting the relationship as shown in Table 8.1 and Fig. 8.3.

Quadratic equations

Consider two quadratic total cost functions

$$T = 2q^2 - 4q + 9 \qquad (1)$$

and

$$T = q^2 + q + 3 \qquad (2)$$

It is required to find the values of q giving the same total costs in each case, i.e. to solve

$$2q^2 - 4q + 9 = q^2 + q + 3$$

or

$$2q^2 - 4q + 9 - q^2 - q - 3 = 0$$

giving

$$q^2 - 5q + 6 = 0$$

To find the values of q that will make this expression zero, it is first written as

$$(q-2)(q-3) = 0$$

This is easily shown to be the same as the original expression by multiplying out the brackets to get

$$q^2 - 2q - 3q + 6 = q^2 - 5q + 6$$

It can now be seen that zero is obtained when either $q=2$ or $q=3$; i.e. if 2 or 3 units are made then the costs are the same.

To determine these values it was necessary to solve a *quadratic equation*, the general form of which is

$$ax^2 + bx + c = 0$$

Sometimes quadratic equations can be solved by *factors*. This is done as follows. Firstly rewrite the quadratic equation as

$$x^2 + (b/a)x + (c/a) = 0$$

or

$$x^2 + mx + n = 0$$

where

$$m = b/a \qquad \text{and} \qquad n = c/a$$

If factors p and q exist, this means that the quadratic can be written as

$$(x+p)(x+q)=0$$

i.e.

$$(x+p)(x+q)=x^2+mx+n$$

Multiplying the factors out gives

$$(x+p)(x+q)=x^2+px+qx+pq$$
$$=x^2+(p+q)x+pq$$

and so

$$x^2+(p+q)x+pq=x^2+mx+n$$

Hence,

$$p+q=m \quad \text{and} \quad pq=n$$

Therefore, we must find two numbers p and q such that

$$p+q=m$$

and

$$pq=n$$

The most straightforward way of doing this is to firstly list all the pairs of numbers that multiply together to give n and then pick from these a pair that add together to give m.

Example
Solve

$$x^2+7x+12=0$$

It is required that

$$(x+p)(x+q)=x^2+7x+12$$

where

$$p+q=7 \text{ and } pq=12$$

List all the possible values for $pq=12$:

$p=1, q=12$	$p=-1, q=-12$
$p=2, q=6$	$p=-2, q=-6$
$p=3, q=4$	$p=-3, q=-4$

Choose a pair of these such that

$$p+q=7$$

i.e.

$$p=3, \ q=4$$

Then

$$x^2+7x+12=0$$

is

$$(x+3)(x+4)=0$$

Hence

$$x=-3 \text{ or } x=-4$$

Example
Solve

$$x^2-3x-10=0$$

It is required that

$$(x+p)(x+q)=x^2-3x-10$$

where

$$p+q=-3 \quad \text{and} \quad pq=-10$$

List all the possible values for $pq=-10$:

$$p=-1, \ q=10 \qquad p=1, \ q=-10$$
$$p=-2, \ q=5 \qquad p=2, \ q=-5$$

Choose a pair of these such that

$$p+q=-3$$

i.e.

$$p=2, \ q=-5$$

Then

$$x^2-3x-10=0$$

is

$$(x+2)(x-5)=0$$

Hence

$$x=-2 \quad \text{or} \quad x=5$$

When the factors cannot easily be found by this method recourse must be made to the *quadratic formula*. In fact, this formula can be used any time to solve a quadratic equation.

The quadratic formula

It is required to solve

$$ax^2 + bx + c = 0$$

or

$$x^2 + (b/a)x + c/a = 0$$

Notice that

$$\left(x + \frac{b}{2a}\right)^2 = x^2 + \frac{b}{2a}x + \frac{b}{2a}x + \frac{b^2}{4a^2}$$

$$= x^2 + \frac{b}{a}x + \frac{b^2}{4a^2}$$

or

$$x^2 + \frac{b}{a}x = \left(x + \frac{b}{2a}\right)^2 - \frac{b^2}{4a^2}$$

Then

$$x^2 + \frac{b}{a}x + \frac{c}{a} = 0$$

becomes

$$\left(x + \frac{b}{2a}\right)^2 - \frac{b^2}{4a^2} + \frac{c}{a} = 0$$

or

$$\left(x + \frac{b}{2a}\right)^2 = \frac{b^2}{4a^2} - \frac{c}{a}$$

$$= \frac{b^2 - 4ac}{4a^2}$$

Hence

$$x + \frac{b}{2a} = \pm \sqrt{\left(\frac{b^2 - 4ac}{4a^2}\right)}$$

because there is a positive and a negative square root for any positive number, i.e.

$$x + \frac{b}{2a} = \pm \frac{\sqrt{(b^2 - 4ac)}}{2a}$$

or

$$x = -\frac{b}{2a} \pm \frac{\sqrt{(b^2 - 4ac)}}{2a}$$

Hence the required values of x can be found by

$$x = \frac{-b \pm \sqrt{(b^2 - 4ac)}}{2a}$$

Notice that, since it is possible to find the square root of only a non-negative number, the quadratic equation

$$ax^2 + bx + c = 0$$

has a solution only if

$$b^2 - 4ac \geqslant 0$$

i.e.

$$b^2 \geqslant 4ac$$

If

$$b^2 > 4ac$$

then the quadratic equation has two different solutions, but if

$$b^2 = 4ac$$

then the two solutions to the quadratic equation are the *same*.

Consider the quadratic formula applied to a second example of equal total costs.

Suppose

$$T = 0.1q^2 + 65q + 1{,}100 \tag{1}$$

and

$$T = 0.06q^2 + 74q + 1{,}300 \tag{2}$$

Then the quantities equating these two costs are given by

$$0.1q^2 + 65q + 1{,}100 = 0.06q^2 + 74q + 1{,}300$$

or

$$0.04q^2 - 9q - 200 = 0$$

i.e. in the quadratic formula $a=0.04$, $b=-9$, $c=-200$, so

$$q\frac{-(-9)\pm\sqrt{[(-9)^2-(4)(0.04)(-200)]}}{(2)(0.04)}$$

$$=\frac{9\pm\sqrt{(81+32)}}{0.08}$$

$$=\frac{9\pm\sqrt{113}}{0.08}$$

$$=\frac{9\pm10.63}{0.08}$$

$$=\frac{19.63}{0.08}\text{ or }-\frac{1.63}{0.08}$$

$$=245.4\text{ or }-20.4$$

As a production quantity -20.4 is meaningless, the costs are the same when 245.4 units are produced.

Break-even point

As was done before with the linear cost function, it is useful to look again at the profit-and-loss situation with a quadratic total cost function.

Suppose we have a total cost function

$$T=aq^2+bq+c$$

for the production of a product that sells at £p per unit. Then, as before, the revenue function is given by

$$R=pq$$

For break-even we have

$$T=R$$

i.e.

$$aq^2+bq+c=pq$$

or

$$aq^2+(b-p)q+c=0$$

Hence, the values of q that break even are found by solving another quadratic equation.

For example, if

$$T = 0.02q^2 + 5q + 800$$

and

$$R = 18q$$

then for break even,

$$0.02q^2 + 5q + 800 = 18q$$

or

$$0.02q^2 - 13q + 800 = 0$$

giving

$$q = \frac{13 \pm \sqrt{[169 - (4)(0.02)(800)]}}{0.04}$$

$$= \frac{13 \pm \sqrt{(169 - 64)}}{0.04}$$

$$= \frac{13 \pm \sqrt{105}}{0.04}$$

$$= \frac{13 \pm 10.25}{0.04}$$

$$= \frac{23.25}{0.04} \text{ or } \frac{2.75}{0.04}$$

$$= 581.25 \text{ or } 68.75$$

Therefore, for break even the quantity produced should be 581.25 or 68.75. Now if

$$R > T$$

then a profit is made, but if

$$R < T$$

then a loss is incurred.

From Fig. 8.4 it is seen that, to make a profit, between 68.75 and 581.25 units should be produced. However, if less than 68.75 units or more than 581.25 units are produced a loss is incurred.

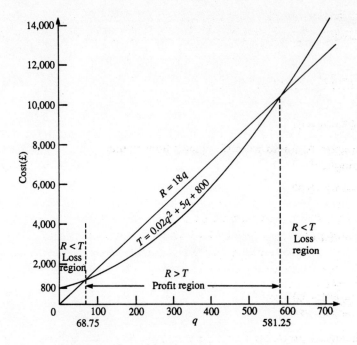

Fig. 8.4 Profit and loss regions.

Demand function

It is often assumed that the quantity sold of a product is related to its price, in such a way that the cheaper it becomes the more will be sold. Usually the relationship is taken to be linear. That is

$$p = a - bq$$

Notice that b is assumed to be positive here, so that the gradient is *negative*, to indicate that as q increases, p decreases.

If we are again interested in break-even analysis our revenue function is now

$$R = pq$$
$$= (a - bq)q$$
$$= aq - bq^2$$

Assuming a linear total cost function

$$T = mq + c$$

we get break even when

$$R = T$$

or

$$aq - bq^2 = mq + c$$

i.e.

$$bq^2 + (m - a)q + c = 0$$

and q can again be found from the quadratic formula.
For example, if

$$p = 10 - 0.02q$$

and

$$T = 600 + 2q$$

Then

$$R = pq$$
$$= (10 - 0.02q)q$$
$$= 10q - 0.02q^2$$

and break even is given by

$$R = T$$

or

$$10q - 0.02q^2 = 600 + 2q$$

i.e.

$$0.02q^2 - 8q + 600 = 0$$

$$q = \frac{8 \pm \sqrt{[64 - (4)(0.02)(600)]}}{0.04}$$

$$= \frac{8 \pm \sqrt{[64 - 48]}}{0.04}$$

$$= \frac{8 \pm \sqrt{16}}{0.04}$$

$$= \frac{8 \pm 4}{0.04}$$

$$= \frac{12}{0.04} \text{ or } \frac{4}{0.04}$$

$$= 300 \text{ or } 100$$

Therefore, if between 100 and 300 units are produced a profit is made, but if less than 100 or more than 300 units are produced a loss is incurred.

The *profit function* is given by

$$P = R - T$$
$$= aq - bq^2 - mq - c$$
$$= (a - m)q - bq^2 - c$$

The *maximum profit* is given by

$$P = \frac{(a - m)^2}{4b} - c$$

when

$$q = \frac{a - m}{2b}$$

But, again, the proof of these results is beyond the scope of this book.

However, applying these formulae to our example, we have $a = 10$, $b = 0.02$ (remember we described the demand relationship as $p = a - bq$ to emphasise that its gradient was negative), $c = 600$, $m = 2$. Hence

$$P = \frac{(10 - 2)^2}{(4)(0.02)} - 600$$

$$= \frac{(8)^2}{0.08} - 600$$

$$= \frac{64}{0.08} - 600$$

$$= 800 - 600$$
$$= 200$$

and

$$q = \frac{10 - 2}{(2)(0.02)}$$

$$= \frac{8}{0.04}$$

$$= 200$$

Therefore, a maximum profit of £200 is achieved when 200 units are produced.

9

Regression and correlation

Introduction

In many business situations it is useful to be able to relate one measurement to another. For instance, it may be required to relate overall costs to the number of employees. The simplest relationship is a straight line or linear equation. There are many methods for finding an equation to fit a set of data. A simple method is to draw a scatter diagram and draw on a line by eye. This can be a hit-and-miss approach and more formal methods are also available. These are called *regression techniques*.

One of the more common reasons for fitting an equation is so that it can be used for predicting what will happen given certain changes. To assess how good these predictions might be, some indication of how close our data is to a straight line relationship is needed. The *correlation coefficient* is used for this purpose.

Scatter diagrams

In any situation where a relationship between two measurements is to be found the starting point should be a scatter diagram. The scatter diagram gives an indication of what sort of equation is appropriate. For example, suppose a company wishes to relate packaging time to the number of items being packaged. If the company collected the data given in Table 9.1 then the appropriate scatter diagram is as shown in Fig. 9.1.

To draw the scatter diagram it is necessary to decide which measurement goes on which axis. The vertical or *y*-axis is usually used for the measurement to be predicted. It is the axis for the *dependent* variable. The horizontal or *x*-axis is used for the measurement that can be set or fixed. This is the *independent* variable. In Table 9.1 the time taken to package the items results from the number of items being packaged so 'time taken' is the dependent or *y*-variable, 'number of items' is the independent or *x*-variable. Further, our interest is in forecasting the time taken to package a number of items rather than the number of items, so again indicating 'time taken' is the *y*-variable.

Table 9.1. Packaging time for varying
numbers of items

Packaging time (min)	Number of items
65	10
62	9
42	6
33	5
24	3
44	8
69	12
90	14
26	4
86	13

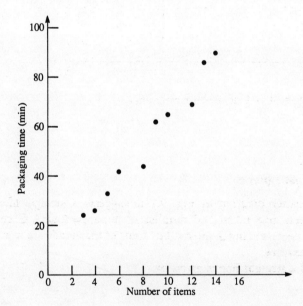

Fig. 9.1 Scatter diagram of packaging times against number of items packaged.

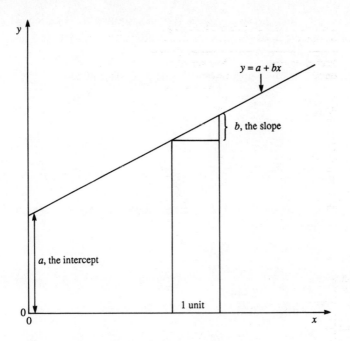

Fig. 9.2 Intercept and slope of a straight line.

Line fitting by least squares

Looking at the scatter diagram in Fig. 9.1 it suggests a straight-line relationship between time taken and number of items packaged. Such relationships were discussed in Chapter 7, but some of the details are now repeated for convenience.

The equation of a straight line is given by

$$y = a + bx$$

where a is the intercept and b is the slope of the fitted line. The intercept is the place where the line cuts the y-axis. The slope is the amount the y-value changes for a one unit change in the x-value. These are illustrated in Fig. 9.2. The aim, then, in fitting a straight line, is to find the 'best' values of a and b.

The method of least squares is a general method which can be used for fitting straight lines or any other form of equation. It is based on minimising the spread of points around the fitted line.

The fitted line is chosen so that the vertical differences between the line and each point (as shown in Fig. 9.3), when squared and added, give the smallest total. Without going through the algebra, the values of a and b can be found by either of two methods.

Method 1. Calculate a and b directly from the formulae

$$b = \frac{n\Sigma x_i y_i - \Sigma x_i \Sigma y_i}{n\Sigma x_i^2 - (\Sigma x_i)^2}$$

and

$$a = \frac{\Sigma y_i}{n} - \frac{b\Sigma x_i}{n}$$

For the packaging data in Table 9.1 the calculations are as shown in Table 9.2. Using these results

$$b = \frac{(10)(5,359) - (84)(541)}{(10)(840) - (84)(84)}$$

$$= \frac{53,590 - 45,444}{8,400 - 7,056}$$

$$= \frac{8,146}{1,344}$$

$$= 6.061$$

Now, substituting this result in the second equation

$$a = \frac{541}{10} - \frac{(6.061)(84)}{10}$$

$$= 54.1 - 50.9125$$
$$= 3.19 \text{ (to 2 dp)}$$

so the least squares regression equation is

$$y = 3.19 + 6.061x$$

Method 2. Solve two simultaneous equations, known as the normal equations

$$na + b\Sigma x_i = \Sigma y_i$$
$$a\Sigma x_i + b\Sigma x_i^2 = \Sigma x_i y_i$$

Using the results already calculated the equations to be solved are

$$10a + 84b = 541 \tag{1}$$

$$84a + 840b = 5,359 \tag{2}$$

Table 9.2

x	y	x^2	xy
3	24	9	72
4	26	16	104
5	33	25	165
6	42	36	252
8	44	64	352
9	62	81	558
10	65	100	650
12	69	144	828
13	86	169	1,118
14	90	196	1,260
84	541	840	5,359

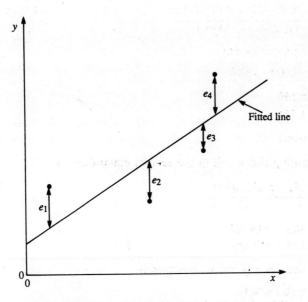

Fig. 9.3 Differences between points and the fitted line.

Multiply equation (1) by 10, then subtract equation (2) to obtain

$$100a + 840b = 5{,}410$$
$$\underline{84a + 840b = 5{,}359}$$
$$16a \qquad\quad = \; 51$$

so that

$$a = 3.19$$

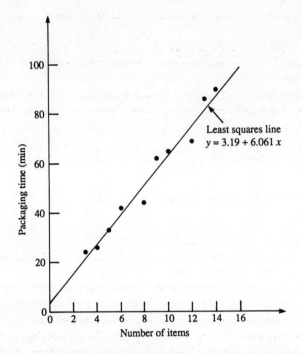

Fig. 9.4 Least squares fitted line for the packaging times.

Substituting the result back in equation (1) gives

$$10\tfrac{51}{16} + 84b = 541$$
$$84b = 509.125$$
$$b = 6.061$$

so that the least squares regression line is (as before)

$$y = 3.19 + 6.061x$$

This line is superimposed on the original points in Fig. 9.4 and, as can be seen, is close to these points.

Interpretation and uses of the fitted line

The fitted line describes in mathematical terms the relationship between an independent variable, denoted by x, and a dependent variable, denoted by y.

The regression line is called the regression of y upon x, so if a straight-line relationship of savings upon income were fitted, x would be income and y would be savings.

When choosing which variable should be x and which should be y, remember that y will be the variable to be predicted, the variable that results from the other.

The form of the equation says that the dependent variable y is a constant plus a multiple of the independent variable x. This means that within the context of a particular business problem we can attempt to give an interpretation to the constant value (intercept) and the multiple of x (slope). In the packaging times example, the relationship calculated can be written in words as

time taken $= 3.19 + 6.061 \times$ number of items

The constant could be interpreted as a fixed quantity. It is in the equation regardless of how many items are packaged. In this example it is a fixed time so might be interpreted as the necessary preparation time for collecting together materials etc. prior to packaging.

The multiple is used with the independent variable and for every unit increase in the independent variable there is an increase in the dependent variable equal to the multiple. It is a variable quantity or quantity per unit. In this example it is multiplied by the number of items being packaged so could be interpreted as the time to package an individual item. Every extra item packaged adds the multiple to the time taken.

With the figures calculated

$$a = 3.19, \qquad b = 6.061$$

the preparation time might be estimated at 3.19 minutes and the time to package a single item as 6.061 minutes.

The equation itself can be used to predict the most likely value for y if x equals a certain value. If an estimate of how long it would take to package 7 items is required, then $x = 7$ is substituted in the fitted line to obtain

$$y = 3.19 + (6.061)(7)$$
$$= 45.6 \text{ minutes}$$

so the predicted packaging time for 7 items is 45.6 minutes.

As 7 items is within the range of the data used to determine the fitted line, this is called an *interpolation*, as defined in Chapter 7. If the line is used to predict outside the range of the original data it is called *extrapolation*. For 25 items the equation gives

$$y = 3.19 + (6.061)(25)$$
$$= 154.7 \text{ minutes}$$

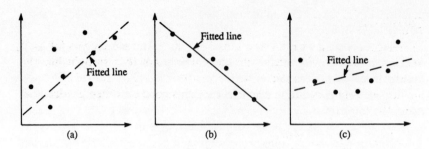

Fig. 9.5 Scatter diagrams and fitted lines.

As 25 items is outside the range of the original data this prediction is an extrapolation as mentioned in Chapter 7.

When making predictions using the fitted straight line it is necessary to consider how reliable the predictions are likely to be. The first consideration is how well the line fits the data.

Figure 9.5(a) shows a scattered set of data which does not really suggest any relationship. A straight line can be fitted but is only a poor representation of the data. It does not follow the data closely and so would not be expected to give reliable predictions. In diagram (b) the fitted line has a negative slope and follows the data very closely. This suggests that any predictions from this fitted line will be reliable. Finally in diagram (c) the fitted line is quite close to all the points but does not follow their pattern. Any predictions from this fitted line could be improved. A curve should be fitted by curvilinear regression but this is beyond the scope of the present text.

To check formally the 'closeness' or 'goodness of fit' of a straight line equation to a set of data, measures called correlation coefficients can be calculated and these will be discussed in the next sections.

As well as considering how closely the fitted line follows the data it is necessary also to look at what sort of prediction is being made. If the prediction is for a value inside the range of the original data, then as long as the line is a good fit the prediction should be reliable. If we are extrapolating much more care must be taken. However closely the fitted line follows the data there is no guarantee that the straight-line relationship will continue outside the range of the data available. Any extrapolation for values well outside the data available is at best a tentative estimate. When the time to package 25 items was estimated earlier, 25 is well above the highest data value used, so little reliability can be expected of this prediction. If it had been required to predict the time for 15 items then, as this is just outside the range of the data, reasonable confidence in any prediction is possible. The further the value for which a prediction is required lies outside the range of the data the less reliable any prediction will be.

Correlation

Correlation is a measure of how closely a pair of measurements follow a *linear relationship*. The nearer the data points are to a straight line the higher the correlation is said to be. Correlation is measured by the *Pearson product moment correlation coefficient* (*r*), this coefficient being calculated using the formula

$$r = \frac{n\Sigma x_i y_i - \Sigma x_i \Sigma y_i}{\sqrt{[n\Sigma x_i^2 - (\Sigma x_i)^2][n\Sigma y_i^2 - (\Sigma y_i)^2]}}$$

This coefficient can take any value from -1 to $+1$. The figure has two characteristics, its sign and its size. A positive value of *r* indicates that the fitted line has a positive slope, i.e. as one measurement increases the other increases. A negative value of *r* indicates that the fitted line has a negative slope, i.e. as one measurement increases the other decreases. This is the only significance of the sign.

The size of the correlation coefficient, ignoring the sign, indicates how close to a straight line the data is. The higher the correlation the more closely the data follow a straight line. A correlation of $+1$ indicates that the points lie *exactly* on a straight line with a positive or upward slope. A correlation near to $+1$ indicates the points lie nearly on a straight line. As the correlation gets smaller the scatter around the fitted line increases. A correlation of 0 indicates no correlation or a random scatter of points. A correlation of -1 indicates the points lie *exactly* on a straight line with a negative or downward slope. A correlation of near -1 indicates the points lie nearly on a straight line. Again, as the value gets smaller the scatter around the fitted line increases.

In Fig. 9.6 various examples of correlations for scatter diagrams are given.

To find the Pearson product moment correlation coefficient for the packaging times data in Table 9.1 the calculations are (see Table 9.3):

$$r = \frac{(10)(5,359) - (84)(541)}{\sqrt{[(10)(840) - (84)(84)][(10)(34,367) - (541)(541)]}}$$

$$= \frac{53,590 - 45,444}{\sqrt{(8,400 - 7,056)(343,670 - 29,681)}}$$

$$= \frac{8,146}{\sqrt{(1,344)(50,989)}}$$

$$= \frac{8,146}{8,278.24}$$

$$= 0.984$$

Table 9.3

x	y	x^2	y^2	xy
3	24	9	576	72
4	26	16	676	104
5	33	25	1,089	165
6	42	36	1,764	252
8	44	64	1,936	352
9	62	81	3,844	558
10	65	100	4,225	650
12	69	144	4,761	828
13	86	169	7,396	1,118
14	90	196	8,100	1,260
84	541	840	34,367	5,354

a very high positive correlation confirming the earlier view that the data lie very close to the fitted straight line.

The square of the correlation coefficient is called the *coefficient of determination*. Its value, when converted to a percentage, measures how much of the total variation has been explained by the fitted line. In the packaging times example the coefficient of determination is

$$r^2 = (0.984)^2 = 0.968 = 96.8\%$$

indicating that 96.8% of the variation in packaging times is explained by the straight-line equation. Without a straight-line equation the mean of packaging times would be used for estimation. The total variation is the variation around this mean as shown in Fig. 9.7.

The nearer the coefficient of determination is to 100% the better the straight line is at explaining y, the dependent variable.

Rank correlation

When working out correlations there are situations when the two measurements are not truly numerical. As long as the results can be placed in rank order for each of the measurements the *Spearman rank correlation* can be calculated. This correlation coefficient is also sometimes used in place of the Pearson product moment correlation coefficient since it is easier to calculate. It is given by the formula

$$r_s = 1 - \frac{6 \sum_{i=1}^{n} d_i^2}{n(n^2 - 1)}$$

where the d_i are the differences in rankings for each measurement.

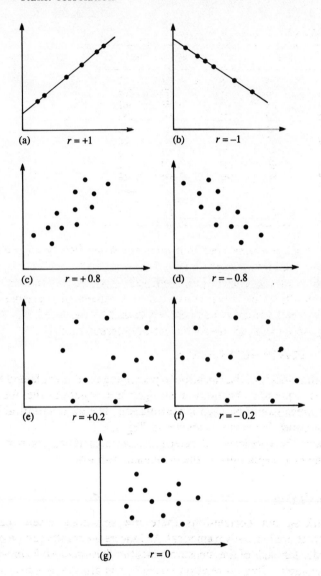

Fig. 9.6 Examples of different correlations.

Table 9.4. Magazine assessments

| | Car | | | | | | | |
	A	B	C	D	E	F	G	H
Magazine 1	8	3	1	7	2	6	5	4
Magazine 2	2	1	6	8	3	5	4	7

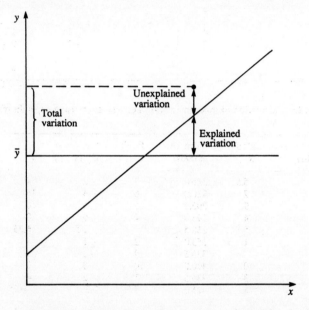

Fig. 9.7 Total variation and variation explained by the fitted lines.

Two consumer magazines placed 8 cars in order of their value for money. The results were (1 = best, 8 = worst) as shown in Table 9.4. By calculating the rank correlation an indication of any similarity (or otherwise) of opinion between the two magazines can be found. The calculations are laid out in Table 9.5, which gives

$$r_s = 1 - \frac{(6)(78)}{(8)(64-1)}$$

$$= 1 - 0.929$$
$$= 0.072$$

a very low correlation indicating there is no similarity between the rankings given by the magazines.

Table 9.5. Ranking of magazine assessments

Car	Magazine 1 rank x	Magazine 2 rank y	$d = (x - y)$	d^2
A	8	2	6	36
B	3	1	2	4
C	1	6	−5	25
D	7	8	−1	1
E	2	3	−1	1
F	6	5	1	1
G	5	4	1	1
H	4	7	−3	9
				78

Table 9.6. Calculation of rank correlation between advertising expenditure and sales

Advertising (£'000s)	Rank x	Sales (£'000s)	Rank y	$d = (x - y)$	d^2
20.5	5.5	325.0	7.5	−2	4
18.0	2	310.0	6	−4	16
23.0	9	305.0	5	4	16
20.0	4	295.0	4	0	0
20.5	5.5	268.5	3	2.5	6.25
16.5	1	255.0	2	−1	1
22.0	7	335.5	9	−2	4
25.0	10	400.0	10	0	0
18.5	3	236.5	1	2	4
22.5	8	325.0	7.5	0.5	0.25
					51.50

The rank correlation can range from −1 to +1 just the same as the Pearson coefficient. In this example a rank correlation near +1 would have indicated the two magazines held similar views on value for money. If the rank correlation had been near −1 this would have indicated opposing views from the two magazines.

If the rank correlation is calculated in place of the Pearson coefficient it is only an approximation. If the correlation between advertising and sales based on ten months' figures, as given in Table 9.6, is required, then if rank correlation is to be used the figures for advertising and for sales must first be ranked separately.

Some values are equal (called ties). The ranks these cover are averaged, so for advertising two figures of 20.5 are ranked 5.5 since they cover the ranks 5 and 6.

$$r_s = 1 - \frac{(6)(51.5)}{(10)(100-1)}$$
$$= 1 - 0.312$$
$$= 0.688$$

a reasonable positive correlation indicating some relationship between advertising and sales.

Cause, effect and correlation

There is a temptation when a high correlation is obtained to take this as evidence of a *causal relationship*, a relationship where one measurement is the direct cause of another measurement. This may well be true, for instance if the correlation between hours worked and output were found to be high it would be legitimate to think of hours worked as the cause with output being the effect. However, if the correlation between hours of sunshine in Blackpool and number of charter flights from Luton Airport is calculated, this gives a high positive correlation. If this were taken as evidence of cause and effect then this would imply that the hours of sunshine in Blackpool directly caused the number of charter flights from Luton Airport. These two measurements are not directly linked but rather both happen to increase in the summer months. This is known as a spurious correlation.

In summary, a cause and effect relationship normally leads to a high correlation (positive or negative) but a high correlation does not necessarily show that a cause and effect relationship exists.

10

Time series

Introduction

Many measurements in business are recorded through time. Any measurement recorded at equal intervals whether it is daily, weekly, monthly, quarterly or annually, is called a *time series*. Examples of time series are monthly sales figures, daily stock levels and quarterly output figures. Time series are of interest for two major reasons. Firstly, studying a time series may aid understanding of what causes the figures to be as they are. Secondly, and more importantly, it is hoped that observing the behaviour of the time series will give an insight into future readings. The idea of extending a time series into the future is known as *forecasting* and is becoming ever more important in planning the development of a business.

Components of a time series

Before attempting to analyse a time series, a picture of the series, a *time-series plot*, should be drawn.

The quarterly sales figures of sweat shirts have been recorded over a four year period in Table 10.1 and are illustrated by the time series plot in Fig. 10.1.

For this plot we can see that the values in the series are generally increasing. In addition to this increase there is a pattern which repeats every four time intervals. This is known as a four-quarterly seasonal pattern.

The figures recorded in a time series can be caused by several factors. In analysing time series there are four specific types of factor, called *components of variation*, which we look for. These are listed below.

1. Trend. The overall or underlying behaviour of a time series is known as *trend*. It is the general movement of the series. Trend can be upward, downward or level and it may be given in the form of an equation or as a series of trend values.
2. Seasonal. Any pattern in a time series which repeats every year, or part of a year, is known as a *seasonal* pattern. The differing behaviour of the

Table 10.1. Quarterly sweat shirt sales (in '000s)

	Q1	Q2	Q3	Q4
Year 1	1.0	0.9	3.3	4.5
2	3.4	3.0	5.9	6.9
3	6.6	6.4	9.0	9.2
4	8.8	8.0	10.7	11.4

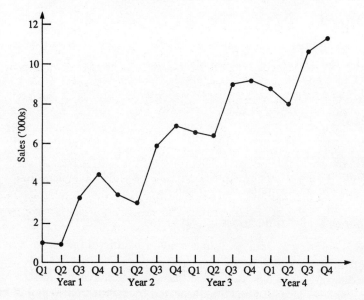

Fig. 10.1 Time series plot of sweat shirt sales figures.

time series at different phases of the pattern is described by a series of *seasonal effects*, one for each time point within the cycle. Notice that the term seasonal has a much wider use than in everyday language. In this context it may be that the seasonal effects are due to the quarters of the year but it is also possible to have a seasonal pattern lasting a week with the days of the week being the seasonal effects.

3. Cyclic. Any repeated pattern which has a pattern extending longer than a year is known simply as a *cycle* or a *business cycle*. Again, a series of *cyclic effects* is used to describe the differing behaviour of the series within the cycle.

4. Irregular or error. Irregular or error variation is the term used to describe any behaviour in a time series which cannot be explained or

predicted. There are two types of variation which make up irregular variation:

(a) natural variation is the random variability that occurs in any recorded measurement;

(b) catastrophic variation is caused by some unexpected occurrence. The occurrence is not predictable in advance but its effect can be seen once it has happened. A strike, a warehouse fire, a competitor ceasing to trade are all possible events that have an effect on the results in a time series.

The reason for making the distinction between seasonal patterns and business cycles is that seasonal cycles are usually caused by such things as climate or social custom. Business cycles, however, are not easily explained apart from their being evidence of changes in economic activity.

The components of variation are denoted by

T = trend
S = seasonal
B = business cycle
E = irregular or error

and in time series analysis these are combined in one of two ways. The components can be added together to form an *additive time series model*. Alternatively, they can be multiplied together to form a *multiplicative time series model*.

The additive model assumes that any seasonal or business cycle effects remain the same size, regardless of the underlying trend values. In other words, they are *absolute effects*. With the multiplicative model, however, it is assumed the seasonal or business cycle effects are a proportion of the underlying trend, so if trend values are low the effects will be small, but if trend values are high the effects will be large. In this case they are *relative or proportional effects*.

A time series plot usually highlights which type of model to use. The choice depends on whether the pattern remains the same size, approximately, or whether the size of the pattern increases as the trend gets larger (or decreases as the trend gets smaller).

In Fig. 10.2(a) and (d) repeating patterns are shown and these are approximately the same size, which suggests that an *additive* model should be used for these series. In Fig. 10.2(b), as the figures get larger the pattern gets larger, so suggesting a *multiplicative* model for this series. In Fig. 10.2(c), as the figures get smaller the pattern gets smaller, so this also suggests a *multiplicative* model for this series. If in any doubt use an additive model. The example in Fig. 10.1 has a trend and a seasonal pattern (the

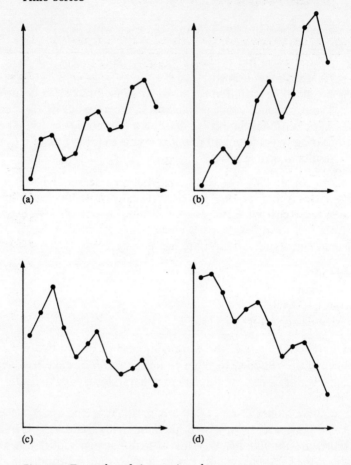

Fig. 10.2 Examples of time series plots.

pattern lasting one year). The pattern stays about the same size, which suggests an additive model. There is no pattern of length greater than a year, so the model for this time series would be written as

$$Y = T + S + E$$

where Y is used for the measurement being recorded. An error term is included since all results will be subject to natural variation. The trend looks like a straight line with a positive slope and the seasonal pattern consists of four quarterly effects.

The aim of time series analysis is to determine, numerically, the various components and effects within a time series.

Table 10.2. Moving average calculations for sweat shirt sales figures

Year	Quarter	Sales	Totals of 4	Centred totals of 8	Trend
1	1	1.0			
	2	0.9			
			9.7		
	3	3.3		20.8	2.6000
			12.1		
	4	4.5		26.3	3.2875
			14.2		
2	1	3.4		31.0	3.8750
			16.8		
	2	3.0		36.0	4.5000
			19.2		
	3	5.9		41.6	5.2000
			22.4		
	4	6.9		48.2	6.0250
			25.8		
3	1	6.6		54.7	6.8375
			28.9		
	2	6.4		60.1	7.5125
			31.2		
	3	9.0		64.7	8.0875
			33.5		
	4	9.2		68.6	8.5750
			35.1		
4	1	8.9		71.9	8.9875
			36.8		
	2	8.0		75.8	9.4750
			39.0		
	3	10.7			
	4	11.4			

Moving average calculations for additive models

In the method of moving averages individual trend values are found for time points rather than finding trend as an equation. This method can be used for any type of time series but is generally used for series containing seasonal or cyclic effects. For seasonal or cyclic series the number of points in a pattern must first be determined. The results in the series are then added in groups of this size, each new total being obtained by moving one time point down the series. In Table 10.2 the calculations for the sweat shirt sales figures are given. The figures are added in blocks of four since there are four time points in each seasonal pattern. Starting at the first result, the total of four is

$$1.0 + 0.9 + 3.3 + 4.5 = 9.7$$

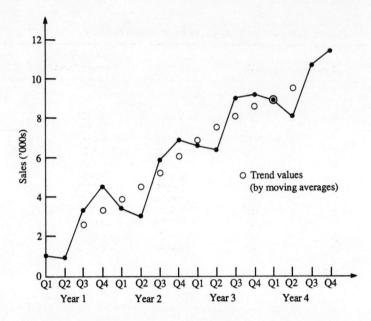

Fig. 10.3 Moving average trend values for sweat shirt sales figures.

then dropping down one result, the next total of four is

$$0.9 + 3.3 + 4.5 + 3.4 = 12.1$$

and this process continues until the last block of four results is reached. These totals are called *moving totals*. Here, as four time points have been combined this total corresponds to halfway between the middle two time points. This is how Table 10.2 has been set out.

As these totals do not correspond to original time points they are added in pairs to obtain centred totals. These centred totals now correspond to original time points as shown. Finally divide by the number of results which were added to give the totals, in this case 8. The figures obtained are *moving averages* and form a series of trend values.

Trend values are obtained for all but the earliest and latest time points. These can then be used to fit a trend line if this is required. Least squares can be used to determine the trend line.

The trend figures in this example are illustrated in Fig. 10.3.

In this example centring was necessary. Whenever the number of time points in a cycle is *even* then centring will be required. However, if the number is *odd* centring will not be required as the totals centre themselves.

Table 10.3. Calculations of detrended values for sweat shirt sales figures

Year	Quarter	Sales	Trend	Detrended (sales-trend)
1	1	1.0	—	—
	2	0.9	—	—
	3	3.3	2.6000	0.7000
	4	4.5	3.2875	1.2125
2	1	3.4	3.8750	−0.4750
	2	3.0	4.5000	−1.5000
	3	5.9	5.2000	0.7000
	4	6.9	6.0250	0.8750
3	1	6.6	6.8375	−0.2375
	2	6.4	7.5125	−1.1125
	3	9.0	8.0875	0.9125
	4	9.2	8.5750	0.6250
4	1	8.9	8.9875	−0.0875
	2	8.0	9.4750	−1.4750
	3	10.7	—	—
	4	11.4	—	—

Finding seasonal effects

Having found trend values or a trend equation the next stage is to
determine the 'ups' and 'downs' that occur within the seasonal pattern, the
seasonal effects. These are found using the detrended figures, which are
found as

$$\text{detrended} = \text{original} - \text{trend}$$

for each time point for which a trend value has been determined. Using the
sales figures column (original figures) and trend values from Table 10.2 the
detrended figures in the sweat shirt example are given in Table 10.3.

These detrended figures are estimates of the seasonal effects. Hence, the
first figure is an estimate of what happens in Quarter 3, i.e. the Quarter 3
sales figures will be 0.7 units above trend. More than one estimate is
available for each quarter, the seventh time point occurs in Quarter 3 and
here the detrended figure is again 0.7 but the last Quarter 3 detrended figure
is 0.9125. These different estimates are averaged as in Table 10.4.

The seasonal effects must add up to zero so if these averages do not total
zero they must be adjusted. This adjustment will be the negative of the total
of the averages, divided by the number of seasonal effects.

Table 10.4. Calculation of seasonal effects for sweat shirt sales figures

	Q1	Q2	Q3	Q4
Year 1	—	—	0.7000	1.2125
2	−0.4750	−1.5000	0.7000	0.8750
3	−0.2375	−1.1125	0.9125	0.6250
4	−0.0875	−1.4750	—	—
Total	−0.8000	−4.0875	2.3125	2.7125
Average	−0.2667	−1.3625	0.7708	0.9042
Adjustment	−0.0115	−0.0115	−0.0115	−0.0115
Seasonal effects	−0.2782	−1.3740	0.7593	0.8927
	= −0.28	= −1.37	=0.76	=0.89

$$\text{Adjustment} = \frac{-(-0.2667 - 1.3625 + 0.7708 - 0.9042)}{4}$$

$$= \frac{-0.0458}{4}$$

$$= -0.0115$$

After adjustment, the averages are the seasonal effects estimates. These are usually quoted to the accuracy of the original figures or to one extra decimal place.

In this example the seasonal effects tell us that, on average, in

Quarter 1 sales will be 0.28 units, i.e. 280, below trend.
Quarter 2 sales will be 1.37 units, i.e. 1,370, below trend.
Quarter 3 sales will be 0.76 units, i.e. 760, above trend.
Quarter 4 sales will be 0.89 units, i.e. 890, above trend.

In summary, the method of moving averages for determining trend values and seasonal effects is as follows:

Step 1. Determine the length of the seasonal pattern.
Step 2. Calculate moving totals.
Step 3. Centre totals if length of pattern is an even number of time points.
Step 4. Calculate moving averages as trend values.
Step 5. Calculate detrended figures.
Step 6. Average detrended figures (with adjustment if necessary) to find seasonal effects.

Table 10.5. Annual turnover figures for XYT PLC (in £m)

Year	Turnover (£m)	Year	Turnover (£m)	Year	Turnover (£m)
1	1.1	4	3.9	7	6.0
2	4.8	5	7.8	8	9.3
3	2.0	6	4.6	9	7.5

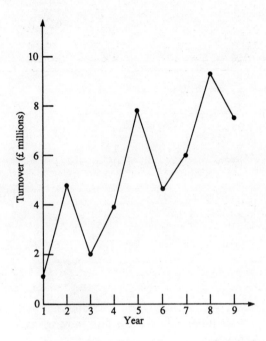

Fig. 10.4 Plot of annual turnover figures for XYT PLC.

Finding cyclic effects

To find cyclic effects moving averages is used in exactly the same way as for finding seasonal effects. The only noticeable difference is that the length of the cycle is not suggested by the way the series has been collected, only by the time series plot.

For the series in Table 10.5 for annual turnover figures, the time series plot is given in Fig. 10.4.

Looking at the plot there is an obvious three-year cycle and the pattern stays about the same size, so the time series model is

$$Y = T + B + E$$

Table 10.6. Moving average calculations for annual turnover figures for XYT PLC

Cycle	Year	Turnover	Totals of 3	Trend	Detrended
1	1	1.1	—	—	—
	2	4.8	7.9	2.63	2.17
	3	2.0	10.7	3.57	−1.57
2	4	3.9	13.7	4.57	−0.67
	5	7.8	16.3	5.43	2.37
	6	4.6	18.4	6.13	−1.53
3	7	6.0	19.9	6.63	−0.63
	8	9.3	22.8	7.60	1.70
	9	7.5	—	—	—

Table 10.7. Calculation of cyclic effects for turnover figures for XYT PLC

	Year of cycle		
	1	2	3
Cycle 1	—	2.17	−1.57
2	−0.67	2.37	−1.53
3	−0.63	1.70	—
Total	−1.30	6.24	−3.10
Average	−0.65	2.08	−1.55
Adjustment	0.04	0.04	0.04
Cyclic effects	−0.61	2.12	−1.51

where the trend looks like a straight line with a positive slope and there is a business cycle of length three time points. The full moving average calculations are given in Table 10.6.

Here, as three figures are being added to obtain totals, no centring is required. The cyclic effects can then be calculated as in Table 10.7.

The adjustment is

$$\text{Adjustment} = \frac{-(-0.65 + 2.08 - 1.55)}{3}$$

$$= 0.04$$

The adjusted figures, the cyclic effects, tell us that the effects in each year of the three year cycle are on average the following:

Turnover will be £0.61m below trend in year 1 of a cycle.
Turnover will be £2.12m above trend in Year 2 of a cycle.
Turnover will be £1.51m below trend in Year 3 of a cycle.

Table 10.8. Annual sales figures for personal computers

Year	Sales (£m)	Year	Sales (£m)	Year	Sales (£m)
1	1.3	6	3.6	11	6.4
2	1.2	7	3.5	12	6.0
3	1.2	8	3.3	13	5.6
4	1.8	9	4.4	14	7.5
5	3.2	10	6.4	15	9.8

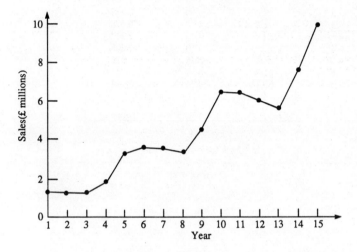

Fig. 10.5 Plot of annual sales figures for personal computers.

Moving average calculations for a multiplicative model

If a multiplicative model is appropriate for a time series, the moving averages can still be used to determine trend values and seasonal or cyclic effects but some changes in the method of calculation are necessary.

If we wish to fit a time series model to the data on sales of personal computers as given in Table 10.8, then start by drawing a time series plot as in Fig. 10.5.

From this plot we can see that there is a five-year pattern with the pattern getting larger as the figures increase. This suggests that the multiplicative model

$$Y = T \times B \times E$$

is appropriate.

Table 10.9. Moving average calculations for personal computer sales figures

Year	Sales (£m)	Totals of 5	Trend	Detrended (Y/T)
1	1.3			
2	1.2			
3	1.2	8.7	1.74	0.690
4	1.8	11.0	2.20	0.818
5	3.2	13.3	2.66	1.203
6	3.6	15.4	3.08	1.169
7	3.5	18.0	3.60	0.972
8	3.3	21.2	4.24	0.778
9	4.4	24.0	4.80	0.917
10	6.4	26.5	5.30	1.208
11	6.4	28.8	5.76	1.111
12	6.0	31.9	6.38	0.940
13	5.6	35.3	7.06	0.793
14	7.5			
15	9.8			

Table 10.10. Calculations of cyclic effects for personal computer sales

	Year of cycle				
	1	2	3	4	5
Cycle 1	—	—	0.690	0.818	1.203
2	1.169	0.972	0.778	0.917	1.208
3	1.111	0.940	0.793	—	—
Total	2.280	1.912	2.261	1.735	2.411
average	1.140	0.956	0.754	0.868	1.206
adjusted	1.175	0.985	0.777	0.895	1.243

The calculations up to and including trend values are exactly the same as for an additive model (see Section 10.3). However, to obtain the detrended figures it is necessary to *divide* the original figures by their corresponding trend figures.

The full set of calculations are given in Table 10.9, the first detrended figure being found as

$$\text{detrended} = 1.2/1.74 = 0.690$$

the second as

$$\text{detrended} = 1.8/2.20 = 0.818$$

and so on.

These detrended figures are the estimates of the cyclic multiplicative effects (sometimes called cyclic indices) and need to be averaged as before. The calculations are given in Table 10.10.

These multiplicative effects should multiply to 1. Here they multiply to 0.8602 so some adjustment is necessary. To adjust multiplicative effects we must multiply each effect by

$$\frac{1}{\sqrt[n]{\text{(product of unadjusted effects)}}}$$

where n is the number of seasonal or cyclic effects so here multiply all unadjusted effects by

$$\frac{1}{\sqrt[5]{0.8602}} = 1.0306$$

The cyclic effect for Year 1 is therefore adjusted to

$$1.0306 \times 1.140 = 1.175$$

and similarly for the remaining years of a cycle.

These multiplicative cyclic effects tell us the following:

In Year 1 of a cycle, sales will be trend multiplied by 1.175 or 17.5% above trend.
In Year 2 of a cycle sales will be 1.5% below trend.
In Year 3 of a cycle sales will be 22.3% below trend.
In Year 4 of a cycle sales will be 10.5% below trend.
In Year 5 of a cycle sales will be 24.3% above trend.

Although moving averages have been used to find trend values, it may be that an equation is required for trend. In this case linear regression can be used but it is generally less reliable for finding trend as the equation found is influenced by any seasonal or cyclic effects present.

Forecasting

One of the main aims of time series analysis is to facilitate prediction of future values. These forecasts are obtained by extrapolating the time series model into the future. Suppose forecasts are required for sales of sweat shirts in each quarter of Year 5, the following year for the results in Table 10.1. The time series model was

$$Y = T + S + E$$

so estimates of trend must be found for each quarter of Year 5. The appropriate seasonal effect can then be added to obtain the forecast. No attempt is made to estimate error since this is the part of a time series that cannot be predicted. Instead, it is assumed to be zero.

If trend values have been found by moving averages, a trend line can be

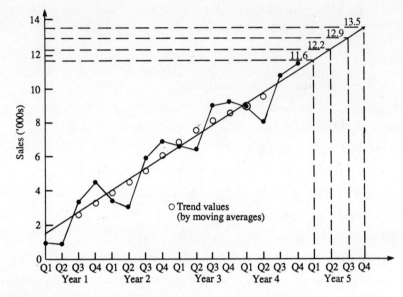

Fig. 10.6 Extrapolation of moving average trend figures.

drawn through the trend values by eye and extended to the appropriate time points.

From Fig. 10.6 the forecasts for trend are:

Year 5   Q1:   11.6
          Q2:   12.2
          Q3:   12.9
          Q4:   13.5

Once trend values have been found the appropriate seasonal effects can be added. The forecasts obtained are

Year 5   Q1: $11.6 + (-0.28) = 11.3 = 11,300$
          Q2: $12.2 + (-1.37) = 10.8 = 10,800$
          Q3: $12.9 + (0.76) = 13.7 = 13,700$
          Q4: $13.5 + (0.89) = 14.4 = 14,400$

to the nearest hundred.

In the example of annual turnover in Table 10.5, if a forecast is required for Year 12, the trend line needs to be extended as in Fig. 10.7.

The forecast is then found by adding the third-year cyclic effect since Year 12 would be the third year of the fourth cycle.

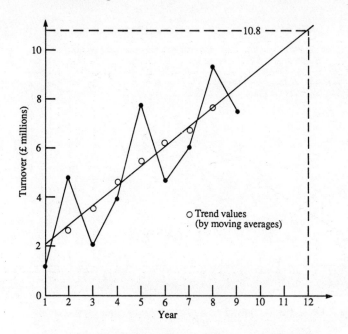

Fig. 10.7 Extrapolation of trend for turnover figures.

Forecast for Year 12 = trend + year 3 effect
                     = 10.8 − 0.51
                     = £10.29 million
                     = £10.3 million (to 1 dp)

Now, if forecasts are required from a multiplicative model the same procedure is used but the trend and seasonal or cyclic effects are multiplied together. For the annual sales in Table 10.8, if forecasts are required for years 16, 17 and 18, trend forecasts are initially needed. These are obtained by eye, as illustrated in Fig. 10.8.

Reading these off, the trend forecasts are:

Year 16   8.6
Year 17   9.2
Year 18   9.8

Then, to obtain the forecasts these figures must be multiplied by the appropriate cyclic effect. As Year 16 is the first year of a cycle, its trend value is multiplied by the first year effect, i.e.

Forecast year 16 = 8.6 × 1.175 = £10.1 million
Forecast year 17 = 9.2 × 0.985 = £9.1 million
Forecast year 18 = 9.8 × 0.777 = £7.6 million   (all results to dp)

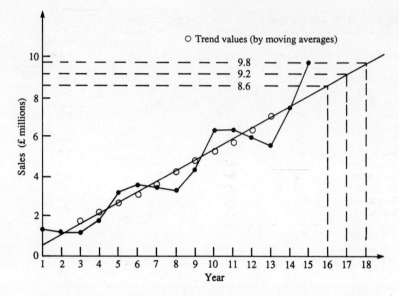

Fig. 10.8 Extrapolation of trend for personal computer sales figures.

Z-charts

Before leaving time series we look at a special chart which is used to illustrate figures collected through time. It consists of three different graphs drawn on the same diagram. The first graph is a simple time series plot. The second graph is a running total or cumulative graph, the final graph being a moving totals graph.

For the production figures in Table 10.11 the cumulative frequencies are calculated for the second year only since this is the year being illustrated. The moving totals are the running total of the present month and the previous eleven months. The z-chart is then drawn as in Fig. 10.9.

These charts can be drawn through the year, building up an overall picture. Using the chart a check can be made against pre-set targets or the chart can be used as a straightforward indication of progress.

In the example a calendar year was used but any twelve-month period of relevance could be used, for example the financial year.

Table 10.11. Production figures over 24 consecutive months from TBX Ltd

Month	Year 1 output	Year 2 output	Cumulative total (Year 2)	Moving totals
January	37	45	45	626
February	51	54	99	629
March	42	48	147	635
April	41	48	195	642
May	53	60	255	649
June	58	59	314	650
July	61	67	381	656
August	60	62	443	658
September	54	60	503	664
October	52	55	558	667
November	58	62	620	671
December	51	54	674	674

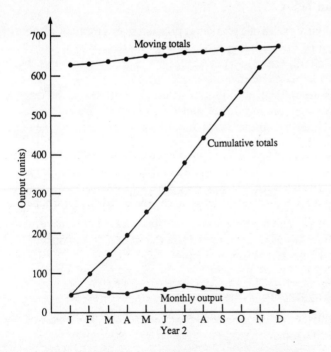

Fig. 10.9 Z-chart for production figures for TBX Ltd.

11

Index numbers

Introduction

An *index number* is a device that attempts to express average changes in economic activity over a period of time. Index numbers are regularly calculated for a wide variety of economic variables, the Index of Retail Prices and the Financial Times Ordinary Share Index being just two examples. Despite the fact that the way in which they are calculated is often criticised, much use is made of them. For example, increases in many people's pensions are linked to the Index of Retail Prices.

The base of an index

Suppose a company's sales of a particular product over a number of months is as shown in Table 11.1. One way of describing the sales pattern would be to represent each month's sales as a percentage of the previous month's. These percentages are indices. We then obtain Table 11.2.

Such indices are difficult to interpret as every variation in the original data shows up twice, up and down, and no overall picture emerges.

It would be better to represent each month's sales as a percentage of the same given month, called the *base*. Here we could recalculate the indices using August as the base (see Table 11.3). However, any other month could be chosen as the base. It is usual to choose a 'typical' value as base, i.e. one that does not exhibit extreme values. This is because, in general terms, we find it more difficult to interpret index numbers that indicate very large percentage changes. This is also one reason why bases are updated every so often. However, a more important reason is that a base in the distant past would have less relevance to recent values.

Price relative aggregate index

A cutlery manufacturer has incurred the costs shown in Table 11.4 for comparable weeks in each year.

Table 11.1. Monthly sales of a product

	Sales (1,000s of cases)
August	24
September	28
October	20
November	27
December	35
January	30

Table 11.2

	Sales	Index
August	24	
September	28 $(28/24) \times 100$	116.7
October	20 $(20/28) \times 100$	71.4
November	27 $(27/20) \times 100$	135.0
December	35 $(35/27) \times 100$	129.6
January	30 $(30/35) \times 100$	85.7

Table 11.3

	Sales	Index
August	24 $(24/24) \times 100$	100
September	28 $(28/24) \times 100$	116.7
October	20 $(20/24) \times 100$	83.3
November	27 $(27/24) \times 100$	112.5
December	35 $(35/24) \times 100$	145.8
January	30 $(30/24) \times 100$	125.0

Table 11.4. A cutlery manager's costs

	Cost(£)	
	1986	1987
Steel (per tonne)	708	734
Silver (per ounce)	5.30	7.50
Electricity (per kilowatt-hour)	0.045	0.052
Labour (per hour)	4.64	4.90

Table 11.5. Calculation of price relatives

	Price relatives	
Steel	734/708	= 1.0367
Silver	7.50/5.30	= 1.4151
Electricity	0.052/0.045	= 1.1556
Labour	4.90/4.64	= 1.0560

To calculate an index by simply summing the costs in 1986 ($= 717.985$) and in 1987 ($= 746.452$), then evaluating

$$\frac{746.452}{717.985} \times 100 = 103.96$$

which gives

1986:   100   1987:   103.96

is meaningless because the resources are all quoted in different units. If, for example, the price of steel was quoted in £ per troy pound, i.e. £84.80 in 1986 and £120.00 in 1987, then the 1987 index is

$$\frac{858.952}{797.485} \times 100 = 107.71$$

The dependence on units could be removed by calculating the *price relatives* of each resource with 1986 as base. This is done by dividing each 1987 price by its corresponding 1986 price to give Table 11.5.

An index for 1987 could then be found by averaging out these price relatives and multiplying by 100, i.e.

$$\frac{(1.0367 + 1.4151 + 1.1556 + 1.0560)}{4} \times 100 = \frac{4.6634}{4} \times 100 = 116.58$$

Despite the fact that this is a more meaningful measure of how costs have risen, it is still not ideal. Might it not be the case that the 5.6% increase in labour costs has more influence on the company's overall costs than the 41.5% increase in the cost of silver? It obviously depends upon the quantities of each resource consumed, and the most useful indices are those that are weighted with the quantities consumed as they are aggregated.

Table 11.6. Resources consumed

Steel	15 tonnes
Silver	50 ounces
Electricity	30,000 kWh
Labour	400 hours

Weighted aggregate indices

Laspeyres index

Suppose that the quantities of the resources consumed during the week in 1986 are as shown in Table 11.6. Then the total cost of these resources in 1986 was

$$(15 \times 708) + (50 \times 5.30) + (30,000 \times 0.045) + (400 \times 4.64)$$
$$= 10,620 + 265 + 1,350 + 1,856 = £14,091$$

However, in 1987 these same resources would cost

$$(15 \times 734) + (50 \times 7.50) + (30,000 \times 0.052) + (400 \times 4.90)$$
$$= 11,010 + 375 + 1,560 + 1,960 = £14,905$$

Then the increase in costs can be represented by

$$\frac{14,905}{14,091} \times 100 = 105.78$$

Therefore, costs have increased overall by 5.78%.

The index we have calculated here is called a *Laspeyres index* (referred to in some texts as a Laspeyre index) and it gives the relative change in the cost of goods in the nth year assuming the same quantities were bought as in the base year.

In general, if P_0 and Q_0 are the prices and quantities in the base year and P_n are the prices in year n, then the

$$\text{Laspeyres index} = \frac{\Sigma P_n Q_0}{\Sigma P_0 Q_0} \times 100$$

An alternative way of evaluating the Laspeyres index is as follows.

The total base cost,

$$C_0 = \Sigma P_0 Q_0$$

Then

$$\text{Laspeyres index} = \frac{\Sigma P_n Q_0}{C_0} \times 100$$

$$= \frac{\Sigma Q_0 P_n}{C_0} \times 100$$

$$= \frac{\Sigma P_0 Q_0 \dfrac{P_n}{P_0}}{C_0} \times 100$$

$$= \Sigma \left(\frac{P_0 Q_0}{C_0} \times \frac{P_n}{P_0} \right) \times 100$$

Now

$$P_0 Q_0 / C_0$$

is the *proportion* of total cost spent on *one* resource in the base year and

$$P_n / P_0$$

is the price relative of that resource. Therefore,

$$\text{Laspeyres index} = 100 \ \Sigma \left(\begin{array}{l} \text{proportion of total} \\ \text{cost spent on} \\ \text{resource in base} \\ \text{year} \end{array} \right) \left(\begin{array}{l} \text{price} \\ \text{relative} \\ \text{of} \\ \text{resource} \end{array} \right)$$

Using this version of the formula we do not need to know exactly how much is spent initially on the resources provided we know the proportions (possibly of a notional £100) spent on each. These proportions are called the *weights*.

A criticism of the Laspeyres index results from its sole use of base year quantities. However, price rises often result in a reduction in quantity consumed and so the total quantity purchased in year n is likely to be less than that purchased in the base year. A way of attempting to avoid this feature is to evaluate instead an alternative index.

Paasche index

With the Paasche index the quantities that are required in the current year are used and their total cost is compared with what they would have cost in the base year.

If Q_n represents the quantities required in year n, then the

$$\text{Paasche index} = \frac{\Sigma P_n Q_n}{\Sigma P_0 Q_n} \times 100$$

Table 11.7. Resources consumed

Steel	13 tonnes
Silver	55 ounces
Electricity	25,000 kWh
Labour	300 hours

In the example, suppose that the quantities of the resources consumed during the week in 1987 are as shown in Table 11.7. Then the total cost of these resources in 1987 will be

$$(13 \times 734) + (55 \times 7.50) + (25{,}000 \times 0.052) + (300 \times 4.90)$$
$$= 9{,}542 + 412.5 + 1{,}300 + 1{,}470 = £12{,}724.50$$

But in 1986 the total cost of these resources would have been

$$(13 \times 708) + (55 \times 5.30) + (25{,}000 \times 0.045) + (300 \times 4.64)$$
$$= 9{,}204 + 291.5 + 1{,}125 + 1{,}392 = £12{,}012.50$$

Then the change in costs can be represented by

$$\frac{12{,}724.50}{12{,}012.50} \times 100 = 105.93$$

The Paasche index can be rewritten, as the Laspeyres index was, as follows. The total cost in year n,

$$C_n = \Sigma P_n Q_n$$

Then the

$$\text{Paasche index} = \frac{\Sigma P_n Q_n}{\Sigma P_0 Q_0} \times 100 = \frac{C}{\Sigma P_0 Q_n} \times 100$$

$$= \frac{100}{\Sigma \dfrac{P_0 Q_n}{C_n}} = \frac{100}{\Sigma \dfrac{P_n Q_n}{C_n} \dfrac{P_0}{P_n}}$$

$$= \frac{100}{\left(\begin{array}{l} \text{proportion of total} \\ \text{cost spent on} \\ \text{resource in} \\ \text{Year } n \end{array} \right) \left(\begin{array}{l} \dfrac{1}{\text{price}} \\ \text{relative of} \\ \text{resource} \end{array} \right)}$$

Table 11.8. Consumer spending

	Weight
Food and catering	213
Alcohol and tobacco	114
Housing and household expenditure	335
Personal expenditure	112
Travel and leisure	226
	1,000

This is obviously more complicated to evaluate than the Laspeyres index and is made more so because the proportions of total cost must be re-evaluated each year.

It is also totally reliant on the quantities consumed in one period and so again does not reliably indicate the changes in cost.

Fisher's ideal index

To try to compensate for the 'extreme' indicators of change in price as given by the Laspeyres and Paasche indices, the *ideal index* is simply a type of 'average' of the two.

$$\text{Ideal index} = \sqrt{[(\text{Laspeyres index}) \times (\text{Paasche index})]}$$

$$= \sqrt{\left[\left(\frac{\Sigma P_n Q_0}{\Sigma P_0 Q_0}\right) \times \left(\frac{\Sigma P_n Q_n}{\Sigma P_0 Q_n}\right)\right]} \times 100$$

In our example we have

$$\text{Ideal index} = \sqrt{(105.78 \times 105.93)}$$
$$= 105.85$$

The retail price index

The General Index of Retail Prices (RPI) is a Laspeyres type index number devised by the Government to attempt to show inflation. As was explained on p. 21 every year the Family Expenditure Survey is used to determine the average amounts spent out of a nominal £1,000 (the *weights*) of a 'typical shopping basket of consumer items'.

In January 1987, when the base year was changed, the 'shopping basket', representing the areas of consumer spending, and weights were as shown in Table 11.8.

Table 11.9. Price relatives for consumer spending

	Price relative
Food and catering	1.037
Alcohol and tobacco	1.030
Housing and household expenditure	1.029
Personal expenditure	1.022
Travel and leisure	1.045

In January 1988 the price relatives of these items, also determined from the Family Expenditure Survey, were as shown in Table 11.9.

Therefore, the RPI for January 1988 was determined thus:

$$RPI = 100 \sum \begin{pmatrix} \text{proportion of total cost} \\ \text{spent on item in base year} \end{pmatrix} \begin{pmatrix} \text{price relative} \\ \text{of item} \end{pmatrix}$$

$$= 100[(0.213 \times 1.037) + (0.114 \times 1.030) + (0.335 \times 1.029)$$
$$+ (0.112 \times 1.022) + (0.226 \times 1.045)]$$
$$= 100[0.221 + 0.117 + 0.345 + 0.115 + 0.236]$$
$$= 100 \ (1.034)$$
$$= 103.4$$

Therefore, inflation was estimated to have risen by 3.4%.

It is worth noting that prior to the change of base in January 1987 the 'shopping basket' had been classified as follows:

Food
Alcoholic drink
Tobacco
Housing
Fuel and light
Durable household goods
Clothing and footwear
Transport and vehicles
Miscellaneous goods
Services
Meals bought and consumed outside the home.

Quantity indices

Sometimes an index may be required that indicates the effect of changes in quantity or volume. Basically the calculation of these indices follows the same procedures as for price indices, but the roles of price and quantity are reversed.

General quantity indices

The Laspeyres quantity index compares the total cost of the base year quantities with the total cost of the current year quantities at base year prices.

Paasche's quantity index compares the total cost of the current year quantities with the total cost of the base year quantities at current year prices. That is,

$$\text{Laspeyres quantity index} = \frac{\Sigma P_0 Q_n}{\Sigma P_0 Q_0} \times 100$$

and

$$\text{Paasche quantity index} = \frac{\Sigma P_n Q_n}{\Sigma P_n Q_0} \times 100$$

Here, from our example, we have Laspeyres quantity index

$$= \frac{(708 \times 13) + (5.3 \times 55) + (0.045 \times 25{,}000) + (4.64 \times 300)}{(708 \times 15) + (5.3 \times 50) + (0.045 \times 30{,}000) + (4.64 \times 400)} \times 100$$

$$= \frac{12{,}012.5}{14{,}091.0} \times 100$$

$$= 85.25$$

and Paasche quantity index

$$= \frac{(734 \times 13) + (7.5 \times 55) + (0.052 \times 25{,}000) + (4.90 \times 300)}{(734 \times 15) + (7.5 \times 50) + (0.052 \times 30{,}000) + (4.90 \times 400)} \times 100$$

$$= \frac{12{,}724.5}{14{,}905.0} \times 100$$

$$= 85.37$$

The ideal quantity index is then

$$= \sqrt{[(\text{Laspeyres quantity index}) \times (\text{Paasche quantity index})]}$$
$$= \sqrt{(85.25 \times 85.37)}$$
$$= 85.31$$

and quantity consumed has fallen by 14.7%.

Index of industrial production

A practical example of a quantity index is the index of industrial production (IIP). Similar to the RPI this is an index number determined by the

Table 11.10. Change in production between 1980 and 1987

	Weight (in 1980)	Relative change in output from 1980 to 1987
Energy and water supply	264	1.39
Metals	25	1.00
Other minerals and mineral products	41	0.83
Chemicals and man-made fibres	68	1.20
Engineering and allied industries	325	0.93
Food, drink and tobacco	99	0.97
Textiles, footwear, clothing and leather	52	0.95
Other manufacturing industries	126	1.03
	1,000	

Government to attempt to show changes in the output of production industries. All such production industries are classified into certain categories and each is given a weighting which is that category's estimated contribution to £1,000 of gross domestic product. Table 11.10 shows how the change in production output between 1980 and 1987 can be estimated.

The IIP is then calculated as a Laspeyres quantity index as follows:

$$\text{IIP} = 100 \sum \begin{pmatrix} \text{weight of industry as a} \\ \text{proportion of £1,000} \end{pmatrix} \begin{pmatrix} \text{relative change in} \\ \text{output of industry} \end{pmatrix}$$

$$= 100 \begin{bmatrix} (0.264 \times 1.39) + (0.025 \times 1.00) + (0.041 \times 0.83) \\ + (0.068 \times 1.20) + (0.325 \times 0.93) + (0.099 \times 0.97) \\ + (0.052 \times 0.95) + (0.126 \times 1.03) \end{bmatrix}$$

$$= 100[0.367 + 0.025 + 0.034 + 0.082 + 0.302 + 0.096]$$
$$= 100 \, (1.085)$$
$$= 108.5$$

Hence, it is estimated that output has risen by 8.5% between 1980 and 1987.

Changing the base

Eventually an index number that continuously increases becomes too large to be meaningful. When this happens it is common to rebase the index and, effectively, start again. On p. 170 this was undertaken with the Index of Retail Prices (RPI) in January 1987.

If we consider the values of such an index that cross such a change of base, how can meaning be derived from them?

Table 11.11. Index of Retail Prices to two bases

	Index of Retail Prices (January 1974 = 100)	
January 1986	379.7	
June 1986	385.8	
January 1987	394.5	100 (Rebase to
June 1987		101.9 January 1987 = 100)
January 1988		103.3
June 1988		106.6

For example, consider the values of the RPI expressed at six-monthly intervals from January 1986 to June 1988 (see Table 11.11). Prior to 1987, the previous time when the base of the RPI was changed was January 1974.

To extract meaning from these figures it was necessary first to evaluate June 1987 to June 1988 assuming the rebasing had not taken place.

From January 1987 to June 1987 the RPI has increased from 100 to 101.9 (i.e. 1.9%). Therefore, on the original 1974 base, the January 1987 value of 394.5 should have increased by 1.9% to a value X_1, that is

$$\frac{X_1}{394.5} = \frac{101.9}{100}$$

or

$$X_1 = \frac{394.5 \times 101.9}{100} = 402.0$$

Similarly, a 3.3% increase, to a value X_2, is experienced by January 1988. Hence

$$\frac{X_2}{394.5} = \frac{103.3}{100}$$

or

$$X_2 = \frac{394.5 \times 103.3}{100} = 407.5$$

and a value X_3 is experienced in June 1988 given by

$$\frac{X_3}{394.5} = \frac{106.6}{100}$$

or

$$X_3 = \frac{394.5 \times 106.6}{100} = 420.5$$

Table 11.12. Index of Retail Prices to a 1974 base

	(January 1974 = 100)
January 1986	379.7
June 1986	385.8
January 1987	394.5
June 1987	402.0
January 1988	407.5
June 1988	420.5

Table 11.13. Index of Retail Prices to a 1986 base

January 1986	$\dfrac{379.7 \times 100}{379.7} = 100$
June 1986	$\dfrac{385.8 \times 100}{379.7} = 101.6$
January 1987	$\dfrac{394.5 \times 100}{379.7} = 103.9$
June 1987	$\dfrac{402.0 \times 100}{379.7} = 105.9$
January 1988	$\dfrac{407.5 \times 100}{379.7} = 107.3$
June 1988	$\dfrac{420.5 \times 100}{379.7} = 110.7$

Therefore, the completed table of RPI values to the 1974 base is as shown in Table 11.12.

To consider the changes in RPI from January 1986 it is necessary to recalibrate to make January 1986 = 100. The results of this are shown in Table 11.13. In particular, it is now possible to estimate that inflation has increased by 10.7% between January 1986 and June 1988.

Deflating index numbers

Consider the index numbers shown in Table 11.14. It is required to determine what has happened to real earnings over the given period. They appear to have increased regularly, but some of the increase is allowing for inflation, as described by the RPI. It is necessary to deflate the Average Earnings Index with the RPI to obtain an Index of Real Earnings.

Firstly, both indices must be rebased to 1983 (see Table 11.15). The Index of Real Earnings is then found by dividing the Average Earnings Index (× 100) by the RPI (see Table 11.16).

Now the index can be interpreted, showing that real earnings have increased steadily from 1983 to 1986 with a large increase in 1987. In particular, we see that real earnings have increased by 15% between 1983 and 1987.

Table 11.14. Average earnings and RPI to different bases

	Average Earnings Index (1980 = 100)	RPI (1974 = 100)
1983	152.8	335.1
1984	162.8	351.8
1985	176.8	373.2
1986	191.2	385.9
1987	206.9	394.5

Table 11.15. Average earnings and RPI to a single base

	Average Earnings Index (1983 = 100)	RPI (1983 = 100)
1983	$\dfrac{152.8 \times 100}{152.8} = 100$	$\dfrac{335.1 \times 100}{335.1} = 100$
1984	$\dfrac{162.8 \times 100}{152.8} = 106.5$	$\dfrac{351.8 \times 100}{335.1} = 105.0$
1985	$\dfrac{176.8 \times 100}{152.8} = 115.7$	$\dfrac{373.2 \times 100}{335.1} = 111.4$
1986	$\dfrac{191.2 \times 100}{152.8} = 125.1$	$\dfrac{385.9 \times 100}{335.1} = 115.2$
1987	$\dfrac{206.9 \times 100}{152.8} = 135.4$	$\dfrac{394.5 \times 100}{335.1} = 117.7$

Table 11.16. Real earnings

	Average Earnings Index	RPI	Real Earnings Index
1983	100	100	$\dfrac{100 \times 100}{100} = 100$
1984	106.5	105.0	$\dfrac{106.5 \times 100}{105.0} = 101.4$
1985	115.7	111.4	$\dfrac{115.7 \times 100}{111.4} = 103.9$
1986	125.1	115.2	$\dfrac{125.1 \times 100}{115.2} = 108.6$
1987	135.4	117.7	$\dfrac{135.4 \times 100}{117.7} = 115.0$

12

Financial mathematics

Introduction

Many of the calculations necessary for the evaluation of investments, interest rates or deterioration can be performed using the standard formulae concerning mathematical progressions and series.

A *progression* is a string of numbers, or *terms*, arranged in a certain order, with each successive number being related to the previous number, or numbers, by some rule.

For example,

1. 50, 60, 70, 80, . . .
2. 50, 500, 5,000, 50,000, . . .
3. 50, 60, 110, 170, 280, . . .

Progression (1) starts with the given value 50 and each successive term is the previous term plus 10.
Progression (2) starts with the given value 50 and each successive term is the previous term multiplied by 10.
Progression (3) starts with the two given values 50 and 60, and each successive term is the sum of the previous two terms.

A *series* is the sum of a progression.

Arithmetic progression

An *arithmetic progression* is one where each successive term is the previous term *plus a given constant*.

Progression (1) above is an example of an arithmetic progression and so is

4. 20, 17, 14, 11, 8, . . .

which starts with the given value 20 and each successive term is the previous term plus (-3).

In general, an arithmetic progression can be written as

$$a, a+d, a+2d, a+3d, a+4d, \ldots$$

where a is the given first term and d is the *common difference.*
In the previous examples (1) has

$$a = 50, d = 10$$

whilst (4) has

$$a = 20, d = -3$$

If the first term is a, the second term $a+d$, third term $a+2d$, notice that the nth term is $a+(n-1)d$. Therefore the 10th term of (1) is

$$50 + (10-1)(10) = 50 + 90 = 140$$

and the 20th term of (4) is

$$20 + (20-1)(-3) = 20 - 57 = -37$$

Simple interest

A useful application of arithmetic progressions is the calculation of *simple interest.*

For example, suppose £500 is invested at 10% per year simple interest. Then the interest in the first year is £500 × 0.10 = £50 and, since the interest is simple, this amount will be added each year. Therefore, we have an arithmetic progression with $a = 500$ and $d = 50$. Hence,

after one year the investment is worth £550
after two years the investment is worth £600
after three years the investment is worth £650

etc., and so after n years the investment is worth $500 + 50n$.

This situation could exist if the interest from the investment was withdrawn each year.

Caution. In all interest calculations pay particular attention to how your problem requires the number of years, n, to be interpreted. If in our given example we require the value of the investment *after 10 years* (i.e. at the end of the 10th year) it will be

$$500 + (10 \times 50) = £1,000$$

but if we require it *at the beginning of the 10th year* we have only had 9 years of interest and then the value will be

$$500 + (9 \times 50) = £950$$

Arithmetic series

Frequently we require the sum of an arithmetic progression. In general terms, the first n terms of such a progression are

$$a, a+d, a+2d, a+3d, \ldots, a+(n-1)d$$

and so the sum of the first n terms, S_n, is

$$S_n = a + (a+d) + (a+2d) + (a+3d) + \ldots + (a+[n-1]d)$$

or

$$S_n = na + d + 2d + 3d + \ldots + [n-1]d$$

Equally, we could write this

$$S_n = na + [n-1]d + [n-2]d + [n-3]d + \ldots + d$$

Adding these last two expressions gives

$$\begin{aligned}
2S_n &= 2na + (d + [n-1]d) + (2d + [n-2]d) + (3d + [n-3]d) \\
&\quad + \ldots + ([n-1]d + d) \\
&= 2na + (d + nd - d) + (2d + nd - 2d) + (3d + nd - 3d) \\
&\quad + \ldots + (nd - d + d) \\
&= 2na + nd + nd + nd + \ldots + nd \\
&= 2na + [n-1]nd \\
&= n(2a + [n-1]d)
\end{aligned}$$

Hence,

$$S_n = \frac{n}{2}(2a + [n-1]d)$$

Note that this could also be written

$$S_n = \frac{n(a + a + [n-1]d)}{2}$$

i.e.

$$S_n = (\text{number of terms}) (\text{average of first and last terms})$$

Therefore, for the series where $a = 50$, $d = 10$,

$$50 + 60 + 70 + 80 + \ldots$$

the sum of the first 3 terms

$$\begin{aligned}
S_3 &= \tfrac{3}{2}([2 \times 50] + [3-1][10]) \\
&= \tfrac{3}{2}(100 + 20) = \tfrac{3}{2}(120) = 180
\end{aligned}$$

and the sum of the first 10 terms

$$S_{10} = \tfrac{10}{2}([2 \times 50] + [10 - 1][10])$$
$$= \tfrac{10}{2}(100 + 90) = 5(190) = 950$$

Further simple interest

Suppose now that £500 is to be invested *annually* in an investment that pays 10% simple interest per annum. Therefore, the total value of the investment at the *beginning* of the

first year is 500
second year is $500 + (500 + 50)$ (2nd year investment plus 1st year investment, now worth 550)
third year is $500 + (500 + 50) + (500 + 100)$
fourth year is $500 + (500 + 50) + (500 + 100) + (500 + 150)$

etc. Therefore, at the beginning of the 12th year, the total value of the investment is found using the S_n formula with $n = 12$, $a = 500$, $d = 50$, i.e.

$$S_{12} = \tfrac{12}{2}([2 \times 500] + [12 - 1][50])$$
$$= 6(1,000 + 550) = 6(1,550) = £9,300$$

Geometric progression

A *geometric progression* is one where each successive term is the previous one *multiplied by a given constant.*

Progression (2) (p. 177) is an example of a geometric progression and so is

5. $8, 4, 2, 1, \tfrac{1}{2}, \tfrac{1}{4}, \ldots$

which starts with the given value 8 and each successive term is the previous one multiplied by $\tfrac{1}{2}$.

In general, a geometric progression can be written as

$$a, ar, ar^2, ar^3, ar^4, \ldots$$

where a is the first term and r is the *common ratio.*

In the previous examples (2) has

$$a = 50, r = 10$$

whilst (5) has

$$a = 8, r = \tfrac{1}{2}$$

If the first term is a, the second term is ar, the third term is ar^2 etc., notice that the nth term is

$$ar^{n-1}$$

Therefore, the 5th term of (2) is

$$50(10)^{5-1} = 50(10)^4 = 50(10,000) = 500,000$$

and the 8th term of (5) is

$$8(1/2)^{8-1} = 8(1/2)^7 = 8(1/128) = 1/16$$

Compound interest

A useful application of geometric progressions is the calculation of *compound interest*. Here, the sum upon which interest is calculated in any year includes the interest earned in the previous year, i.e. interest is not withdrawn at the end of each year as previously, but is re-invested the following year.

For example, suppose £500 is invested at 10% per annum compound interest, then during the first year the interest earned is $500 \times 0.10 = £50$ and so at the beginning of the second year the investment is worth £550. During the second year the interest is $550 \times 0.10 = £55$ and so at the beginning of the third year the investment is worth £605. During the third year the interest is $605 \times 0.10 = £60.50$ and so at the beginning of the fourth year the investment is worth £665.50, etc.

To generalise this, suppose we start with an investment of a and an interest factor of i. By *interest factor* we mean that if the interest rate is $R\%$ per year then $i = R/100$. In other words, if $R = 10\%$ then $i = 0.10$, and if $R = 5\%$ then $i = 0.05$, etc. Then, at the start of the 1st year we have

$$a$$

at the start of the 2nd year we have

$$a + ai = a(1+i)$$

at the start of the 3rd year we have

$$a(1+i) + a(1+i)i = a(1+i)^2$$

at the start of the 4th year we have

$$a(1+i)^2 + a(1+i)^2 i = a(1+i)^3$$

and, in general, at the start of the nth year, the value of the investment is

$$a(1+i)^{n-1}$$

In the example $a = 500$, $i = 0.10$, so at the beginning of the 7th year the value of the investment is

$$500(1+0.10)^{7-1} = 500(1.1)^6 = 500(1.77156)$$
$$= £885.78$$

Table 12.1. Compound interest

Year	5%	10%	15%	20%
0	1.00000	1.00000	1.00000	1.00000
1	1.05000	1.10000	1.15000	1.20000
2	1.10250	1.21000	1.32250	1.44000
3	1.15763	1.33100	1.52088	1.72800
4	1.21551	1.46410	1.74901	2.07360
5	1.27628	1.61051	2.01136	2.48832
6	1.34010	1.77156	2.31306	2.98598

Note that some relevant powers of 1.1 can be found in Table 12.1, which gives values of $(1+i)^n$ for various values of i and n. Usually, however, the relevant powers have to be found with the aid of more general tables or a calculator.

Note also that the 'value at the beginning of the 7th year' means the same as the 'value after 6 years', therefore, as before, choose the value of n in such calculations with great care.

Geometric series

Again, we frequently require the sum of a geometric progression. In general terms, the first n terms of such a progression are

$$a, ar, ar^2, ar^3, \ldots, ar^{n-1}$$

and so the sum of the first n terms, S_n, is

$$S_n = a + ar + ar^2 + ar^3 + \ldots + ar^{n-1}$$

To find an expression for S_n write down S_n again:

$$S_n = a + ar + ar^2 + ar^3 + \ldots + ar^{n-1} \tag{1}$$

Then multiply this expression throughout by r:

$$rS_n = ar + ar^2 + ar^3 + ar^4 + \ldots + ar^n \tag{2}$$

Subtracting (2) from (1) gives

$$S_n - rS_n = a - ar^n$$

or

$$(1-r)S_n = a(1-r^n)$$

i.e.

$$S_n = \frac{a(1-r^n)}{(1-r)}$$

A special case arises when $-1 < r < 1$. Under these circumstances r^n approaches zero as n approaches infinity and it is possible to talk about the sum to infinity of the geometric series and find

$$S_\infty = \frac{a}{(1-r)} \qquad (-1 < r < 1)$$

For example, when $a = 50$, $r = 10$, giving the series

$$50 + 500 + 5{,}000 + \ldots$$

then

$$S_4 = \frac{50(1 - 10^4)}{1 - 10} = \frac{50(1 - 10{,}000)}{1 - 10}$$

$$= \frac{50\ (9{,}999)}{9} = 50\ (1{,}111)$$

$$= 55{,}550$$

and, when $a = 8$, $r = \frac{1}{2}$, giving the series

$$8 + 4 + 2 + 1 + \tfrac{1}{2} + \ldots$$

$$S_8 = \frac{8(1 - [0.5]^8)}{1 - [0.5]} = \frac{8(1 - 0.0039)}{0.5}$$

$$= \frac{8(0.9961)}{0.5} = 15.9375$$

and

$$S_\infty = \frac{8}{1 - 0.5}$$

$$= \frac{8}{0.5}$$

$$= 16$$

Further compound interest

Suppose this time that £500 is to be invested *annually* in an investment that pays 10% compound interest per annum. Then the total value of the investment at the beginning of the 1st year is

$$500$$

After 1 year, or at the beginning of the 2nd year it is

$$500 + 500(1.1)$$

[2nd year investment plus 1st year investment now worth 500(1.1)]
After 2 years, or at the beginning of the 3rd year it is

$$500 + 500(1.1) + 500(1.1)^2$$

After 3 years, or at the beginning of the 4th year, it is

$$500 + 500(1.1) + 500(1.1)^2 + 500(1.1)^3$$

etc.

Therefore, after 5 years, or at the beginning of the 6th year, the total value of the investment is found using the S_n formula with $n = 6$, $a = 500$, $r = 1.1$:

$$S_6 = \frac{500(1 - [1.1]^6)}{1 - [1.1]} = \frac{500([1.1]^6 - 1)}{[1.1] - 1}$$

$$= \frac{500(1.77156 - 1)}{0.1} = \frac{500(0.77156)}{0.1}$$

$$= £3,857.80$$

Discounting

If money is capable of earning interest, then its absolute value some years in the future will be greater than its present value. Suppose investment is possible at 8% per annum, then £100 now will be worth £108 after one year.

Conversely, however, if it is required to have £108 available in one year's time only £100 is needed to be available at the present time, which is invested.

Suppose £100 is required in one year's time, then it is possible to calculate how much needs to be invested at the present time, X, by

$$X(1.08) = 100$$
$$X = (1/1.08) \times 100 = (0.9259) \times 100$$
$$= £92.59$$

If £100 is required in 2 years' time, it would be necessary to invest an amount at the present time given by

$$X(1.08)^2 = 100$$
$$X = (1/1.08)^2 \times 100 = (0.8573) \times 100$$
$$= £85.73$$

The calculation of the present value of sums of money required in the future is called *discounting*.

Table 12.2. Discount factors

Year	5%	10%	15%	20%
0	1.00000	1.00000	1.00000	1.00000
1	0.95238	0.90909	0.86957	0.83333
2	0.90703	0.82645	0.75614	0.69444
3	0.86384	0.75131	0.65752	0.57870
4	0.82270	0.68301	0.57175	0.48225
5	0.78353	0.62092	0.49718	0.40188
6	0.74622	0.56447	0.43233	0.33490

In general terms the *present value* of a sum A required in n years time with an interest factor of i is

$$P = \frac{A}{(1+i)^n}$$

Again, tables exist to help with discounting. Suppose it is required to find the present value of £8,000 required in 4 years' time with a discount rate of 15%, then Table 12.2 could be used to obtain the required value of $1/(1+i)^n$ and hence

$$P = 8,000 \left(\frac{1}{1.15} \right)^4$$

$$= 8,000(0.57175)$$
$$= £4,574$$

Annuities

An *annuity* is a constant annual income purchased for a fixed amount at the beginning.

Suppose an annual income of A is required for each of the next n years from an annuity with an interest factor of i. Then the amount that must be paid for this P is determined by adding together the present values of A for each of the next n years, i.e.

$$P = \frac{A}{(1+i)} + \frac{A}{(1+i)^2} + \frac{A}{(1+i)^3} + \ldots + \frac{A}{(1+i)^n}$$

Let

$$r = \frac{1}{1+i}$$

then

$$P = Ar + Ar^2 + Ar^3 + \ldots + Ar^n$$
$$= Ar(1 + r + r^2 + \ldots + r^{n-1})$$
$$= \frac{Ar(1 - r^n)}{1 - r}$$

because this is simply the summation of a geometric series. Therefore,

$$P = A \frac{1}{(1+i)} \left[\frac{1 - \dfrac{1}{(1+i)^n}}{1 - \dfrac{1}{(1+i)}} \right]$$

$$= A \frac{1}{(1+i)} \left[\frac{1 - \dfrac{1}{(1+i)^n}}{\dfrac{(1+i-1)}{(1+i)}} \right]$$

$$= A \frac{1}{(1+i)} \left[\frac{1 - \dfrac{1}{(1+i)^n}}{\dfrac{i}{(1+i)}} \right]$$

$$= A \frac{1}{(1+i)} \left[1 - \frac{1}{(1+i)^n} \right] \frac{(1+i)}{i}$$

that is

$$P = \frac{A}{i} \left[1 - \frac{1}{(1+i)^n} \right]$$

This is called the *present value of an annuity*.

The present value of a unit annuity is often denoted as a_n hence

$$a_n = \frac{1}{i} \left(1 - \frac{1}{(1+i)^n} \right)$$

Therefore, the amount required to pay an income of £1,000 annually for the next 12 years with an interest rate of 10% is given by

$$P = 1{,}000 a_{12}$$

$$P = \frac{1{,}000}{0.1} \left(1 - \frac{1}{(1.1)^{12}} \right)$$

Table 12.3. a_a = Present value of annuity

Year	5%	10%	15%	20%
1	0.95238	0.90909	0.86957	0.83333
2	1.85941	1.73554	1.62571	1.52778
3	2.72325	2.48685	2.28323	2.10648
4	3.54595	3.16987	2.85498	2.58873
5	4.32948	3.79079	3.35216	2.99061
6	5.07569	4.35526	3.78448	3.32551

$$= (10,000)(1 - 0.31863) \text{ (by calculator)}$$
$$= (10,000) (0.68137)$$
$$= £6,813.70$$

If this annuity was bought from an insurance company, presumably they would add an amount to this to be the profit that they themselves would require.

Tables, such as Table 12.3 which gives values of

$$a_n = \frac{1}{i}\left(1 - \frac{1}{(1+i)^n}\right)$$

can often be used to aid the calculation. For example, the amount required to pay an income of £1,200 annually for the next 6 years with an interest rate of 15% is given by

$$P = 1,200 a_6$$
$$= 1,200 \ (3.78448)$$
$$= £4,541.38$$

Similarly, we could ask what annual income a lump sum investment of £10,000 could pay for each of the next 5 years with an interest rate of 20%, i.e.

$$10,000 = \frac{A}{0.20}\left(1 - \frac{1}{(1.20)^5}\right)$$

$$= A a_5$$
$$= A(2.99061)$$

Giving

$$A = \frac{10,000}{2.99061}$$

$$= 3,343.80$$

Therefore, such an investment would pay an annual income of £3,343.80.

A special case occurs when an annuity is to continue paying an income indefinitely. Then n approaches infinity and $1/(1+i)^n$ approaches zero. Then

$$P = \frac{A}{i}$$

Such an annuity is called a *perpetual annuity*.

Therefore, a lump sum of £10,000 invested now at 15% would give an annual income given by

$$10,000 = \frac{A}{0.15}$$

$$A = 10,000 \times 0.15 = 1,500$$

i.e. an annual income of £1,500.

Mortgages and loans

Mortgage and loan repayments can be calculated using these same annuity formulae. In this case the lender is letting the borrower have the present lump sum P at the beginning of the period and, in effect, is investing in the borrower over the length of the loan with an interest factor i, with the borrower agreeing to pay back with regular payments A. Then, as before

$$P = \frac{A}{i}\left[1 - \frac{1}{(1+i)^n}\right]$$

For example, suppose a loan of £30,000 was required at an interest rate of 15% to be repaid annually over 20 years. Then the annual repayment is given by

$$30,000 = \frac{A}{0.15}\left[1 - \frac{1}{(1.15)}20\right]$$

$$4,500 = A(1 - 0.0611) \text{ (by calculator)}$$
$$4,500 = 0.9389A$$
$$A = 4,792.84$$

Hence £4,792.84 must be paid back each year.

Non-annual repayments

Loans are not usually repaid annually, but are repaid quarterly, monthly, or even weekly. The same formulae can still be used to determine the amount of the repayments, but n should then refer to the number of repayment periods and i to the interest factor averaged over each repayment period. Then, suppose in the previous example where £30,000 was borrowed over 20 years at 15%, the repayments were to be made each calendar month. Then there are $20 \times 12 = 240$ repayment periods and the period interest factor $= 0.15/12 = 0.0215$. The monthly repayment is then determined from

$$30{,}000 = \frac{A}{0.0125}\left[1 - \frac{1}{(1.0125)}240\right]$$

$$375 = A(1 - 0.05072) \text{ (by calculator)}$$
$$375 = 0.94928A$$
$$A = \frac{375}{0.94928} = 395.04$$

Hence, the loan is repaid at £395.04 each month.

Sinking funds

A *sinking fund* is an investment fund into which a constant annual sum is added to give a lump sum payment at some time in the future.

In general terms, an annual payment of A will give a lump sum P in n years time at an interest factor i given by

$$
\begin{aligned}
P \quad &= A + A(1+i) + A(1+i)^2 + \ldots + A(1+i)^{n-1}\\
&= A[1 + (1+i) + (1+i)^2 + \ldots + (1+i)^{n-1}]\\
&= \left[\frac{1-(1+i)^n}{1-(1+i)}\right]\\
&= A\left[\frac{(1+i)^n - 1}{(1+i)-1}\right]\\
&= A\left[\frac{(1+i)^n - 1}{i}\right]
\end{aligned}
$$

that is

$$P = \frac{A[(1+i)^n - 1]}{i}$$

Note that this assumes that the first payment is made at the end of the first year and the last payment is made when the lump sum is required.

The *future value of a unit annuity* is denoted by

$$s_n = \left[\frac{(1+i)^n - 1}{i}\right]$$

Table 12.4. s_n = Future value of an annuity

Year	5%	10%	15%	20%
1	1.00000	1.00000	1.00000	1.00000
2	2.05000	2.10000	2.15000	2.20000
3	3.15250	3.31000	3.47250	3.64000
4	4.31013	4.64100	4.99338	5.36800
5	5.52563	6.10510	6.74238	7.44160
6	6.80191	7.71561	8.75374	9.92992

Hence

$$P = As_n$$

Therefore, to obtain £10,000 in 10 years time at an interest rate of 9%, the amount paid each year is given by

$$10,000 = As_{10}$$

$$10,000 = \frac{A[(1.09)^{10} - 1]}{0.09}$$

$$= \frac{A(2.36736 - 1)}{0.09} \text{ (by calculator)}$$

$$= \frac{A(1.36736)}{0.09} = A(15.19289)$$

Then

$$A = \frac{10,000}{15.19289} = 658.20$$

Hence, £658.20 must be paid each year.

Once again, tables can be used to aid these calculations. Table 12.4 gives values of

$$s_n = \left[\frac{(1 + i)^n - 1}{i} \right]$$

Hence, if £5,000 is required in 6 years time an annual payment A must be paid given by

$$5,000 = As_6$$
$$= A(6.80191)$$

Then

$$A = \frac{5,000}{6.80191} = 735.09$$

that is, £735.09 must be paid annually.

Net present value of an investment

Many investment decisions in business require an annual outlay of cash for a number of years to achieve an annual return. For example, in the launching of a new product, market research and possibly the purchase of new equipment must be undertaken initially before production begins and the annual production costs must be incurred. The returns will then be the annual revenues earned by the new product.

Therefore if such an investment is to be considered over a period of n years with an interest factor of i, then if C_0 is the immediate cost and R_0 is the immediate return, C_1 is the first-year cost, assumed payable at the end of the first year, and R_1 is the first-year return, assumed received at the end of the first year, etc., then the present value of costs is given by

$$PC_n = C_0 + \frac{C_1}{(1+i)} + \frac{C_2}{(1+i)^2} + \ldots + \frac{C_n}{(1+i)^n}$$

and the present value of the income is given by

$$PR_n = R_0 + \frac{R_1}{(1+i)} + \frac{R_2}{(1+i)^2} + \ldots + \frac{R_n}{(1+i)^n}$$

The *net present value of the investment* is given by

$$PR_n - PC_n = (R_0 - C_0) + \frac{(R_1 - C_1)}{(1+i)} + \ldots + \frac{(R_n - C_n)}{(1+i)^n}$$

Naturally, if $PR_n - PC_n > 0$, then the investment is profitable and could be undertaken, but if $PR_n - PC_n < 0$, then the investment is unprofitable and should not be undertaken.

Here, i is interpreted as the interest factor that capital required for the project could be invested at to produce the cash outlays as required. It is usually called the *cost of capital*.

Example
Suppose a new product will cost £20,000 to launch and will then incur production costs of £2,000 each year. The revenue from the product will be £5,000 per year. Evaluate the net present value of the investment over a 10-year period if the cost of capital is 10%.

Costs are

$$C_0 = 20,000, \ C_1 = \ldots = C_{10} = 2,000$$

Revenue is

$$R_0 = 0, \ R_1 = \ldots = R_{10} = 5,000$$

Then

$$PR_{10} - PC_{10} = (-20,000) + \frac{(3,000)}{(1.1)} + \frac{(3,000)}{(1.1)^2} + \ldots + \frac{(3,000)}{(1.1)^{10}}$$

$$= (-20,000) + \frac{(3,000)}{(1.1)} \left[1 + \frac{1}{(1.1)} + \ldots + \frac{1}{(1.1)^9} \right]$$

$$= (-20,000) + (3,000) \left[\frac{1 - \dfrac{1}{(1.1)^{10}}}{1 - \dfrac{1}{(1.1)}} \right]$$

$$= (-20,000) + \frac{(3,000)}{(1.1)} \left[1 - \frac{1}{(1.1)^{10}} \right] \left[\frac{(1.1)}{(1.1 - 1)} \right]$$

$$= (-20,000) + \frac{(3,000)}{(0.1)} (1 - 0.38554) \quad \text{(by calculator)}$$

$$= (-20,000) + (30,000)(0.61446)$$
$$= (-20,000) + (18,434)$$
$$= -£1,566$$

Therefore, the new product does not look worthwhile. However, if the product could be considered to have a life of 12 years, then

$$PR_{12} - PC_{12} = (-20,000) + \frac{(3,000)}{(1.1)} \left[\frac{1 - \dfrac{1}{(1.1)^{12}}}{1 - \dfrac{1}{(1.1)}} \right]$$

$$= (-20,000) + \frac{(3,000)}{(0.1)} \left[1 - \frac{1}{(1.1)^{12}} \right]$$

$$= (-20,000) + (30,000)(1 - 0.31863)$$
$$= (-20,000) + (30,000)(0.68137)$$
$$= (-20,000) + (20,441)$$
$$= £441$$

In other words, it is now just worth considering.

Internal rate of return

The value of i used in the above formulae obviously has a considerable influence on the net present value of a project under consideration. However, it is usually extremely difficult to estimate this with any accuracy.

Often, therefore, the issue is addressed in reverse – it is required to know what the cost of capital should be to make the project break even, i.e. the value of i to give

$$PR_n = PC_n$$

or

$$(R_0 - C_0) + \frac{(R_1 - C_1)}{(1+i)} + \ldots + \frac{(R_n - C_n)}{(1+i)^n} = 0$$

This value of i is called the *internal rate of return* (IRR) and the higher it is, the more profitable the project will be.

Because of the difficulty of solving high-degree polynomial equations, internal rates of return are not easy to determine.

For example, suppose a project will have a life cycle of just 2 years. It will cost £400 to set up, £100 to run in the first year and £80 to run in the second year. It will return £300 at the end of each year.

Then, to find the IRR we solve

$$(-400) + \frac{(200)}{(1+i)} + \frac{(220)}{(1+i)^2} = 0$$

$$(-400)(1+i)^2 + (200)(1+i) + 220 = 0$$
$$(-400)(1 + 2i + i^2) + 200 + 200i + 220 = 0$$
$$-400 - 800i - 400i^2 + 200i + 420 = 0$$
$$400i^2 + 600i - 20 = 0$$

or

$$20i^2 + 30i - 1 = 0$$

using the quadratic formula

$$i = \frac{-30 \pm \sqrt{[(30)^2 - 4(20)(-1)]}}{2(20)}$$

$$= \frac{-30 \pm \sqrt{(900 + 80)}}{40}$$

$$= \frac{-30 \pm \sqrt{980}}{40} = \frac{-30 \pm 31.30}{40}$$

$$= 0.03 \text{ or } -1.53$$

Table 12.5. Interest table of values of $(1+i)^n$ (extended version of Table 12.1)

n	8%	9%	10%	11%	12%	13%	14%	15%
1	1.0800	1.0900	1.1000	1.1100	1.1200	1.1300	1.1400	1.1500
2	1.1664	1.1881	1.2100	1.2321	1.2544	1.2769	1.2996	1.3225
3	1.2597	1.2950	1.3310	1.3676	1.4049	1.4429	1.4815	1.5209
4	1.3605	1.4116	1.4641	1.5181	1.5735	1.6305	1.6890	1.7490
5	1.4693	1.5386	1.6105	1.6851	1.7623	1.8424	1.9254	2.0114
6	1.5869	1.6771	1.7716	1.8704	1.9738	2.0820	2.1950	2.3131
7	1.7138	1.8280	1.9487	2.0762	2.2107	2.3526	2.5023	2.6600
8	1.8509	1.9926	2.1436	2.3045	2.4760	2.6584	2.8526	3.0590
9	1.9990	2.1719	2.3579	2.5580	2.7731	3.0040	3.2519	3.5179
10	2.1589	2.3674	2.5937	2.8394	3.1058	3.3946	3.7072	4.0456
11	2.3316	2.5804	2.8531	3.1518	3.4785	3.8359	4.2262	4.6524
12	2.5182	2.8127	3.1384	3.4984	3.8960	4.3345	4.8179	5.3502

*Remember that if the interest rate is 8%, then $i = 0.08$.

Table 12.6. Discounting table of values of $1/(1+i)^n$ (extended version of Table 12.2)

n	8%	9%	10%	11%	12%	13%	14%	15%
1	0.92593	0.91743	0.90909	0.90090	0.89286	0.88496	0.87719	0.86957
2	0.85734	0.84168	0.82645	0.81162	0.79719	0.78315	0.76947	0.75614
3	0.79383	0.77218	0.75131	0.73119	0.71178	0.69305	0.67497	0.65752
4	0.73503	0.70843	0.68301	0.65873	0.63552	0.61332	0.59208	0.57175
5	0.68058	0.64993	0.62092	0.59345	0.56743	0.54276	0.51937	0.49718
6	0.63017	0.59627	0.56447	0.53464	0.50663	0.48032	0.45559	0.43233
7	0.58349	0.54703	0.51316	0.48166	0.45235	0.42506	0.39964	0.37594
8	0.54027	0.50187	0.46651	0.43393	0.40388	0.37616	0.35056	0.32690
9	0.50025	0.46043	0.42410	0.39092	0.36061	0.33288	0.30751	0.28426
10	0.46319	0.42241	0.38554	0.35218	0.32197	0.29459	0.26974	0.24718
11	0.42888	0.38753	0.35049	0.31728	0.28748	0.26070	0.23662	0.21494
12	0.39711	0.35553	0.31863	0.28584	0.25667	0.23071	0.20756	0.18691

Therefore, the IRR $= 0.03$, i.e. 3% (the negative value need not be considered).

If it is required to consider a longer-term problem, suppose a project will cost £17,000 to set up and then £2,000 per year for each of the next 10 years, but it will return £5,000 per year over the period. Then to find the IRR we must solve

$$(-17,000) + \frac{(3,000)}{(1+i)} + \frac{(3,000)}{(1+i)^2} + \ldots + \frac{(3,000)}{(1+i)^{10}} = 0$$

Let the left-hand side of this equation be denoted by $C(i)$. The only way, in this book to find a value for i is to evaluate $C(i)$ for different chosen values of i using a discounting table. The tables already used (Tables 12.1–12.4) are

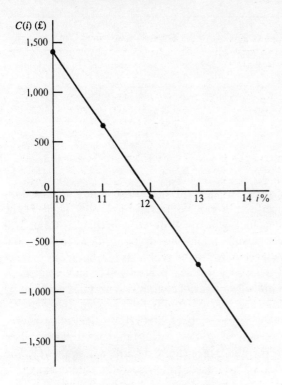

Fig. 12.1 Finding the IRR graphically.

those provided by the ICSA for their examinations. However, they are very limited and so Tables 12.5 and 12.6, which are extended versions of Tables 12.1 and 12.2, are also presented. Table 12.6 will be used here as follows:

$$C(i) = (-17,000) + (3,000)\frac{1}{(1+i)} + \frac{1}{(1+i)^2} + \cdots + \frac{1}{(1+i)^{10}}$$

Using Table 12.6 we find

$C(10) = (-17,000) + (3,000)(6.14456) = -17,000 + 18,433.68 = 1,433.68$
$C(11) = (-17,000) + (3,000)(5.88922) = -17,000 + 17,667.66 = 667.66$
$C(12) = (-17,000) + (3,000)(5.65022) = -17,000 + 16,950.66 = -49.34$
$C(13) = (-17,000) + (3,000)(5.42625) = -17,000 + 16,278.75 = -721.25$
$C(14) = (-17,000) + (3,000)(5.21612) = -17,000 + 15,648.36 = -1,351.64$

It is concluded that the internal rate of return is approximately 12%, by choosing the value nearest zero.

A more accurate value of the IRR could be found graphically, as shown in Fig. 12.1. From this we see that $C(i) = 0$ when $i = 11.9$. Therefore, the IRR equals 11.9%.

13

Probability

Introduction

In business many of the day-to-day operations and planning are based on uncertainties. These uncertainties can be at various levels. There is the problem of whether a machine will break down, whether an order will arrive on time, both of which might be thought of as operational uncertainties. At another level there are the problems of whether a contract tender will be successful, whether a research project will be successful, each of which could be thought of as micro-economic uncertainties. Finally, there are problems of future market trends, changes in the markets themselves, technological changes which might all be thought of as macro-economic uncertainties. Ideally all of these uncertainties should be taken account of but this is only possible if they can be described in some way. The terms 'chance' and 'likelihood' are used quite naturally, simple examples being the following:

1. There is a 1 in 3 chance one of our competitors will withdraw from our market.
2. There is a 60 : 40 chance a better product will be developed in the next year.
3. There is a 20% chance we will be awarded the contract.
4. Five times out of six this type of research project will be successful.

Here the statements have used ratios like 1 in 3 or percentages like 20% to describe the chance of an event happening. To progress further a unified measure of uncertainty or risk is required and the measure used is *probability*.

Outcomes and events

Before dealing with probability itself we need to consider the things we are trying to find probabilities for. In any situation where uncertainty is present there is a set of possible results which can occur. Each distinct result is called an *outcome* and the list of all possible outcomes is called the *outcome set*.

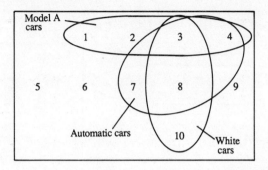

Fig. 13.1 Venn diagram showing events automatic, white and model A cars.

For example if an inspector checks 5 switches to see how many operate correctly, the possible outcomes are

0, 1, 2, 3, 4 or 5

switches operate correctly. This list is the outcome set.

Alternatively, suppose a firm tenders for two different contracts. The outcome set would consist of four outcomes:

1. Contract 1 obtained,   Contract 2 obtained.
2. Contract 1 not obtained, Contract 2 obtained.
3. Contract 1 obtained,   Contract 2 not obtained.
4. Contract 1 not obtained, Contract 2 not obtained.

Often our interest is not in a single outcome but rather a group of outcomes. An *event* is a single outcome or a collection of outcomes. So, in the first example an event might be 'less than three switches operate correctly' or 'between 2 and 5 switches operate correctly'. In the second example an event might be 'one contract tender is successful' or 'both contract tenders are unsuccessful'. There are many other events which could be defined in these examples and a particular outcome might appear in any number of events.

Venn diagrams

Venn diagrams (see p. 1) are pictures used to illustrate outcomes, events and how they interrelate. Suppose that a car showroom has 10 new cars in stock. Cars 1–4 are model A, cars 5–9 are model B and car 10 is model C. Cars 1, 2, 5, 6 and 7 are red, cars 3, 8 and 10 are white whilst cars 4 and 9 are black. Finally cars 1, 2, 5, 6, 9 and 10 are manual whilst cars 3, 4, 7 and 8 are automatics. To illustrate these characteristics and how they overlap, an outcome set or sample space can be drawn as in Fig. 13.1.

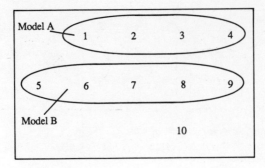

Fig. 13.2 Venn diagram of mutually exclusive events, model A and B
cars.

This Venn diagram shows the following events and how they overlap.

1. Model A cars.
2. White cars.
3. Automatic cars.

Looking at the diagram we see cars 3 and 8 have all three characteristics
specified, car 4 is a model A and automatic, car 7 is automatic, car 10 is
white, cars 1 and 2 are model A and cars 5, 6 and 9 have none of these
characteristics. The shapes used to illustrate each event are called *event
spaces*. In a Venn diagram the size of the event space does not signify its
relative importance and event spaces are not drawn to scale.

Mutually exclusive events

Two events are said to be *mutually exclusive* (see p. 3) if they cannot
happen together. In the new cars' example, the events 'a car is model A' and
'a car is model B' are mutually exclusive since a car cannot be both models
at once. In a Venn diagram such mutually exclusive events have event
spaces which do not overlap. Figure 13.2 shows these two events.

Looking at Fig. 13.1 the event spaces for 'white cars' and 'automatic cars'
overlap so these are not mutually exclusive. In fact, cars 3 and 8 have both
characteristics – they are both white and automatic.

In general, events are denoted by capital letters and if their event spaces
do not overlap they are mutually exclusive. If the event spaces do overlap
the events are not mutually exclusive. For two events *A* and *B* Fig 13.3
illustrates each case.

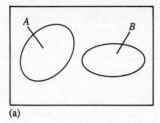 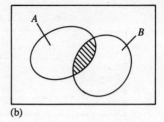

(a)   (b)

Fig. 13.3 Venn diagrams of (a) mutually exclusive and (b) non-mutually
exclusive events.

Independent events

Two events are said to be *independent* if the occurrence or non-occurrence
of one event has no influence or effect on the occurrence of the other event. If
a firm tenders for two contracts with separate organisations the event
'offered first contract' and 'offered second contract' will be independent
since the tenders are being made to two different organisations and being
offered one contract will have no influence on the offering of the other
contract. In contrast, if an organisation has a policy of offering contracts to
firms which have not previously been awarded a contract by the
organisation, then the event 'offered contract' is influenced by the event
'have already been awarded a contract', in this case detrimentally.

Two mutually exclusive events cannot be independent since the occurrence of one means the other cannot happen.

Definitions of probability

There are three ways in which probability can be defined. The first uses a
theoretical approach, the second relies on frequency data and the final
depends on a person's judgement.

Theoretical probability

Some probabilities can be deduced from considering the possible outcomes
and events, and their relative chance of occurring. Suppose 10 people are
entered in a raffle with one ticket each. As long as the raffle is carried out
fairly each person has an equal chance of winning the raffle. It may then be
deduced that the probability a particular person wins the raffle is 0.1. Going
further, if there are 6 men and 4 women entered for the raffle, the probability
that a woman wins the raffle is 0.4.

Table 13.1. Comparison of delivery reliability of UK and overseas suppliers

	UK suppliers	Overseas suppliers	Total
Orders on time	390	860	1,250
Orders late	130	620	750
Total	520	1,480	2,000

Empirical probability

If a particular situation (often called a trial) can be repeated a number of times, then the number of times the event of interest occurs may be counted. The estimated probability for the event is then

$$P \text{ (event)} = \frac{\text{number of trials in which event occurs}}{\text{total number of trials}}$$

Suppose a company has recorded how its suppliers perform in filling orders on time, the figures being given in Table 13.1. This table can be used to find empirical probabilities:

$$P \text{ (order on time)} = \frac{\text{number of orders on time}}{\text{total number of orders}}$$

$$= \frac{1,250}{2,000}$$

$$= 0.625$$

P (order placed with overseas supplier)

$$= \frac{\text{number of orders placed with overseas supplier}}{\text{total number of orders}}$$

$$= \frac{1,480}{2,000}$$

$$= 0.740$$

P (order late and from UK supplier)

$$= \frac{\text{number of orders with UK supplier and late}}{\text{total number of orders}}$$

$$= \frac{130}{2,000}$$

$$= 0.065$$

This method of estimating probabilities relies on having a large number of trials. If only a few trials are available these probabilities can be unreliable. If the popularity of a new product is being investigated it is hardly convincing to claim that the probability that people will prefer the new product is 0.75, if this estimate is based on 6 out of 8 people stating a preference for the new product. If, however, it is based on 300,000 out of 400,000 people stating a preference for the new product, then the estimate looks rather more reliable and some faith can be placed in it.

This type of probability is sometimes called a relative frequency probability since it is based on frequencies.

Subjective probability

There are many situations where neither of the previous two methods is applicable or appropriate to finding a probability. In these cases, if a probability is required, an informed person might be asked to estimate the probability.

If a firm wishes to know whether the demand for a new product will exceed 200 units per month then, starting from a theoretical view, there is no reason why this probability should be a certain value. Secondly, the product cannot be launched several times and the number of times when demand exceeds 200 units be counted. The only realistic approach is to ask someone who has experience of the product's market or of similar launches what their estimate of the probability would be. Perhaps the firm's marketing manager or an independent market researcher could be asked.

Probability can range from a value of 0 up to 1. If the probability of an event is 0, then this indicates it is impossible for the event to happen. At the other end of the scale if the probability of an event is 1 this indicates the event is certain to happen.

Total probability equals 1, so if all the possible outcomes of a trial are listed with their probabilities, the probability total will be 1. This can be useful when the events of interest are *complementary* events. Complementary events are mutually exclusive events which together cover all possible outcomes. A typical example of complementary events is the following:

Event A: Firm is awarded contract.
Event B: Firm is not awarded contract.

Complementary events can be illustrated in a Venn diagram as shown in Fig. 13.4.

$\bar{A}$ is used to represent the complementary event to A and because total probability equals 1, this leads to the first law of probability, which can be written as

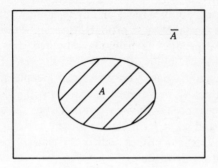

Fig. 13.4 Venn diagram of complementary events A and $\bar{A}$.

$$P(A) + P(\bar{A}) = 1$$

This is called the *total law of probability*.

Probabilities are quoted as decimal figures but can easily be converted to ratios or percentages. For example a probability of 0.2 is the same as a 1 in 5 chance which in turn is the same as a percentage chance of 20%.

Addition law of probability

This is the second law of probability and allows combined probabilities to be found where the probability of one event *or* another event happening, or both happening, is required. If the events are mutually exclusive the addition law of probability for events A and B is given by

$$P(A \text{ or } B) = P(A) + P(B)$$

or, in set-theory notation

$$P(A \cup B) = P(A) + P(B)$$

and can be illustrated by the shaded areas in Fig. 13.5.

If the probabilities that certain companies are awarded a particular contract are as given in Table 13.2, then the probability that a firm in London is awarded the contract is the probability that Firm A or Firm D is awarded the contract. Since firm A or D being awarded the contract are mutually exclusive events

$$\begin{aligned} P(A \text{ or } D) &= P(A) + P(D) \\ &= 0.2 + 0.1 \\ &= 0.3 \end{aligned}$$

as shown in Fig. 13.6.

Table 13.2. Chances of four firms being awarded a contract

Firm	Location	Probability
A	London	0.2
B	Manchester	0.4
C	Birmingham	0.3
D	London	0.1

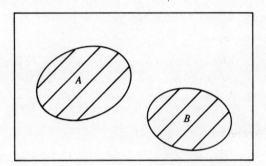

Fig. *13.5* Venn diagram illustrating law for mutually exclusive events.

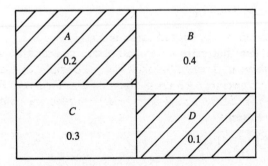

Fig. *13.6* Venn diagram of event firms *A* or *D* being awarded the contract.

Table 13.3. Numbers of employees in departments of a firm by their age

	Age				
	Under 21	21–35	35–50	51–65	Total
Accounts	17	33	10	5	65
Sales	5	54	17	9	85
Production	6	56	31	12	105
Research	2	27	12	4	45
Total	30	170	70	30	300

A different situation arises if a table with frequencies is given. In Table 13.3 the number of employees, by age, is given in each of four departments within a firm. The probability of an employee being under 21 is

$$P \text{ (under 21)} = \frac{30}{300}$$

$$= 0.1$$

The probability of an employee being 21 or over can then be found as

$$P \text{ (21 or over)} = 1 - P \text{ (under 21)}$$
$$= 1 - 0.1$$
$$= 0.9$$

The probability that an employee is from the accounts department or sales department is

$$P \text{ (accounts or sales)} = P \text{ (accounts)} + P \text{ (sales)}$$

$$= \frac{65}{300} + \frac{85}{300}$$

$$= 0.5$$

When events are not mutually exclusive, then the addition law of probability becomes

$$P(A \text{ or } B) = P(A) + P(B) - P(A \text{ and } B)$$

or in set-theory notation

$$P(A \cup B) = P(A) + P(B) - (A \cap B)$$

where the probability of A and B is the probability of overlap between events A and B. This is illustrated in Fig. 13.7. It can be seen that if the overlap between A and B (the shaded area) were not subtracted it would be counted twice.

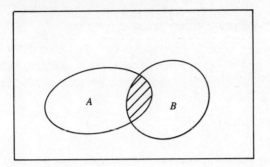

Fig. 13.7 Venn diagram of two non-mutually exclusive events *A* and *B*.

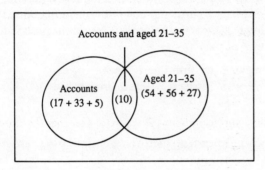

Fig. 13.8 Venn diagram showing overlap of the events 'aged 21–35' and
'accounts'.

For Table 13.3, if the probability that an employee worked in accounts or
was aged 21–35 is required, then

P (accounts or aged 21–35)
$= P$ (accounts) $+ P$ (aged 21–35) $- P$ (accounts and aged 21–35)
$= \dfrac{65}{300} + \dfrac{70}{300} - \dfrac{33}{300}$

$= 0.34$

or by using the Venn diagram in Fig. 13.8,

$$P \text{ (accounts or aged 21–35)} = \frac{17 + 33 + 5 + 10 + 54 + 56 + 27}{300}$$

$$= \frac{102}{300}$$

$$= 0.34$$

Multiplication law of probability

This is the third law of probability and allows us to find probabilities when we are interested in the probability of one event *and* another event happening. If the events are independent, then the multiplication law for events A and B is given by

$$P(A \text{ and } B) = P(A) \times P(B)$$

or in set-theory notation

$$P(A \cap B) = P(A) \times P(B)$$

Suppose a factory has two separate production lines. If the probability that the first line breaks down on a particular day is 0.1, the probability that the second line breaks down on a particular day is 0.2, then the probability that both break down on a particular day is

$$
\begin{aligned}
P &\text{ (line 1 breaks down and line 2 breaks down)} \\
&= P \text{ (line 1 breaks down)} \times P \text{ (line 2 breaks down)} \\
&= 0.1 \times 0.2 \\
&= 0.02
\end{aligned}
$$

If the events are not independent then the multiplication law must be modified. For the example of employees in Table 13.3 suppose it is required to find the probability that an employee is from production and is aged 51–65, then this can be read off from the table directly as

$$P \text{ (production and age 51–65)} = \frac{12}{300}$$

$$= 0.04$$

Using the simple multiplication law gives an incorrect answer since the events 'production employee' and 'aged 51–65' are not independent. To deal with situations where the events are not independent it is necessary to use *conditional* probability. A conditional probability is one where account is taken of the influence one event can have on another event happening. In a raffle if a person has two out of ten tickets entered, the probability that the person wins first prize is

$$P \text{ (first drawn)} = \frac{2}{10}$$

$$= 0.2$$

The probability the person then wins the second prize is

$$P \text{ (second drawn given first drawn)} = \frac{2-1}{10-1}$$

$$= 0.1111$$

since as the person has won first prize, he or she has only one ticket left in the draw and there are now only 9 tickets left altogether.

Conditional probabilities are those for event A given event B has happened or for event B given event A has happened. These are denoted by

$$P \text{ (event } A \text{ given event } B) = P(A \mid B)$$
$$P \text{ (event } B \text{ given event } A) = P(B \mid A)$$

the vertical lines representing 'given that'.

The general multiplication law can be written in two ways:

$$P(A \text{ and } B) = P(A)P(B \mid A)$$

or

$$P(A \text{ and } B) = P(B)P(A \mid B)$$

Alternatively, in set-theory notation, these are:

$$P(A \cap B) = P(A)P(B \mid A)$$

or

$$P(A \cap B) = P(B)P(A \mid B)$$

Returning to the employee example in Table 13.3, to find the probability that an employee works in production and is aged 51–65 either formula can be used:

$$P \text{ (production and aged 51–65)}$$
$$= P \text{ (production) } P \text{ (aged 51–65 given production)}$$

Now P (aged 51–65 given production) is calculated as

$$\frac{\text{Number of employees aged 51–65 and working in production}}{\text{Number of employees working in production}}$$

$$= \frac{12}{105}$$

Hence

$$P \text{ (production and aged 51–65)} = \frac{105}{300} \times \frac{12}{105}$$

$$= 0.04 \text{ (as before)}$$

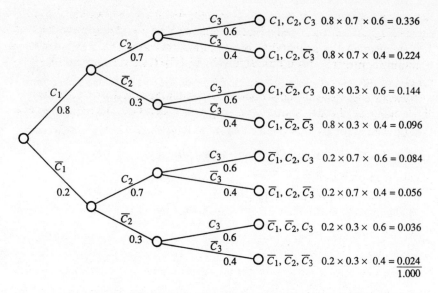

Fig. 13.9 Probability tree of outcomes of tendering for three contracts.

Using the alternative formula gives

P (production and aged 51-65)
$= P$ (aged 51-65) P (production given aged 51-65)

$$= \frac{30}{300} \times \frac{12}{30}$$

$$= 0.04$$

(again as before).

Either version can be used when the events are characteristics but if one event follows another event then only one version will be usable.

Probability tree diagram

An alternative method of illustrating probability problems is a tree diagram. The tree diagram shows all the possible outcomes with their probabilities. Suppose a firm tenders for three contracts. If the probability of success for the first contract is 0.8, for the second contract is 0.7 and for the third contract is 0.6, then the outcomes of all three tenders can be illustrated by the tree diagram in Fig. 13.9. In the tree diagram C_1 represents 'contract 1 awarded' and $\overline{C}_1$ represents 'contract 1 not awarded' to the firm and similarly for C_2 and C_3. All the possible outcomes are shown by the diagram and their individual probabilities are calculated at the ends.

If we wanted the probability of obtaining contracts 1 and 3 but not obtaining contract 2, this is represented by $C_1, \overline{C_2} \cdot C_3$ and its probability is 0.144.

Next suppose we want the probability of obtaining exactly two contracts. By looking at the diagram, there are three outcomes which meet our requirements:

$$\overline{C_1}, C_2, C_3 \qquad C_1, \overline{C_2}, C_3 \qquad C_1, C_2, \overline{C_3}$$

which have probabilities

$$0.224 \qquad 0.144 \qquad 0.084$$

so the probability of obtaining exactly two contracts is

$$0.224 + 0.144 + 0.084 = 0.452$$

If we want the probability of obtaining contract 1 but not contract 3, then we require every outcome containing both C_1 and $\overline{C_3}$, which are

$$C_1, C_2, \overline{C_3} \qquad C_1, \overline{C_2}, \overline{C_3}$$

with probabilities

$$0.224 \qquad 0.096$$

so the required probability is

$$0.224 + 0.096 = 0.320$$

Finally, if we want the probability of obtaining contract 2 or contract 3 but not both, then we require each outcome with C_2 or C_3 but not both, which are

$$C_1, C_2, \overline{C_3} \qquad C_1, \overline{C_2}, C_3 \qquad \overline{C_1}, C_2, \overline{C_3} \qquad \overline{C_1}, \overline{C_2}, C_3$$

with probabilities

$$0.224 \qquad 0.144 \qquad 0.056 \qquad 0.036$$

so the probability required is

$$0.224 + 0.144 + 0.056 + 0.036 = 0.460$$

14

Probability distributions

Introduction

The probability laws in the previous chapter were useful for finding probabilities when we were dealing with combinations of two events. However, their extension to more than two events is not always as simple. One way round this problem is to draw a tree diagram, but these become unmanageable if the number of events is large. An alternative is to use probability distributions. Theoretical probability distributions are summaries, in a formula or set of tables, of the probabilities for the repeated occurrence of an event.

Probability distributions and expected values

A probability distribution, in its simplest form, is a list of outcomes and their associated probabilities. An example is given in Table 14.1 for the colours of new cars.

In Fig. 13.9 the tree diagram showed the probabilities of each combination of contracts awarded. This could be summarised into a probability distribution of how many contracts were awarded, this being shown in Table 14.2. A question which naturally arises is how many contracts can the firm expect to be awarded? To find expectations the following formula is used:

$$\text{expected value (EV)} = \Sigma \; \text{Prob}(x)x$$
$$= \Sigma px$$

so for the contracts' example, the expected number awarded is

$$(0.024)(0) + (0.118)(1) + (0.452)(2) + (0.336)(3)$$
$$= 2.1 \text{ contracts}$$

The expected value is the average number of contracts the firm could expect to be awarded in the long run if the situation were repeated a large number of times.

If a frequency table is given it can be converted into a probability

Table 14.1. Probability distribution for colour of new car

Colour of car	Probability
Red	0.3
Green	0.1
White	0.2
Blue	0.1
Black	0.2
Other	0.1

Table 14.2. Probability distribution for number of contracts awarded

Number of contracts awarded		Probability
0	0.024	0.024
1	0.096 + 0.056 + 0.036	0.188
2	0.224 + 0.144 + 0.084	0.452
3	0.336	0.336
		1.000

Table 14.3. Relative frequencies and expected value for number of orders

Number of orders per day, x	Number of days f	Probability p	px
0	2	0.02	0.00
1	17	0.17	0.17
2	42	0.42	0.84
3	19	0.19	0.57
4	12	0.12	0.48
5	7	0.07	0.35
6 or more	1	0.01	0.06
	100	1.00	2.49

distribution by dividing each frequency by total frequency. In Table 14.3 a frequency table is given for the number of orders arriving at a factory per day. The frequencies are then converted to probabilities by dividing by 100, the total frequency. The expected value is then found by calculating the product of the probability (p) column and the x column. Just as for calculating the mean the same rules for determining x when there are open-ended classes or when there are intervals apply. Here the expected number of orders arriving is 2.49 orders per day.

Any probability distribution found from a frequency table is usually called an *empirical* probability distribution.

Binomial distribution

The binomial distribution is a theoretical distribution which has many applications within the sphere of business. The binomial distribution is a discrete distribution, giving the probability of an event happening a number of times. It assumes that there are only two mutually exclusive events of interest, one called 'success', the other called 'failure'. In a series of trials these are the only possible results and the probability of a success is the same in each trial. Using the binomial distribution the probability of a specified number of successes in a number of trials can be calculated.

The binomial distribution is given by the formula

$$\text{Prob }(r \text{ successes}) = \frac{n!}{r!(n-r)!} p^r (1-p)^{n-r}$$

where p is the probability of a success in a single trial, n is the number of trials and ! stands for factorial. A factorial is calculated by multiplying each successive integer up to and including the factorial required, so $5! = 1 \times 2 \times 3 \times 4 \times 5 = 120$. (Note $0! = 1$.)

The expression

$$\frac{n!}{r!(n-r)!}$$

is sometimes denoted by ^nC_r and is the number of different ways (combinations) in which r successes can be obtained from n trials.

If a company tenders for 5 contracts and the probability of being awarded an individual contract is 0.7, then the binomial distribution can be used to calculate the probability of being awarded a specified number of contracts.

If a success is defined as being awarded a contract, then $p = 0.7$. The total number of trials is the number of contracts tendered for, so $n = 5$. The probability of being awarded no contracts ($r = 0$) is then

$$P(0) = \frac{5!}{0!(5-0)!} (0.7)^0 (0.3)^5$$

$$= (0.3)^5$$
$$= 0.00243$$

Similarly, we can calculate the probabilities for each number of contracts being awarded.

For one contract ($r = 1$)

$$P(1) = \frac{5!}{1!(5-1)!}(0.7)^1(0.3)^4$$

$$= 5(0.7)(0.3)^4$$
$$= 0.02835$$

For two contracts $(r=2)$

$$P(2) = \frac{5!}{2!(5-2)!}(0.7)^2(0.3)^3$$

$$= 10(0.7)^2(0.3)^3$$
$$= 0.13230$$

For three contracts $(r=3)$

$$P(3) = \frac{5!}{3!(5-3)!}(0.7)^3(0.3)^2$$

$$= 10(0.7)^3(0.3)^2$$
$$= 0.30870$$

For four contracts $(r=4)$

$$P(4) = \frac{5!}{4!(5-4)!}(0.7)^4(0.3)^1$$

$$= 5(0.7)^4(0.3)^1$$
$$= 0.36015$$

For five contracts $(r=5)$

$$P(5) = \frac{5!}{5!(5-5)!}(0.7)^5(0.3)^0$$

$$= (0.7)^5$$
$$= 0.16807$$

These can be summarised and listed in a probability distribution as in Table 14.4, and this probability distribution can be illustrated by Fig. 14.1.

Further illustrations of the binomial distribution are given for $n=8$ and values of $p=0.2, 0.5, 0.8$ in Fig. 14.2.

The binomial distribution is often used in sampling associated with quality control. As an example, consider a batch of switches where 10% of the switches do not work correctly. If 10 switches are checked it is possible to find the following probabilities:

1. None are faulty.
2. Two are faulty.
3. Two or less are faulty.

Table 14.4. Binomial probabilities

Number of contracts awarded	Binomial probability
0	0.00243
1	0.02835
2	0.13230
3	0.30870
4	0.36015
5	0.16807
	1.00000

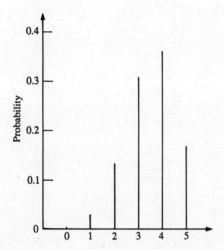

Fig. 14.1 Binomial probabilities for contracts awarded.

It is known that $p = 0.1$ and $n = 10$. Using the binomial distribution:

1. $$P(0) = \frac{10!}{0!(10-0)!} (0.1)^0 (0.9)^{10}$$

    $$= (0.9)^{10}$$
    $$= 0.3487$$

2. $$P(2) = \frac{10!}{2!(10-2)!} (0.1)^2 (0.9)^8$$

    $$= 45(0.1)^2 (0.9)^8$$
    $$= 0.1937$$

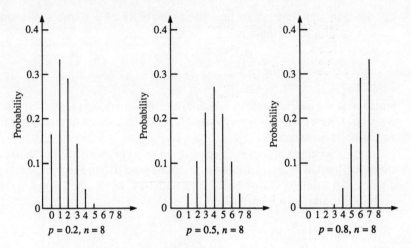

Fig. 14.2 Binomial distributions.

3. $$P(2 \text{ or less}) = P(0) + P(1) + P(2)$$

$$= 0.3487 + \frac{10!}{1!(10-1)!}(0.1)^1(0.9)^9 + 0.1937$$

$$= 0.3487 + 0.3874 + 0.1937$$
$$= 0.9298$$

In summary, the binomial distribution is used for finding probabilities for a number of successes out of a number of trials provided the following requirements are met:

1. The trials are independent.
2. The probability of a success is the same in each trial.
3. The number of trials is known.
4. There are only two possible outcomes of a trial, termed success and failure.

Poisson distribution

The Poisson distribution, like the binomial distribution, is a discrete distribution. It is used when events happen at an average rate but each individual event occurs randomly. This means that there is no such thing as a trial but rather that an event can occur at any time or place. The Poisson distribution can be used to find the probability of a number of events occurring, and its formula is

$$P(r \text{ successes}) = \frac{m^r}{r!} e^{-m}$$

where m is the average rate at which events occur and e is a mathematical constant (like π) which is approximately equal to 2.71828 and is called the *exponential constant*.

Suppose a car salesroom sells one car, on average, per day. If sales are at random, then the Poisson distribution can be used to find the probability of a particular number of cars being sold on a day. In this case $m = 1$, so the probability that no cars are sold on a day is

$$P(0) = \frac{(1)^0}{0!} e^{-1}$$

$$= e^{-1}$$
$$= 0.3679$$

Similarly, for one car sold on a day

$$P(1) = \frac{(1)^1}{1!} e^{-1}$$

$$= e^{-1}$$
$$= 0.3679$$

and for two cars

$$P(2) = \frac{(1)^2}{2!} e^{-1}$$

$$= \tfrac{1}{2} e^{-1}$$
$$= 0.1839$$

This process can be continued for any number of cars sold in a day. Generally, the calculations are continued until the probabilities become negligible. In this case the distribution obtained is given in Table 14.5. As any number of car sales is theoretically possible the last interval is an open-ended interval.

An alternative way of calculating the probabilities is to use a relationship between successive probabilities:

$$P(r+1 \text{ successes}) = \frac{mP(r \text{ successes})}{r+1}$$

Table 14.5. Poisson probabilities for number of
cars sold

Number of cars sold	Probability
0	0.3679
1	0.3679
2	0.1839
3	0.0613
4	0.0153
5	0.0031
6	0.0005
over 6	0.0001
	1.0000

For illustration, in Table 14.5, to obtain the probability of 3 cars sold from
the probability of 2 cars sold

$$P(3 \text{ cars sold}) = \frac{(m)P(2 \text{ cars sold})}{3}$$

$$= \tfrac{1}{3}(0.1839)$$
$$= 0.0613$$

(as before).

In Fig. 14.3 illustrations of Poisson distributions with three different
values of m are given.

In summary, a Poisson distribution is used for finding probabilities for a
number of events occurring in an interval provided the following conditions
are satisfied:

1. Events occur at random.
2. Events occur at a fixed and known mean rate.

Normal distribution

Both distributions dealt with so far have been for discrete variables. A
different type of problem arises with continuous variables. Suppose that a
shop manager wishes to know what the chance is that a packet of tea,
chosen at random, has a weight between 115 g and 120 g. In order to answer
this type of question a distribution is needed which can be used for
continuous measurements. The most commonly used is the *normal*
distribution. This distribution is bell-shaped and symmetrical about the

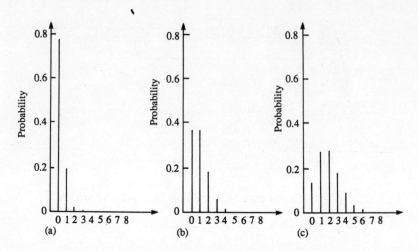

Fig. 14.3 Poisson distributions: (a) $m = 0.25$; (b) $m = 1$; (c) $m = 2$.

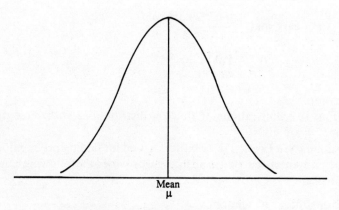

Fig. 14.4 Normal distribution curve.

mean. A typical normal distribution curve shape is given in Fig. 14.4. Its shape depends on two characteristics, the mean and the standard deviation. The mean specifies where the curve is located and the standard deviation specifies how dispersed or closely grouped the curve is. Figure 14.5 shows the curve shape for small and large standard deviations.

The normal distribution is widely used in statistics since many physical measurements can be assumed to follow a normal distribution. These measurements include length, width, weight, volume and time.

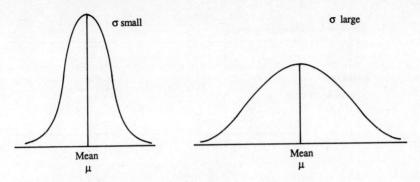

Fig. 14.5 Normal distribution curves for small and large σ.

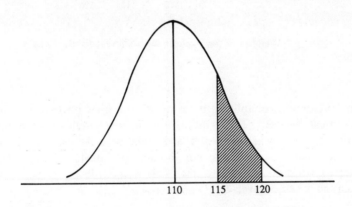

Fig. 14.6 Normal distribution for weights of tea packets.

It is not possible to find probabilities for a particular value of a measurement but rather probabilities for ranges of values are determined. To find these probabilities the area under the normal distribution curve must be found. If, in the tea packet example, the mean weight of a packet of tea is 110 g and its standard deviation is 5 g, the probability of a packet having weight between 115 g and 120 g is represented by the shaded area in Fig. 14.6.

Table 14.6. Standardising limits

	Lower	Upper
Limit (x)	115 g	120 g
Standardised limit (z)	$\dfrac{115-110\,g}{5}$	$\dfrac{120-110\,g}{5}$
	$=1$	$=2$

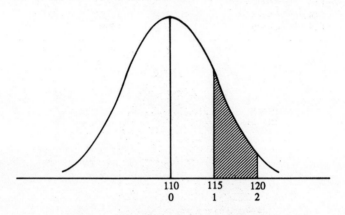

Fig. 14.7 Weights of tea packets with standardised values.

To find these probabilities a set of standardised normal distribution tables must be used. These tables are the probabilities for a normal distribution with mean 0 and standard deviation 1. As every different type of measurement has its own mean and standard deviation these must be converted to standardised values. This standardising is achieved by calculating z-values given by

$$z = \frac{x - \mu}{\sigma}$$

where μ is the mean, σ is the standard deviation and x is the value to be standardised. The z-values are often known as standardised normal variates. For the tea packet weight example there are two limits, so there are two values to be standardised (see Table 14.6).

Since μ, the mean, equals 110 g and σ, the standard deviation, equals 5 g Fig. 14.6 can be modified as in Fig. 14.7 with the standardised limits included.

Table 14.7. Areas to the left for the standardised normal curve

z	Area to left of z	z	Area to left of z
0.00	0.5000	1.96	0.9750
0.25	0.5987	2.00	0.9772
0.50	0.6915	2.25	0.9878
0.75	0.7734	2.33	0.9901
1.00	0.8413	2.50	0.9938
1.25	0.8944	2.58	0.9951
1.50	0.9332	2.75	0.9970
1.64	0.9495	3.00	0.9987
1.75	0.9599	3.09	0.9990

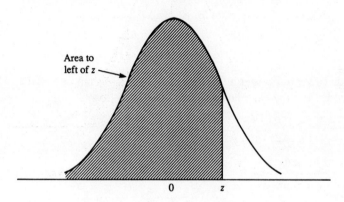

Fig. 14.8 Normal curve areas given in Table 14.7.

Notice that the mean, when standardised, is always zero. The probability required is

$$P(115 < x < 120)$$

which is the same as

$$P(1 < z < 2)$$

if the standardised values are used. Using normal or z-tables we can now find this probability. A selection of z-values and corresponding probabilities are given in Table 14.7, the probabilities being for values less than or equal to the z-value, i.e. the area to the left of the z-value as illustrated in Fig. 14.8.

More extensive tables of the normal distribution can be found in published sets of statistical tables.

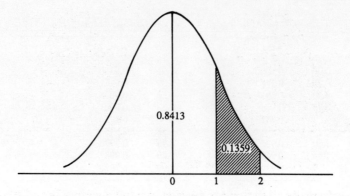

Fig. 14.9 Normal curve for tea packet weights.

If the probability that a tea packet weighs less than or equal to 120 g is required, then the calculation required is as follows:

$$P(x < 120)$$
$$= P(z < 2)$$

and then looking up $z = 2$ in the normal tables gives

probability $= 0.9772$

Similarly, if the tea packet is to be less than or equal to 115 g in weight:

$$P(x < 115)$$
$$= P(z < 1)$$

Looking up $z = 1$ in the normal tables gives

probability $= 0.8413$

In our example, the tea packet is to be between 115 and 120 g in weight and from Fig. 14.7 we can see that this probability is given by the difference of the two probabilities already calculated:

$$P(115 < x < 120)$$
$$= P(1 < z < 2)$$
$$= P(z < 2) - P(z < 1)$$
$$= 0.9772 - 0.8413$$
$$= 0.1359$$

as shown in Fig. 14.9.

The tables only give probabilities for positive values of z. If we wanted to

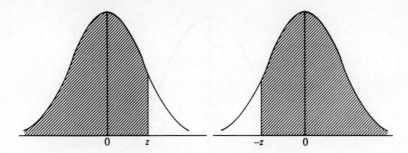

Fig. 14.10 Symmetry of the normal curve.

know the probability that a tea packet weighs between 95 g and 105 g, then standardising gives

$$P(95 < x < 105)$$

$$= P\left(\frac{95 - 110}{5} < z < \frac{105 - 110}{5}\right)$$

$$= P(-3 < z < -1)$$

and the z-values are negative. To use the tables we must make use of the symmetry of the normal distribution. As can be seen in Fig. 14.10,

$$P(<z) = P(> -z)$$

In other words, the normal distribution for $z < 0$ is a mirror image of that for $z > 0$.

If, then, the probability that a packet of tea weighs more than 95 g is required,

$$P(x > 95)$$
$$= P(z > -3)$$
$$= P(z < 3)$$

so looking up $z = 3$ in the tables gives

probability $= 0.9987$

Similarly, the probability that a packet of tea weighs over 105 g is given by

$$P(x > 105)$$
$$= P(z > -1)$$
$$= P(z < 1)$$

so from the tables

probability $= 0.8413$

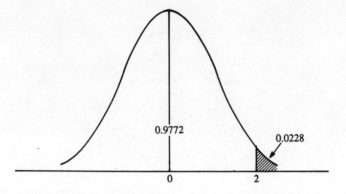

Fig. 14.11 Standardised normal curve for tea packet weights.

To obtain the probability of a packet of tea weighing between 95 and 105 g the difference between these two probabilities is needed:

$$P(95 < x < 105)$$
$$= P(-3 < z < -1)$$
$$= P(z > -3) - P(z > -1)$$
$$= P(z < 3) - P(z < 1)$$
$$= 0.9987 - 0.8413$$
$$= 0.1574$$

It is also possible to make use of the fact that total probability is 1. If the probability that a packet of tea weighs over 120 g is required, then

$$P(x > 120)$$
$$= P(z > 2)$$
$$= 1 - P(z < 2)$$
$$= 1 - 0.9772$$
$$= 0.0228$$

as illustrated in Fig. 14.11.

Now consider finding the probability that a packet of tea weighs between 100 g and 125 g. When the z-values are found, then

$$P(100 < x < 125)$$
$$= P\left(\frac{100 - 110}{5} < z < \frac{125 - 110}{5}\right)$$
$$= P(-2 < z < 3)$$

one negative and one positive limit. In Fig. 14.12 it is seen that if $z = 3$ is looked up in the tables the shaded area is obtained plus the unshaded area

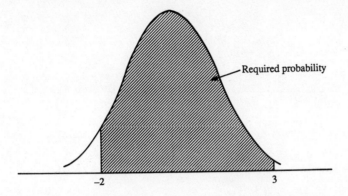

Fig. 14.12 Standardised normal curve for tea packet weights.

at the left end or tail. The left tail is what is *excluded* when 2 is looked up in the tables, so it can be found by subtracting the table value for $z = 2$ from 1. This result, in turn, can be subtracted from the table value for $z = 3$. Put formally,

$$P(100 < x < 125)$$
$$= P(-2 < z < 3)$$
$$= P(z < 3) - P(z < -2)$$
$$= P(z < 3) - [1 - P(z > -2)]$$
$$= P(z < 3) - [1 - P(z < 2)]$$
$$= 0.9987 - [1 - 0.9772]$$
$$= 0.9987 - 0.0228$$
$$= 0.9759$$

Example

An electrical component has length 450 millimetres (mm) with a standard deviation of 20 mm. Find the probability that a particular component has each of the following lengths:

1. Less than 460 mm.
2. Greater than 420 mm.
3. Between 455 and 475 mm.
4. Between 415 and 430 mm.
5. Between 425 and 465 mm.
6. Less than 435 mm.
7. Greater than 470 mm.

Solutions. It is known that $\mu = 450$, $\sigma = 20$ (see Fig. 14.13(a)–(g)).

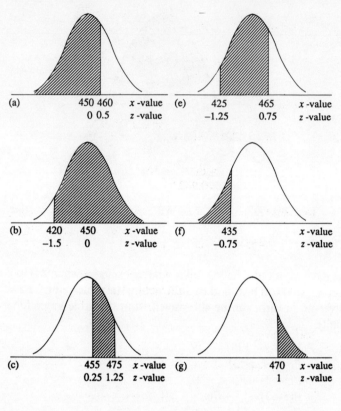

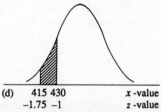

Fig. 14.13 Probabilites for various ranges of x.

1. $$P(x < 460) = P\left(z < \frac{460 - 450}{20}\right)$$
$$= P(z < 0.5)$$
$$= 0.6915$$

(See (a).)

2. $$P(x > 420) = P\left(z > \frac{420 - 450}{20}\right)$$
$$= P(z > -1.5)$$
$$= 0.9332$$

(See (b).)

3. $$P(455 < x < 475) = P\left(\frac{455 - 450}{20} < z < \frac{475 - 450}{20}\right)$$
$$= P(0.25 < z < 1.25)$$
$$= 0.8944 - 0.5987$$
$$= 0.2957$$

(See (c).)

4. $$P(415 < x < 430) = P\left(\frac{415 - 450}{20} < z < \frac{430 - 450}{20}\right)$$
$$= P(-1.75 < z < -1)$$
$$= P(1 < z < 1.75)$$
(by symmetry)
$$= 0.9599 - 0.8413$$
$$= 0.1186$$

(See (d).)

5. $$P(425 < x < 465) = P\left(\frac{425 - 450}{20} < z < \frac{465 - 450}{20}\right)$$
$$= P(-1.25 < z < 0.75)$$
$$= P(z < 0.75) - [1 - P(z < 1.25)]$$
$$= 0.7734 - [1 - 0.8944]$$
$$= 0.6678$$

(See (e).)

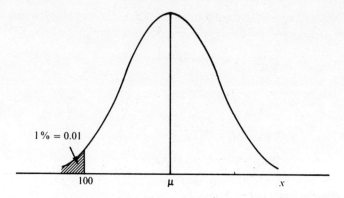

Fig. 14.14 Normal distribution for weights of tea packets.

6.
$$P(x<435)=P\left(z<\frac{435-450}{20}\right)$$
$$=P(z<-0.75)$$
$$=1-P(z>0.75)$$
$$=1-0.7734$$
$$=0.2266$$

(See (f).)

7.
$$P(x>470)=P\left(z>\frac{470-450}{20}\right)$$
$$=P(z>1)$$
$$=1-P(z<1)$$
$$=1-0.8413$$
$$=0.1587$$

(See (g).)

So far the normal distribution has been used to find probabilities. It can be used in reverse to determine appropriate values for the mean or standard deviation when a specification is given based on probabilities. Suppose in the tea packets' example, because of legal requirements, no more than 1% of packets on sale must weigh less than 100 g. This is shown diagrammatically in Fig. 14.14.

If the standard deviation remains at 5 g, then the mean will have to be adjusted. In fact, it will need to be raised since with a mean of 110 g 2.27% of packets will weigh less than 100 g.

The z-value which corresponds to a tail area of 1% or 0.01 is the negative of the z-value corresponding to a table value of 0.99. The nearest to this in Table 14.7 is $z = 2.33$, which has a table value of 0.9901. Hence, the appropriate z-value is -2.33.

When we standardise, the limit for 100 g is

$$z = \frac{100 - \mu}{5}$$

Putting these equal gives

$$-2.33 = \frac{100 - \mu}{5}$$

$$-11.65 = 100 - \mu$$
$$\mu = 100 + 11.65$$
$$= 111.65 \text{ g.}$$

The mean would need to be raised from 110 g to 111.65 g if the legal requirement is to be met.

If instead the mean is kept at 110 g, then the standard deviation has to be changed. The z-value is calculated as

$$z = \frac{100 - 110}{\sigma}$$

and putting this equal to -2.33 we have

$$-2.33 = \frac{100 - 110}{\sigma}$$

$$-2.33\sigma = -10$$
$$= 4.29 \text{ g}$$

so the legal requirement would be met if the standard deviation were reduced from 5 g to 4.29 g.

Normal approximation to the binomial distribution

The calculations for the binomial distribution are quite straightforward when the number of trials n is fairly small. However, as n gets larger the calculations become more complex and lengthy. To find the probability that a box of 1,000 switches contains over 34 faulty switches, the binomial calculations would involve several separate binomial probability calculations. Provided n is large and p is neither too small nor too large, this problem can be avoided by using the normal distribution as an approximation to the binomial distribution.

To use the normal distribution a mean and standard deviation are needed and are given by

$$\text{mean } \mu = np$$
$$\text{standard deviation } \sigma = \sqrt{[np(1-p)]}$$

This normal distribution can be used for $n > 30$ and provided both np and $n(1-p) > 5$. The nearer p is to 0.5 the better the approximation will be.

For the box of switches' example, if the probability that an individual switch will be faulty is 0.05, to find the probability of over 34 faulty switches out of 1,000 the procedure is as follows:

$$\text{mean } \mu = 1{,}000 \times 0.05$$
$$= 50$$
$$\text{standard deviation } \sigma = \sqrt{[1{,}000 \times 0.05 \times (1-0.05)]}$$
$$= \sqrt{47.5}$$
$$= 6.892$$

It is reasonable to use a normal approximation since $n > 30$ and both np and $n(1-p)$ are over 5. The probability $P(x > 34)$ is required, but because a continuous distribution (normal) is being used to approximate a discrete distribution (binomial), a continuity correction must be incorporated. This is an adjustment of 0.5 in the limit. As the probability of 'greater than 34' is required, it is calculated as $P(x > 34.5)$, in other words all the continuous values that would be rounded to integers greater than 34. Hence

$$P(x > 34.5)$$
$$= P\left(z > \frac{34.5 - 50}{6.892}\right)$$
$$= P(z > -2.25)$$
$$= 1 - 0.0122$$
$$= 0.9878$$

If a mail order firm has received 600 orders which should be despatched within 7 days and from past experience knows that, on average 9% of orders are despatched late, what is the chance of the following events?

1. Less than 43 orders will be sent out late.
2. 51 or more orders will be sent out late.

Using the normal approximation

$$\mu = 600 \times 0.09$$
$$= 54$$
$$\sigma = \sqrt{[600 \times 0.09 \times (1-0.09)]}$$
$$= \sqrt{49.14}$$
$$= 7.01$$

1. For less than 43 orders sent out late:

$$P(x < 42.5)$$

$$= P\left(z < \frac{42.5 - 54}{7.01}\right)$$

$$= P(z < -1.64)$$
$$= 1 - 0.9495$$
$$= 0.0505$$

2. For 51 or more orders sent out late:

$$P(x > 50.5)$$

$$= P\left(z > \frac{50.5 - 54}{7.01}\right)$$

$$= P(z > -0.5)$$
$$= 0.6915$$

15

Hypothesis testing

Introduction

Much of business activity concerns making decisions. When statistical data is available this can be used to help the decision maker. It has already been seen how data can be summarised into statistical measures or 'statistics' such as the sample mean. These summaries are guesses or estimates at the underlying or population values and are known as *point* estimates. If this information is to be used to aid decision making some idea is needed of how reliable an estimate is. A different but related problem occurs when there is reason to believe a population parameter should be a certain value. It is required to check whether the data supports our theory. This chapter outlines the methods available to deal with these types of problem.

Standard error of the sample mean

When the sample mean is calculated from a set of data it is an estimate of the population mean. If another set of data of the same size is collected, another sample mean can be collected and this process can be continued so that a distribution is built up of sample means. This distribution is known as the *sampling distribution of the sample mean*. The sample means are not expected to be exactly the same as each other or the same as the population mean. It is hoped, however, that the sample mean values are close to the population mean. The measure of dispersion from the sample mean is called the *standard error of the sample mean* and indicates how good the estimate is likely to be. The smaller the value of this standard error the more reliance can be placed on our estimate.

The standard error of the sample mean is denoted by s.e. $(\bar{x})$ and is calculated as

$$\text{s.e. } (\bar{x}) = \frac{\sigma}{\sqrt{n}}$$

where σ is the true standard deviation of the individual data values. If the true standard deviation is unknown and we have a large sample size, the standard error of the sample mean can be found as

$$\text{s.e. } (\bar{x}) = \frac{s}{\sqrt{n}}$$

where s is the sample standard deviation. It is to be expected that the sample mean will become more reliable as the sample size increases. A sample mean based on one million results might be expected to be better than a sample mean based on 5 results. The calculation of the standard error of the sample mean involves dividing by the square root of the sample size so the measure of dispersion for the sample mean does indeed get smaller for larger sample sizes.

Confidence intervals for the population mean

When sample data is averaged this sample mean, $\bar{x}$, is used as an estimate of the population mean, μ. The standard error of the sample mean then gives an indication of the reliability of this estimate. However, if a range of possible true values is required for the mean, an interval must be quoted. A *confidence interval* is a stated interval in which the true value for the mean is expected to lie with a certain probability or confidence. The limits of this confidence interval depend on the confidence required, and are found as

$$x \pm z_{\alpha/2} \frac{\sigma}{\sqrt{n}}$$

where the lower limit is found using the negative sign and the upper limit is found using the positive sign. The value $z_{\alpha/2}$ is a value obtained from the normal tables where the probability of being 'greater than z' is $\alpha/2$. The resulting confidence interval has probability $1-\alpha$ or confidence $100 \times (1-\alpha)\%$, confidence usually being quoted as a percentage.

If a company records how many personal computers it sells each month over 6 successive months as

1,200, 1,350, 1,050, 1,720, 1,450, 1,600

and it is known from past experience that the standard deviation of sales is 100 units per month, then the sample mean is

$$\bar{x} = \frac{8,370}{6}$$

$$= 1,395$$

personal computers sold per month.

The standard error of the sample mean is

$$\text{s.e. } (\bar{x}) = \frac{100}{\sqrt{6}}$$

$$= 40.82$$

If it is required to know, with 95% confidence, the possible values of the underlying mean monthly sales, a 95% confidence interval is required. The appropriate z-value corresponds to a 'greater than' probability of 0.025 or a 'less than' probability of 0.975. Hence, from Table 14.6,

$$z_{\alpha/2} = 1.96$$

and the confidence limits are given by

$$1,395 \pm (1.96)\frac{100}{\sqrt{6}}$$

$$= 1,395 \pm 80.02$$
$$= 1,315, \quad 1,475 \qquad \text{(to nearest integer)}$$

It is thus stated with 95% confidence that the true mean lies between 1,315 and 1,475 personal computers sold per month.

When quoting a confidence interval the ideal is a narrow interval and a high confidence. However, increasing the confidence required means the interval must be extended. In the example of monthly sales if 99% confidence is specified rather than 95%, the required z-value corresponds to a 'less than' probability of 0.995, which from Table 14.6 gives $z = 2.58$. The confidence limits are then

$$1,395 \pm (2.58)\frac{100}{\sqrt{6}}$$

$$= 1,395 \pm 105.33$$
$$= 1,290, \quad 1,500 \qquad \text{(to nearest integer)}$$

a wider interval. Generally, a 95% confidence interval is quoted unless a specific confidence is required.

The z-test for an assumed mean

Following from the idea of a confidence interval the question arises as to whether an assumed value for a mean is reasonable or supported by the data collected. A check can be made by finding a confidence interval and seeing whether the assumed mean lies within the interval. If it is required to determine whether 1,425 personal computers sold per month is a reasonable assumption for the mean, we can see that this value is within the 95% confidence interval and so is a possible value for the true mean.

A more formal approach is to carry out a statistical test. All statistical tests follow the same five steps:

1. Choose a null hypothesis (denoted by H_0).
2. Choose an alternative hypothesis (denoted by H_1).
3. Choose a significance level (denoted by α).
4. Calculate a test statistic.
5. Compare test statistic to a critical value obtained from tables and draw conclusions.

The null hypothesis is the starting idea or theory and involves specifying a particular assumed value for the mean. It is called the null hypothesis because it is often chosen to represent 'no change'. If the mean length of a component has been 10 cm in the past a reasonable start is to assume this is still the mean length.

The alternative hypothesis is what will be concluded if the test shows the null hypothesis is unacceptable. The alternative hypothesis is a more general hypothesis and when testing an assumed mean one of three main alternatives will be used:

1. The mean is greater than the assumed mean.
2. The mean is less than the assumed mean.
3. The mean is different to the assumed mean.

The question to be answered determines which one we choose. If in doubt use (3) since it is the most general alternative.

The significance level is the level of risk considered acceptable for concluding our assumed mean is wrong when it is actually correct. As uncertainty is involved 100% certainty is impossible, but large risks are undesirable. Usually, a significance level of 5% is used ($\alpha = 0.05$).

A test statistic is a number calculated from the data and used to decide whether the null hypothesis or alternative hypothesis should be accepted.

To carry out a test of an assumed mean the steps are as follows:

1. H_0: mean $= \mu_0$
2. H_1: mean $> \mu_0$
    or
    mean $< \mu_0$
    or
    mean $\neq \mu_0$

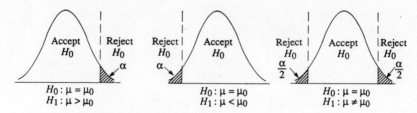

Fig. 15.1 Tests for an assumed mean.

3.   Choose significance level α.
4.   Calculate

$$z = \frac{\bar{x} - \mu}{\sigma / \sqrt{n}}$$

5.   Compare calculated z-value to the appropriate value from the normal tables.

The tests for each of the alternatives can be illustrated as in Fig. 15.1.

The first two tests are called *one-tail* tests since the alternatives considered lie on only one side of the assumed mean. The third test is called a *two-tail* test since a sample mean well below or well above the assumed mean would suggest the true mean is different from the assumed mean.

For the first alternative the borderline or *critical value* for the test is given by z_α where the tail area is α. Similarly, for the second alternative the critical value is $-z_\alpha$ using the symmetry of the tables. Finally, the two critical values for the third alternative are $\pm z_{\alpha/2}$.

For a 5% significance level these critical values can be found from Table 14.7. For the first alternative a 'less than' probability of 0.95 is required, so the z-value is 1.64. Similarly for the second alternative the z-value is -1.64. For the third alternative a 'less than' probability of 0.975 is required, leading to z-values ± 1.96.

If the test statistic falls on or outside a critical value (indicated by the shaded areas), the result is called *significant* and leads us to reject the null hypothesis or starting idea. There is evidence that the data does not support the assumed mean. Any other value of the test statistic is *not significant* and the null hypothesis is assumed to be true. The data gives support for the assumed mean.

To choose the correct alternative hypothesis it is necessary to consider the question to be answered. Questions like

'Has the mean increased?'
'Is the mean greater than . . .?'

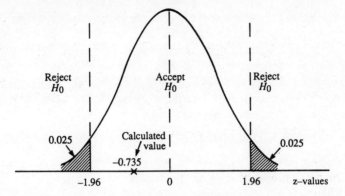

Fig. 15.2 Two-tail test for assumed monthly personal computer sale.

suggest the first alternative should be used. Questions like

'Has there been a drop in the mean?'
'Is the mean less than . . .?'

suggest the second alternative should be used. Finally, questions like

'Has the mean changed?'
'Is the mean different to . . .?'

suggest the third alternative should be used. If there is no clear indication of which alternative would be most appropriate the third alternative should be used.

In the personal computer sales' example it is required to know whether average sales of 1,425 per month was a reasonable assumption. The null hypothesis is that the mean is 1,425 ($\mu_0 = 1,425$). As there is no specific statement concerning what the alternative might be, the most general alternative is chosen (i.e. the two-tail alternative $\mu_0 \neq 1,425$). Choose the standard significance level of 0.05 since there is no indication that the test should use a particular value of α. Calculate the test statistic as

$$z = \frac{\bar{x} - \mu_0}{\sigma/\sqrt{n}}$$

$$= \frac{1,395 - 1,425}{100/\sqrt{6}}$$

$$= -0.735$$

The critical values for this two-tail test are

$$z = \pm 1.96$$

so the diagram which illustrates this test is as shown in Fig. 15.2.

As the calculated value lies in the unshaded area this tells us that H_0, the null hypothesis, is to be accepted; in other words, the assumed mean of 1,425 personal computers sold per month is reasonable. This is the same conclusion as was obtained using the confidence interval, as expected.

Now suppose a quality inspector suspects that a component has an average width in excess of its stipulated average width, 2 cm. Based on the following nine component widths from a random sample:

$$2.06, \ 1.99, \ 2.05, \ 2.04, \ 2.02, \ 1.98, \ 2.00, \ 2.03, \ 2.01$$

and knowing from past experience that the standard deviation of the width is 0.02 cm, what conclusions can be drawn?

To test the inspector's suspicions it is necessary to carry out a statistical test. The test should have 'greater than' as its alternative since the suspicion is that the mean is above what it should be. The test is set out as follows:

1. $H_0: \mu = 2$
2. $H_1: \mu > 2$
3. $\alpha = 0.05$
4. $z = \dfrac{\bar{x} - \mu}{\sigma/\sqrt{n}}$

And since

$$\bar{x} = \frac{18.18}{9}$$

$$= 2.02 \, \text{cm}$$

$$z = \frac{2.02 - 2.00}{0.02/\sqrt{9}}$$

$$= 3$$

The critical value is $z = 1.64$, so this is a significant result, since z is outside the critical value (i.e. $3 > 1.64$). This is shown in Fig. 15.3.

The conclusion is that the mean is not 2 cm but is greater than 2 cm, so supporting the inspector's suspicions.

Standard error for a sample proportion

There are many cases where the measurement of interest is not a direct physical measurement but rather how many people or items have a certain characteristic or *attribute*. This information is usually given as a proportion as we saw in Chapter 13. Typically, we make statements such as

'75% of people prefer Whizoe to Sooper'

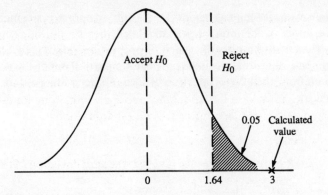

Fig. 15.3 One-tail test for assumed width of components.

As with the mean, we need some indication of the reliability of any such estimate of a proportion.

A population proportion, π, is estimated by the sample proportion, p, where

$$p = \frac{\text{number of items with attribute}}{\text{total number of items}}$$

This sample proportion has a standard error, the standard error of a sample proportion given by

$$\text{s.e. } (p) = \sqrt{\frac{\pi(1 - \pi)}{n}}$$

if the true proportion, π, is known, or more usually

$$\text{s.e. } (p) = \sqrt{\frac{p(1 - p)}{n}}$$

when the true proportion π is unknown.

Confidence intervals for a population proportion

If a range of possible values for the underlying or population proportion is required, then a confidence interval can be found in the same way as for the mean. The limits of a $100(1 - \alpha)\%$ confidence interval for a proportion are given by

$$p \pm z_{\alpha/2} \sqrt{\frac{p(1 - p)}{n}}$$

where the z-value is found as before. This is only an approximate method so when the limits of the interval are calculated they should be checked to ensure they are in the possible range of proportion values 0 to 1.

If a company finds that during a particular month 80 out of 100 accounts are paid on time, then the proportion of accounts generally paid on time is estimated by

$$p = \frac{80}{100}$$

$$= 0.8$$

The standard error of this sample proportion is then

$$\text{s.e.}(p) = \sqrt{\frac{(0.8)(1-0.8)}{100}}$$

$$= 0.04$$

A 95% confidence interval for the population proportion is

$$0.8 \pm (1.96)(0.04)$$
$$= 0.8 \pm 0.0784$$
$$= 0.7216,\ 0.8784$$

so there is 95% confidence that the true proportion of accounts paid on time will be between 0.7216 and 0.8784.

The z-test for an assumed proportion

To decide whether an assumed value for a population proportion is reasonable we can use confidence intervals or a formal statistical test. The test used is similar to the test for an assumed mean. The steps are as follows:

1. H_0: proportion $= \pi$
2. H_1: proportion $> \pi$
     or: proportion $< \pi$
     or: proportion $\neq \pi$
3.   Choose significance level α.
4.   Calculate

$$z = \frac{p - \pi}{\sqrt{\dfrac{\pi(1-\pi)}{n}}}$$

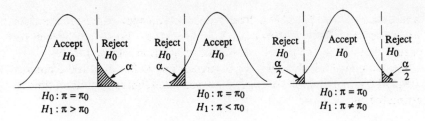

$H_0 : \pi = \pi_0$
$H_1 : \pi > \pi_0$

$H_0 : \pi = \pi_0$
$H_1 : \pi < \pi_0$

$H_0 : \pi = \pi_0$
$H_1 : \pi \neq \pi_0$

Fig. 15.4 Tests for an assumed proportion.

5. Compare calculated value to

z_α (for first alternative)
$-z_\alpha$ (for second alternative)
$\pm z_{\alpha/2}$ (for third alternative)

and draw conclusions just as in the z-test for an assumed mean.

Diagrammatically, the three test situations are shown in Fig. 15.4.

Suppose the company checking the proportion of accounts settled on time believes this proportion is generally 0.75 or 75%. To test this theory the steps are as follows:

1. $H_0 : \pi = 0.75$
2. $H_1 : \pi \neq 0.75$
3. $\alpha = 0.05$
4. $z = \dfrac{p - \pi}{\sqrt{\dfrac{\pi(1 - \pi)}{n}}}$

    $= \dfrac{0.8 - 0.75}{\sqrt{\dfrac{(0.75)(0.25)}{100}}}$

    $= 1.15$

A diagram of this test is shown in Fig. 15.5. The calculated result is seen to be within the unshaded area, so the result is not significant. There is no evidence that the proportion is different from 0.75 or 75%.

Referring back to the confidence interval for these data 0.75 is within the limits of the interval, which suggests 0.75 is a possible population proportion value, in agreement with this test.

In fact, a confidence interval is the equivalent of a two-tailed test provided the confidence (as a probability) is $1 - \alpha$ (the significance level).

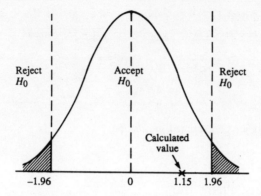

Fig. 15.5 Two-tail test for assumed proportion of accounts settled on time.

Standard error of the difference of two sample means

A situation which often occurs in a business context is the need to compare two sets of results to see whether they have different underlying means. Before formally working out confidence intervals or carrying out significance tests, the standard error of the difference between two sample means is needed. This is given by

$$\text{s.e.}(\bar{x}_1 - \bar{x}_2) = \sqrt{\left(\frac{\sigma_1^2}{n_1} + \frac{\sigma_2^2}{n_2}\right)}$$

where $\bar{x}_1$ is the first sample mean, $\bar{x}_2$ is the second sample mean, n_1 is the first sample size, n_2 is the second sample size, σ_1 is the known standard deviation for results in the first sample and σ_2 is the known standard deviation for results in the second sample. If the standard deviations are unknown but the sample sizes n_1, n_2 are large, then the standard error can be calculated as

$$\text{s.e.}(\bar{x}_1 - \bar{x}_2) = \sqrt{\left(\frac{s_1^2}{n_1} + \frac{s_2^2}{n_2}\right)}$$

where s_1, s_2 are the respective sample standard deviations.

Confidence interval for difference between two means

If a range of possible values for the true difference between two means is required, then a confidence interval can be found using the method already seen. The limits of a $100(1-\alpha)\%$ confidence interval for the difference between two means are given by

$$(\bar{x}_1 - \bar{x}_2) \pm z_{\alpha/2} \sqrt{\left(\frac{\sigma_1^2}{n_1} + \frac{\sigma_2^2}{n_2}\right)}$$

if σ_1, σ_2 are known or

$$(\bar{x}_1 - \bar{x}_2) \pm z_{\alpha/2} \sqrt{\frac{s_1^2}{n_1} + \frac{s_2^2}{n_2}}$$

if σ_1, σ_2 are unknown but the two sample sizes are large.

Suppose a company wishes to compare output from two machines to see whether hourly machine production differs. The company has recorded output figures over 10 hours for machine 1, giving a mean output of 210 items per hour, and has recorded output figures over 8 hours for machine 2, giving a mean output of 200 items. If it is known that the standard deviation of output per hour from machine 1 is 20 items and for machine 2 is 25 times, then the standard error for the difference in mean output is given by

$$\text{s.e.}(\bar{x}_1 - \bar{x}_2) = \sqrt{\left(\frac{20^2}{10} + \frac{25^2}{8}\right)}$$
$$= 10.87$$

A 95% confidence interval for the true difference between mean outputs from the two machines is then given by

$$(210 - 200) \pm (1.96)(10.87)$$
$$= 10 \pm 21.29$$
$$= -11.29, \quad 31.29$$

Now care must be taken in the interpretation of these limits. The conclusion is that the interval ranges from a difference of -11.29 to a difference of $+31.29$. In order words, we are 95% confident that the true difference could be anything from -11.29 (the mean of output from machine 1 is 11.29 less than the mean of output from machine 2) to 31.29 (the mean of output from machine 1 is 31.29 greater than the mean of output from machine 2).

The z-test for the difference between two means

To decide whether two means can be assumed as equal or different in some way we can carry out a z-test in much the same way as the tests we have already seen. The test is as follows:

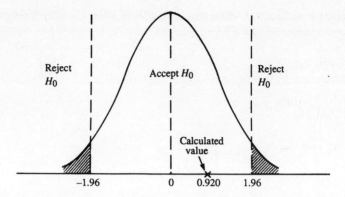

Fig. 15.6 Two-tail test for comparing means of machine outputs.

1. H_0: two means are equal, i.e. $\mu_1 = \mu_2$.
2. H_1: first mean exceeds second mean, i.e. $\mu_1 > \mu_2$.
    or: first mean is lower than second mean, i.e. $\mu_1 < \mu_2$.
    or: two means are different, i.e. $\mu_1 \neq \mu_2$.
3. Choose significance level α.
4. Calculate

$$z = \frac{\bar{x}_1 - \bar{x}_2}{\sqrt{\dfrac{\sigma_1^2}{n_1} + \dfrac{\sigma_2^2}{n_2}}}$$

5. Compare calculated value to

    z_α for first alternative
    $-z_\alpha$ for second alternative
    $\pm z_{\alpha/2}$ for third alternative
    and draw conclusions in the same way as for the previous z-tests.

Suppose the company comparing output from the two machines wishes to know whether the outputs can be assumed equal. To test this theory the steps are as follows:

1. H_0: $\mu_1 = \mu_2$
2. H_1: $\mu_1 \neq \mu_2$
3. $\alpha = 0.05$
4. $z = \dfrac{210 - 200}{10.87}$
    $= 0.920$

A diagram to illustrate this test is shown in Fig. 15.6. It is seen that the calculated result is within the unshaded area, so the result is not significant. This tells us there is no statistical evidence of a difference between the two mean outputs.

Referring back to the confidence interval for this example it is seen that zero is within the limits of the interval, which suggests it is possible that the mean outputs are equal, in agreement with this test, as would be expected.

Standard error of the difference between two sample proportions

Just as it was possible to extend the ideas of confidence intervals and significance tests for comparing two means, so the same can be done to allow comparison of two proportions. The standard error of the difference between two sample proportions is given by

$$\text{s.e.}(p_1 - p_2) = \sqrt{\left(\frac{\pi_1(1-\pi_1)}{n_1} + \frac{\pi_2(1-\pi_2)}{n_2}\right)}$$

where p_1 is the first sample proportion, p_2 is the second sample proportion, n_1 is the first sample size, n_2 is the second sample size, π_1 is the true first proportion and π_2 is the true second proportion.

More usually π_1, π_2 are unknown, so the standard error is given by

$$\text{s.e.}(p_1 - p_2) = \sqrt{\left(\frac{p_1(1-p_1)}{n_1} + \frac{p_2(1-p_2)}{n_2}\right)}$$

Confidence interval for the difference between two proportions

If a range of possible values for the true difference between two proportions is required, then a confidence interval can be found in the usual way, so that a $100(1-\alpha)\%$ confidence interval for the difference between two proportions is given by

$$(p_1 - p_2) \pm z_{\alpha/2} \sqrt{\left(\frac{p_1(1-p_1)}{n_1} + \frac{p_2(1-p_2)}{n_2}\right)}$$

(Note that the standard error with unknown true proportions is used since if the proportions were known there would be no need for the confidence interval!)

Suppose a bank wishes to compare its proportion of bad debtors in two industrial sectors. Its records show that in sector 1, 10 out of 120 companies are bad debtors whilst in sector 2, 25 out of 200 companies are bad debtors.

The standard error for the difference in the two sample proportions is

$$\sqrt{\left(\frac{p_1(1-p_1)}{n_1}+\frac{p_2(1-p_2)}{n_2}\right)}$$

$$=\sqrt{\left[\frac{\left(\frac{10}{120}\right)\left(1-\frac{10}{120}\right)}{120}+\frac{\left(\frac{25}{200}\right)\left(1-\frac{25}{200}\right)}{200}\right]}$$

$$=0.0344$$

A 95% confidence interval for the true difference in proportions of bad debtors in the two sectors is then

$$\left(\frac{10}{120}-\frac{25}{200}\right)\pm(1.96)(0.0344)$$

$$=-0.0417\pm0.0674$$
$$=-0.1091,\quad 0.0257$$

This tells us that with 95% confidence the true difference in proportion is between -0.1091 (the proportion in sector 1 is 0.1091 lower than the proportion in sector 2) and 0.0257 (the proportion in sector 1 is 0.0257 higher than the proportion in sector 2). Finally, remember that these results are proportion figures, not percentages. If percentages are required, then the proportions must be multiplied by 100.

The z-test for the difference between two proportions

To decide whether two proportions can be assumed to be equal or different in some way a z-test can again be used, based on the familiar five steps:

1. H_0: proportions are equal, i.e. $\pi_1=\pi_2$.
2. H_1: first proportion exceeds second proportion, i.e. $\pi_1>\pi_2$.
   or: first proportion is less than second proportion, i.e. $\pi_1<\pi_2$.
   or: proportions are different, i.e. $\pi_1\neq\pi_2$.
3. Choose the significance level α.
4. Calculate

$$z=\frac{p_1-p_2}{\sqrt{\left(\frac{p_1(1-p_1)}{n_1}+\frac{p_2(1-p_2)}{n_2}\right)}}$$

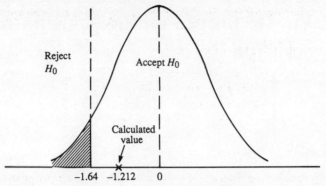

Fig. 15.7 One-tail test for comparing proportions of bad debtors.

5. Compare the calculated value to

z_α for first alternative
$-z_\alpha$ for second alternative
$\pm z_{\alpha/2}$ for third alternative

and draw conclusions as for the previous z-tests.

In the bank bad debtor example to test whether the proportions of bad debtors in each sector can be assumed equal or whether the proportion in sector 2 exceeds that in sector 1, the test is as follows:

1. $H_0: \pi_1 = \pi_2$
2. $H_1: \pi_1 < \pi_2$
3. $\alpha = 0.05$

4. $z = \dfrac{\left(\dfrac{10}{120}\right) - \left(\dfrac{25}{200}\right)}{0.0344}$

$= \dfrac{-0.0417}{0.0344}$

$= -1.212$

Since this is a one-tail test and it is being checked whether the second proportion can be assumed to be the greater, the critical value is $-z_\alpha$, i.e. -1.64.

The test is illustrated in Fig. 15.7 and it is seen that the calculated result is in the unshaded area, so the result is not significant. There is no statistical evidence that the proportion of bad debtors in sector 2 exceeds that in sector 1.

16

Linear programming – graphical solution

Introduction

Decision making is often made more complicated than it might otherwise be by the existence of multiple conditions, or constraints, on the ranges of possible values that the recommended answer to the problem can take. These constraints frequently conflict with one another and making sure that any potential answer to the problem takes account of each individual condition is a major aspect of the decision making. The best of these possible answers is usually required.

Such a problem can often be formulated as a *mathematical programming problem*. Much the largest subset of mathematical programming problems is a class of problems called *linear programming* problems. It is these that will be considered here. The best way to describe the features of a typical linear programming problem is through a particular example.

The manufacturer of a particular product produces and packs it in both standard and large size boxes. Each standard size box contains 1 kg of product but each large box contains 2 kg of product. During the production period considered 5,400 kg of product are available for packing. A box of either size takes 1 minute to pack and during the period there are 4,000 minutes of packing time available.

Orders have already been accepted for 1,000 standard size and 500 large size boxes and company policy dictates that the number of small boxes packed should be at least as many as the number of large boxes packed. The profit on a small box is £3 and the profit on a large box is £5. How many of each size of box should be packed to maximise the manufacturer's total profit?

In solving any such problem, the first issue to be resolved is to rigorously define the variables around which the model is to be constructed. It should always be remembered that the variables are *numbers* and as such must always have *units*. The variables often encapsulate the information needed by those who have to put into practice the requirements of the decision makers.

Here it is required to know how many of each size of box is to be packed. These, therefore, are the variables.

Let x be the number of standard size boxes packed and let y be the number of large size boxes packed.

Since each small box produces £3 profit, x standard boxes will produce £3x profit. Similarly, y large boxes will produce £5y profit. Therefore, the total profit will be

$$P = 3x + 5y$$

This must be maximised and is called the *objective function*.

Let us now consider the weight of product that is packed. Each standard box contains 1 kg of product and so x standard boxes will contain a total of x kg of product. Similarly, each large box contains 2 kg of product and so y large boxes contain 2y kg of product. Therefore, the total product packed is $x + 2y$ and this cannot exceed the amount of product available, 5,400 kg. (Not all of it needs to be packed, but this represents the maximum possible.) Hence

$$x + 2y \leqslant 5,400$$

Each box takes 1 minute to pack and so x standard boxes take x minutes and y large boxes take y minutes. The total time taken to pack is then $x + y$ and there are a maximum of 4,000 minutes available for packing. Hence

$$x + y \leqslant 4,000$$

The number of standard boxes packed must be at least as many as those that have been pre-ordered. (More could be packed, however.) Hence

$$x \geqslant 1,000$$

Similarly, the number of large boxes packed must be at least as many as those that have been pre-ordered, hence

$$y \geqslant 500$$

The number of standard boxes should be at least as many as the number of large boxes (i.e. it cannot be smaller). Hence

$$x - y \geqslant 0$$

For completeness we will include two additional constraints:

$$x \geqslant 0 \quad \text{and} \quad y \geqslant 0$$

These are called the *non-negativity conditions* and state that no variable can ever take a negative value. Logically, these form part of most linear programming problems and *must* form part of any problem to be solved by the standard solution method for linear programming problems, the *simplex method*. Note that the non-negativity conditions are redundant here because of the existence of the more powerful constraints $x \geqslant 1,000$ and $y \geqslant 500$.

The problem is, therefore, to maximise

$$P = 3x + 5y$$

subject to

$$x + 2y \leqslant 5,400$$
$$x + y \leqslant 4,000$$
$$x \geqslant 1,000$$
$$\geqslant 500$$
$$x - y \geqslant 0$$
$$x, y \geqslant 0$$

This is a typical *linear programming* problem. It is an example of *linear* programming because the objective function and every constraint all have *linear* form. This means that there is no power of x or y greater than one (no squared, cubed terms etc.) and there are no product terms.

A typical linear programming problem, therefore, has a linear objective function to be maximised or minimised together with a set of linear constraints involving '$\geqslant$', '$\leqslant$', or '$=$'. Usually the constraints are inequalities, but it is quite in order for a constraint to be an equation, although our current example has none of this type.

Graphical solution of a linear programming problem

As has already been mentioned, the standard solution procedure for linear programming problems is the simplex method, which will be outlined in the next section. However, linear programming problems with only two variables can also be solved by graphical means. Some simple three-variable problems can also be solved graphically.

The first step is to set up axes to represent the two variables in the problem. Upon these, each constraint must be depicted. Consider one of the constraints

$$x + y \leqslant 4,000$$

This can be split into two parts

$$x + y = 4,000 \qquad \text{and} \qquad x + y < 4,000$$

The first of these, $x + y = 4,000$, can be shown graphically as a straight line (see Fig. 16.1).

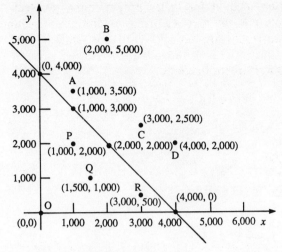

Fig. 16.1 The line x + y = 4,000.

For each point on the line, if $x + y$ is evaluated the result is 4,000.

However, $x + y$ can be evaluated at any point. Let us consider what values we get when we evaluate it at points *not* lying on the line.

Consider points A, B, C, D which all lie *above* the line.

For A: (1,000, 3,500), $x + y = 1,000 + 3,500 = 4,500$
For B: (2,000, 5,000), $x + y = 2,000 + 5,000 = 7,000$
For C: (3,000, 2,500), $x + y = 3,000 + 2,500 = 5,500$
For D: (4,000, 2,000), $x + y = 4,000 + 2,000 = 6,000$

Note that all these values are different, but they are all *greater* than 4,000.

Now consider points O, P, Q, R which all lie *below* the line.

For O: (0, 0), $x + y \ = 0 + 0$ $= 0$
For P: (1,000, 2,000), $x + y = 1,000 + 2,000 = 3,000$
For Q: (1,500, 1,000), $x + y = 1,500 + 1,000 = 2,500$
For R: (3,000, 500), $x + y \ = 3,000 + 500 \ = 3,500$

Note that all these values are again different, but these are all *less* than 4,000.

This then is the key to showing an inequality graphically.

$$x + y \leqslant 4,000$$

is all the points lying on the line $x + y = 4,000$, together with all the points lying below that line. This is shown by shading out all the points *not* required, i.e. those above the line – see Fig. 16.2.

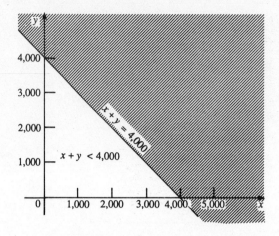

Fig. 16.2 The region $x + y \leqslant 4{,}000$.

A similar procedure is followed with each other constraint. For

$$x + 2y \leqslant 5{,}400$$

draw the line by considering where it crosses the axes. When $x = 0$ (the y-axis) $2y = 5{,}400$, i.e. $y = 2{,}700$. When $y = 0$ (the x-axis) $x = 5{,}400$.

Consider one point *not* lying on the line, such as $(0, 0)$. At this point $x + 2y = 0 + 0 = 0$, which is on the *less than* side of the line. This happens to be the side we require and so we shade out the *other* side (see Fig. 16.3).

Similarly

$$x \geqslant 1{,}000 \qquad \text{and} \qquad y \geqslant 500$$

are represented as shown in Fig. 16.4.

When

$$x - y \geqslant 0$$

is considered, notice that the line is harder to draw than the previous ones, because there is only one intercept of the axes, i.e. when $x = 0$, then $y = 0$.

To draw this line the origin is used as one point and a sensible value of x is chosen to give a second point; e.g. when $x = 2{,}000$, $2{,}000 - y = 0$, i.e. $y = 2{,}000$. (See Fig. 16.5.)

To determine the side of the line required, select a point not on the line, such as $(2{,}000, 0)$. At this point

$$x - y = 2{,}000 - 0 = 2{,}000$$

which is *greater than* 0. Therefore, this is the side required.

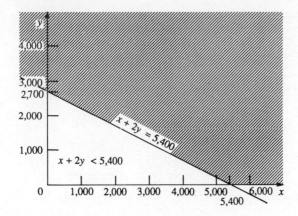

Fig. 16.3 The region $x + 2y \leqslant 5,400$.

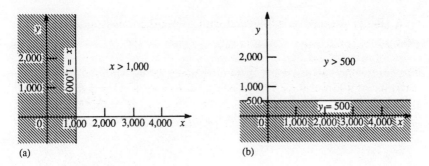

Fig. 16.4 The regions (a) $x \geqslant 1,000$; (b) $y \geqslant 500$.

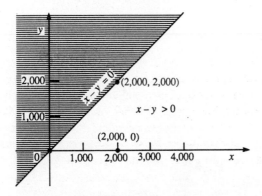

Fig. 16.5 The region $x - y \geqslant 0$.

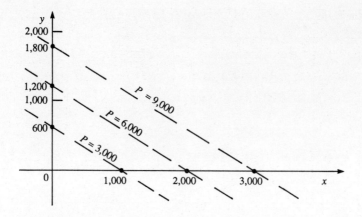

Fig. 16.6 The lines P = 3,000, 6,000 and 9,000.

All the constraints have now to be superimposed upon one another. Any solution (a point on the graph, giving values to the variables) satisfying *every* constraint is called a *feasible solution*. Once we have superimposed all the constraints, we are left with an unshaded region, which contains all the feasible solutions. This is called the *region of feasibility*, and is shown later in Fig. 16.7.

Now consider the representation of the objective function,

$$P = 3x + 5y$$

As it stands, a graph cannot be drawn, as this can be done only for equations (or inequalities with known values of P). But P can be given some value, e.g. 6,000, and the line drawn which represents the equation

$$3x + 5y = 6,000$$

However, P could equally well be given *any* other value, and for each different value a different line obtained. It can be seen (Fig. 16.6) that the lines so drawn are parallel.

Superimposing some of these parallel objective function lines on to the region of feasibility gives Fig. 16.7.

The point required is the one giving maximum profit. To do this place a ruler along one of the sample objective function lines drawn across the region of feasibility and, by sliding it across the region, imagine all the other lines parallel to this one in the direction that increases profit. The aim is to move as far as possible across the region without actually leaving it. Observe that this happens at point A.

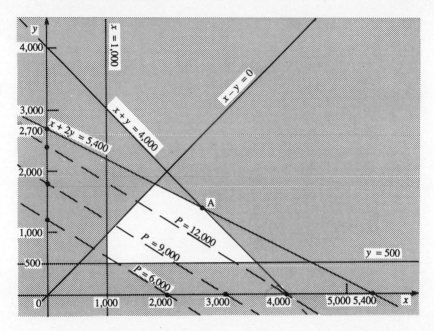

Fig. 16.7 The region of feasibility: finding the optimum point.

Point A, therefore, gives the values of the variables that maximise total profit.

By observation from the graph or, more accurately, from solving the pair of simultaneous equations

$$x + y = 4,000$$
$$x + 2y = 5,400$$

it is found that at A

$$x = 2,600 \quad \text{and} \quad y = 1,400$$

Hence, to maximise total profit, the manufacturer should produce 2,600 standard size boxes and 1,400 large size boxes. When this is done, the maximum profit is then

$$3x + 5y = (3 \times 2,600) + (5 \times 1,400) = 7,800 + 7,000$$
$$= £14,800$$

This is, therefore, the *optimum solution* we have been seeking. Note that at this optimum solution, two of the constraints (total weight of product and packing time) are met exactly. The other constraints are not met exactly and, therefore, have spare capacity. The practical implication of this is that all the available product has been packed and all the packing time has been used up.

Further considerations

Obviously, the method of solving linear programming problems described above is not suitable for larger problems. However, the graphical representation of this problem can be used to establish principles that will lead to a more general method of solution.

Extreme points

An extreme point is a point of intersection of constraint lines that lies within the region of feasibility. In other words, it is a 'corner point' of the region. Look at the graph again (Fig. 16.7) and imagine where the optimum solutions to different objective functions would occur. It is easy to see that *the optimum solution to a linear programming problem must occur at an extreme point.*

Uniqueness

Usually, therefore, a linear programming problem has a unique solution. The only exception to this is if the objective function was actually parallel to a constraint line. In our current example, this would have occurred if the unit profits had been £2 for x and £4 for y, giving an objective function

$$P = 2x + 4y$$

Under these circumstances, it is then possible for two extreme points A and B (in a two-dimensional example – see Fig. 16.8) to give the same optimum value to the objective function. Note that, in addition, all the points on the constraint line joining these two extreme points also give this same optimum value. We describe this situation by saying that this linear programming problem has a *non-unique solution.*

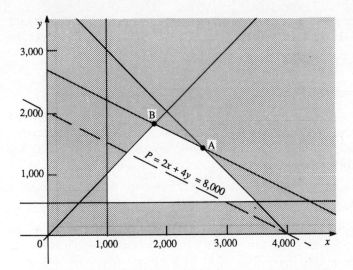

Fig. 16.8 The region of feasibility: a non-unique solution.

17

Linear programming – the simplex method

Introduction

Refer again to the linear programming problem introduced in Chapter 16. Maximise

$$P = 3x + 5y$$

Subject to

$$x + 2y \leqslant 5,400$$
$$x + y \leqslant 4,000$$
$$x \geqslant 1,000$$
$$y \geqslant 500$$
$$x - y \geqslant 0$$
$$x, y \geqslant 0$$

To proceed further we must convert our system of inequalities into a system of equations. This is done for each individual constraint as follows.

Consider

$$x + 2y \leqslant 5,400$$

Usually the left-hand side of this expression is smaller than the right-hand side. It can be converted to an equation by *adding* something to the left-hand side; we will denote this by '*a*'.

$$x + 2y + a = 5,400$$

It is easy to see that a is in fact a variable, since it can take different values. For example, if no product is packed, $x = 0$ and $y = 0$, giving $a = 5,400$, but if all the available product is packed, giving perhaps, $x = 2,000$ and $y = 1,700$, then $a = 0$. In fact, a indicates, for any solution, how much product remains unpacked, i.e. the *spare* product. Notice also that, at all times, $a \geqslant 0$.

A variable converting an inequality into an equation is called a *slack variable*. To avoid confusion, the variables used originally to describe the problem are called the *original variables*.

For the constraint

$$x \geq 1,000$$

the left-hand side is usually greater than the right-hand side. Therefore, the slack variable should be *subtracted* to create an equation

$$x - c = 1,000$$

In this case, c tells us the *surplus* standard size boxes packed over the pre-order. Such slack variables are often called *surplus variables*, but no such distinction will be made here. Introducing slack variables into every constraint gives the following revised problem: Maximise

$$P = 3x + 5y$$

Subject to

$$x + 2y + a = 5,400$$
$$x + y + b = 4,000$$
$$x - c = 1,000$$
$$y - d = 500$$
$$x - y - e = 0$$
$$x, y, a, b, c, d, e \geq 0$$

Now the slack variables have been introduced, there is an alternative means of identifying each constraint line around the boundary of the region of feasibility.

On the boundary

$$x + 2y = 5,400$$

means that 'the weight of product packed equals the total weight of product available'. This situation could equally well be described as 'the spare product still available for packing equals zero', or

$$a = 0$$

Similarly,

$$x + y = 4,000 \text{ could be written as } b = 0$$
$$x = 1,000 \text{ could be written as } c = 0$$
$$y = 500 \text{ could be written as } d = 0$$
$$x - y = 0 \quad \text{could be written as } e = 0$$

and the region of feasibility could now be defined as in Fig. 17.1.

Since the optimal solution to a linear programming problem must occur at an extreme point, the first task in solving such a problem without the benefit of a graph is the identification of extreme points. However, Fig. 17.1

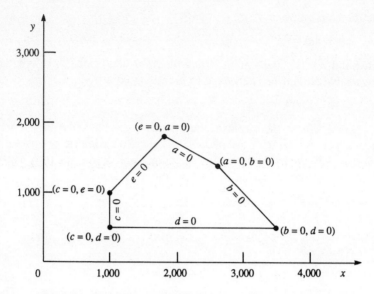

Fig. 17.1 The region of feasibility.

shows a feature of extreme points fundamental to the solution of linear programming problems.

Note, in Fig. 17.1, that at each extreme point *two* variables take *zero value*. Note also that at each extreme point the variables *not* taking *zero value* must be *positive*, as negative variables are not permitted in the region of feasibility. Without proof, which is beyond the scope of this book, we are in a position to make the following observation: *for a problem with two original variables, an extreme point is a point within the region of feasibility where at least two variables take zero value, all the rest being positive.*

Extrapolating this to larger problems, again without proof, we obtain: *for a problem with* n *original variables, an extreme point is a point within the region of feasibility where at least* n *variables take zero value, all the rest being positive.*

This is the key to solving linear programming problems by the simplex method.

The simplex method

Recall again the example problem: Maximise

$$P = 3x + 5y$$

Subject to

$$x + 2y \leqslant 5,400$$
$$x + y \leqslant 4,000$$
$$x \geqslant 1,000$$
$$y \geqslant 500$$
$$x - y \geqslant 0$$
$$x, y \geqslant 0$$

To illustrate the simplex method here, the nature of the problem will first be changed in a rather strange way. This would not be done normally, but is done here because solving problems with '$\geqslant$' constraints, other than the non-negativity conditions, is particularly difficult by hand and is beyond the scope of this book. However, a change in the variables is possible to transform the current problem into one without such '$\geqslant$' constraints, and this revised problem will be used to illustrate the simplex method.

This is simply achieved by considering two new variables X, Y, where

$$X = x - 1,000$$
$$Y = y - 500$$

Then we can substitute

$$x = X + 1,000$$
$$y = Y + 500$$

This revised linear programming problem in the new X, Y variables will, in effect, have moved the origin of the axes from $(0, 0)$ to $(1,000, 500)$. Then

$$3x + 5y$$

becomes

$$3(X + 1,000) + 5(Y + 500)$$
$$= 3X + 3,000 + 5Y + 2,500$$
$$= 3X + 5Y + 5,500$$

Similarly

$$x + 2y \leqslant 5,400$$

becomes

$$(X + 1,000) + 2(Y + 500) \leqslant 5,400$$

or

$$X + 1,000 + 2Y + 1,000 \leqslant 5,400$$

i.e.

$$X + 2Y \leqslant 3,400$$

And

$$x + y \leqslant 4,000$$

becomes

$$(X + 1,000) + (Y + 500) \leqslant 4,000$$

or

$$X + Y + 1,500 \leqslant 4,000$$

i.e.

$$X + Y \geqslant 2,500$$

But

$$x \geqslant 1,000$$

is

$$X + 1,000 \geqslant 1,000$$

i.e.

$$X \geqslant 0$$

And

$$y \geqslant 500$$

is

$$Y + 500 \geqslant 500$$

i.e.

$$Y \geqslant 0$$

Finally

$$x - y \geqslant 0$$

becomes

$$(X + 1,000) - (Y + 500) \geqslant 0$$

i.e.

$$X + 1,000 - Y - 500 \geqslant 0$$

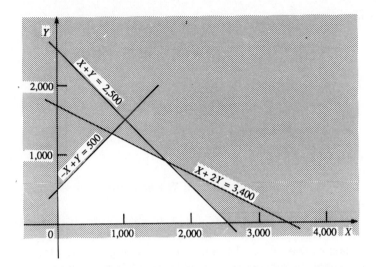

Fig. 17.2 The region of feasibility for the revised problem.

or

$$X - Y + 500 \geqslant 0$$

which can be written

$$-X + Y \leqslant 500$$

Therefore, the revised problem is to

Maximise $P = 3X + 5Y + 5{,}500$

Subject to

$$X + 2Y \leqslant 3{,}400$$
$$X + Y \leqslant 2{,}500$$
$$-X + Y \leqslant 500$$
$$X, \; Y \geqslant 0$$

Graphically the region of feasibility now appears as Fig. 17.2. For solution by the simplex method we must first convert inequalities into equations with the insertion of slack variables A, B, C. The problem is then:

Maximise $P = 3X + 5Y + 5{,}500$

Subject to

$$X + 2Y + A = 3,400$$
$$X + Y + B = 2,500$$
$$-X + Y + C = 500$$
$$X,\ Y,\ A,\ B,\ C \geqslant 0$$

Initial extreme point (basis)

To begin the simplex method we must find an initial extreme point from which the rest of the solution will follow.

Our problem has two original variables X, Y and three slack variables A, B, C giving five variables in total.

From our previous observation, for a problem with two original variables an extreme point is where two variables out of the total have zero value and the rest are positive. Therefore, we are looking for values for X, Y, A, B, and C where two of them are zero and three of them are positive. One such solution is much easier to identify than the others. That is

$$X = 0,\ Y = 0,\ A = 3,400,\ B = 2,500,\ C = 500$$

During the operation of the simplex method, the variables taking zero value and those taking positive values will change. However, at any stage, the set of variables taking *positive* values is called the *basis*. The variables in the basis are called the *basic variables*. The variables that take *zero value*, i.e. those not in the basis, are called the *non-basic variables*.

The iterative procedure

Stage 1. Rewrite the equations with the *basic* variables on the *left, numbers* and *non-basic variables* on the *right*.

$$A = 3,400 - X - 2Y \tag{1}$$

$$B = 2,500 - X - Y \tag{2}$$

$$C = 500 + X - Y \tag{3}$$

$$P = 5,500 + 3X + 5Y$$

Remember that X and Y are currently zero valued and so this is a restatement that $A = 3,400$, $B = 2,500$, $C = 500$.

The current value of P is 5,500. Could this be made any larger? If the value of X was increased from zero to 1, P would increase by 3, but if the value of Y was increased from zero to 1, P would increase by 5. If one allows just one variable increase, the one that gives the largest unit (marginal) increase in P is chosen, i.e. Y.

In other words: *Stage 2*. Select the variable with the *largest positive coefficient* in the *objective function*. In this case, select Y.

Stage 3. In each constraint, determine the *maximum amount* that this selected variable can be increased to.

Here, consider first constraint (1)

$$A = 3,400 - X - 2Y$$

Since the value of X is not currently to be changed, this is effectively

$$A = 3,400 - 2Y$$

It is seen that, as Y increases, A decreases (if $Y = 100$, then $A = 3,200$; if $Y = 1,000$, then $A = 1,400$ etc.). Remembering that no variable can ever take a negative value, the maximum value of Y will be reached when $A = 0$. That is,

$$0 = 3,400 - 2Y$$

or

$$Y = 1,700$$

Similarly, with constraint (2)

$$B = 2,500 - X - Y$$

is effectively

$$B = 2,500 - Y$$

and the maximum value that Y can take is when $B = 0$. That is,

$$Y = 2,500$$

Likewise, with constraint (3)

$$C = 500 + X - Y$$

is effectively

$$C = 500 - Y$$

and the maximum value that Y can take is when $C = 0$. That is,

$$Y = 500$$

The three constraints have, therefore, given us three upper limits on the value of Y:

1,700, 2,500, 500

Stage 4. Select the *maximum possible increase* in this variable that will satisfy *every* constraint.

This will, obviously, be the smallest of these individual constraint increases, i.e. 500. Hence, the amount Y is to be allowed to increase to is

$$Y = 500$$

Letting $Y = 500$ and remembering that X is still zero gives the following values for the other variables:

$$A = 3,400 - 500 = 2,900$$
$$B = 2,500 - 500 = 2,000$$
$$C = 500 - 500 = 0$$

The new set of variable values is then

$$X = 0, \; Y = 500, \; A = 2,900, \; B = 2,000, \; C = 0$$

Note that this gives a *second extreme point*, with two zero-valued variables and three positive-valued variables.

The *basis* is now A, B and Y. The *non-basic variables* are now X and C. Now Y is said to have *entered the basis, replacing* C.

The computation now returns to Stage 1. Again, the equations must be rewritten with the basic variables A, B, Y on the *left* and the non-basic variables X, C on the *right*.

First consider the equation that gave us the limiting increase in Y:

$$C = 500 + X - Y$$

This can be rewritten

$$Y = 500 + X - C$$

As far as the other equations are concerned, we must replace Y on the right-hand side with Xs, Cs and constants. This is achieved by using the rewritten equation, for Y, above. Thus

$$A = 3,400 - X - 2Y$$

becomes

$$A = 3,400 - X - 2(500 + X - C)$$

or

$$A = 3,400 - X - 1,000 - 2X + 2C$$

i.e.

$$A = 2,400 - 3X + 2C$$

Next

$$B = 2,500 - X - Y$$

becomes

$$B = 2,500 - X - (500 + X - C)$$

or

$$B = 2,500 - X - 500 - X + C$$

i.e.

$$B = 2,000 - 2X + C$$

and

$$P = 5,500 + 3X + 5Y$$

becomes

$$P = 5,500 + 3X + 5(500 + X - C)$$

or

$$P = 5,500 + 3X + 2,500 + 5X - 5C$$

i.e.

$$P = 8,000 + 8X - 5C$$

The rewritten set of equations is therefore

$$A = 2,400 - 3X + 2C \tag{1}$$

$$B = 2,000 - 2X + C \tag{2}$$

$$Y = 500 + X - C \tag{3}$$

$$P = 8,000 + 8X - 5C$$

Return to Stage 2. It is seen that P can be increased further by increasing X from zero. (X has the largest positive coefficient in the objective function.)

Return to Stage 3. From (1) X can be increased to 800 (when A becomes zero). From (2) X can be increased to 1,000 (when B becomes zero). From (3) note that as X increases Y also increases (if $X = 100$, $Y = 600$ and if $X = 1,000$, $Y = 1,500$ etc.). Therefore X can increase to infinity and Y can never become zero.

Hence, the possible increases in X are 800, 1,000, ∞.

Return again to Stage 4. The maximum possible increase in X that satisfies every constraint is

$$X = 800$$

Then, remembering that C remains zero, the values of the variables are now

$$X = 800, \; Y = 1{,}300, \; A = 0, \; B = 400, \; C = 0$$

We have yet another extreme point and another basis. X has entered the basis and A has left it.

Returning once more to Stage 1, the equations must now be rewritten with X, Y, B on the left and A and C on the right. Rewriting first the equation that gave the chosen increase in X one can obtain from

$$A = 2{,}400 - 3X + 2C$$

firstly

$$3X = 2{,}400 + 2C - A$$

and then

$$X = 800 + \tfrac{2}{3}C - \tfrac{1}{3}A$$

The whole set of equations becomes

$$X = 800 + \tfrac{2}{3}C - \tfrac{1}{3}A$$
$$B = 2{,}000 - 2(800 + \tfrac{2}{3}C - \tfrac{1}{3}A) + C$$
$$Y = 500 + (800 + \tfrac{2}{3}C - \tfrac{1}{3}A) - C$$
$$P = 8{,}000 + 8(800 + \tfrac{2}{3}C - \tfrac{1}{3}A) - 5C$$

or

$$X = 800 + \tfrac{2}{3}C - \tfrac{1}{3}A \tag{1}$$

$$B = 400 - \tfrac{1}{3}C + \tfrac{2}{3}A \tag{2}$$

$$Y = 1{,}300 - \tfrac{1}{3}C - \tfrac{1}{3}A \tag{3}$$

$$P = 14{,}400 + \tfrac{1}{3}C - \tfrac{8}{3}A$$

Once more returning to Stage 2, it is seen that P can be increased still further by increasing C from zero.

As in Stage 3, it is seen that the maximum possible increases in C from each constraint is as follows:

From (1) C could increase to infinity (X increases as C increases).
From (2) C could increase to 1,200 (when $400 - \tfrac{1}{3}C = 0$, i.e. $B = 0$).
From (3) C could increase to 3,900 (when $1{,}300 - \tfrac{1}{3}C = 0$, i.e. $Y = 0$).

As in Stage 4, it is found the maximum possible increase in C that satisfies every constraint is the smallest of (∞, 1,200, 3,900), i.e.

$$C = 1{,}200$$

and, remembering that A is still zero, the new values of the variables are

$$X = 1,600, \ Y = 900, \ A = 0, \ B = 0, \ C = 1,200$$

yet another extreme point, where B has left the basis to be replaced by C.

Returning once more to Stage 1, the equations must now be rewritten with X, Y, C on the *left* and A and B on the *right*.

Rewriting first the equation that gave the chosen increase in C one can obtain from

$$B = 400 - \tfrac{1}{3}C + \tfrac{2}{3}A$$

that

$$\tfrac{1}{3}C = 400 + \tfrac{2}{3}A - B$$

or

$$C = 1,200 + 2A - 3B$$

The whole set of equations becomes

$$X = 800 + \tfrac{2}{3}(1,200 + 2A - 3B) - \tfrac{1}{3}A$$
$$C = 1,200 + 2A - 3B$$
$$Y = 1,300 - \tfrac{1}{3}(1,200 + 2A - 3B) - \tfrac{1}{3}A$$
$$P = 14,400 + \tfrac{1}{3}(1,200 + 2A - 3B) - \tfrac{8}{3}A$$

or

$$X = 1,600 + A - 2B$$
$$C = 1,200 + 2A - 3B$$
$$Y = 900 - A - B$$
$$P = 14,800 - 2A - B$$

However, this time returning to Stage 2, it is seen that P can be increased no further. The negative coefficients for A and B in the equation for P imply that P would *decrease* if any increase was made in A or B. It follows that the *maximum possible value* for P has been reached.

The maximising condition is therefore: *Stage 5*. The *maximum* value of the objective function is obtained when *all the coefficients of the objective function are less than or equal to zero*.

The *optimum solution* to this problem is therefore

$$X = 1,600, \ Y = 900, \ A = 0, \ B = 0, \ C = 1,200,$$

giving $P = 14,800$.

Returning to the original variables one can obtain

$$x = X + 1,000 = 1,600 + 1,000 = 2,600$$
$$y = Y + 500 = 900 + 500 = 1,400$$

That is, 2,600 standard size boxes and 1,400 large size boxes should be packed to produce a maximum profit of £14,800, as found before by the graphical solution method.

Interpretation of the final objective function

The final objective function

$$P = 14,800 - 2A - B$$

provides more information than just the maximum profit that can be achieved.

Notice that if A is given the value 1, then the profit is

$$P = 14,800 - 2 = 14,798$$

In other words, £2 profit is lost.

The starting point was 5,400 kg of product and slack variable A gave a measure of spare product. Therefore, if A is forced to equal 1, 1 kg of product is deliberately not packed, resulting in a loss of £2 profit. Hence the marginal value of product is £2 and if *more* product could be obtained to pack an *extra* £2 per kg could be earned. However, that assumes the extra product was obtained free. As it will have to be purchased, it is seen that it is not worth paying more than £2 per kg for it. If extra product can be obtained for less than £2 per kg, then it should be bought, but if extra product would cost more than £2 per kg, then it is not worth buying.

Similarly, the -1 coefficient of B in the final objective function implies that the maximum price that should be paid for extra packing time is £1 per minute (or £60 per hour). If extra packing time can be obtained for less than £60 per hour then it should be bought, but if it would cost more than £60 per hour then it should not.

Additionally, suppose the profit margins on the two products had originally been £3 for standard size boxes and £2 for large size boxes. The optimal solution could then be found, by the same method as before, to be

$$A = 900 - Y + B$$
$$X = 2,500 - Y - B$$
$$C = 3,000 - 2Y - B$$
$$P = 11,500 - Y - 3B$$

that is

$$X = 2,500, \ Y = 0, \ A = 900, \ B = 0, \ C = 3,000$$

and so to obtain the new maximum profit of £11,500 3,500 standard size boxes and the minimum quantity possible, 500, large size boxes should be produced.

Notice that now only large boxes are produced, because this is enforced by $y \geqslant 500$ constraint.

If 1 extra unit of Y were produced (1 additional large size box) £1 of profit would be lost. Therefore, to make large boxes worth packing, their price should be raised by £1 to give a profit of £3, the same as standard size boxes.

Therefore, the final objective function can give the amount by which the price of an uneconomic product should be raised to make it worth producing, and the maximum price that should be paid for extra quantities of a resource that has run out.

In the revised problem, above, the maximum price that should be paid for extra packing time is now £3 per minute (£180 per hour), and now nothing should be paid for extra product because we have 900 kg of product left over ($A = 900$).

Glossary

Accuracy   The difference between an observed result and the true result.

Aggregate index   An index calculated over a range of commodities.

Alternative hypothesis   A specific or general alternative to the theory originally assumed in a statistical test.

Annuity   A constant annual income purchased for a fixed amount at the beginning.

Arithmetic mean   The simple average of a set of numbers, being all the numbers summed and then divided by the number of numbers present. Sometimes known simply as the *mean*.

Arithmetic progression   A progression where each successive term is the previous term plus a given constant.

Arithmetic series   The sum of an arithmetic progression.

Average   A summary measure used to indicate the size of figures in a set of data.

Bar chart   A diagram used to illustrate categorical data.

Base of an index   Period that the index for each subsequent period is expressed as a percentage of.

Bias   A tendency for observed results to consistently over- or underestimate a true value.

Binomial distribution   A discrete probability distribution used to determine the probability of a specified number of 'successes' in n trials where it is assumed the probability of a 'success' in an individual trial is constant.

Break-even point   Production quantity for which total production cost equals total revenue.

Business cycle   A pattern observed in a time series which repeats after a period exceeding a year.

Census   An investigation taking in the whole of a population.

Class interval   A range of values used to categorise data.

Class limits   The upper and lower limits of a class interval.

Coefficient of determination   The square of the correlation coefficient, showing the proportion of total variation explained by a regression equation.

Coefficient of quartile deviation   A measure of spread based on the first and third quartiles.

Coefficient of variation   The size of the standard deviation in relation to the mean, usually given as a percentage.

Common difference   The constant difference between successive terms of an arithmetic progression.

Complement of a set   The set of all elements that do not belong to the set.

Compound interest   The interest paid on an investment at the end of a period is added to the amount invested for the next period.

Conditional probability   The probability of an event happening given that another event has happened.

Confidence interval   An interval of values in which the true value of a measurement is expected to lie with a stated confidence (the confidence coefficient).

Constraints   The limiting conditions of a mathematical programming problem.

Continuous variable   A variable which can take any value within a certain range.

Correlation coefficient   A measure of how closely the relationship between two variables follows a straight line.

Cost of capital   The interest factor that the capital required for a project could be invested at to produce the cash outlay required.

Critical value   The value(s) of a test statistic used to decide whether the null or alternative hypothesis is accepted in a statistical test.

Cumulative frequency   The total number of observations up to and including a certain value.

Cumulative frequency curve   A graph illustrating cumulative frequencies.

Cyclic effect   A numerical value for the influence of a business cycle at a time point within the cycle.

Data (s. datum)   Recorded observations of a variable.

Decile   Values of a distribution corresponding to the ten percentage points, e.g. the seventh decile corresponds to the 70% point of the distribution.

Demand function   A function relating the quantity sold of a product to its price.

Dependent variable   In regression, the variable which results from the independent variable; it is the variable to be predicted.

Detrended series   The values of a time series after the trend values have been removed.

Discounting   Determining the present value of sums of money required in the future.

Discrete variable   A variable which can only take certain values (usually integer values) e.g. counts.

Element   An item in a set.

Empirical distribution   The observed distribution of a set of data which has been collected.

Empty set   A set with no elements.

Estimation   The methods used whereby sample results are converted into estimates of the true or population values.

Event   An outcome or combination of outcomes in a statistical trial.

Event space   An illustration within a Venn diagram used to represent an event.

Expected value   The value that a variable will average in the long run.

Exponential function   A mathematical constant equal to 2.7182818.

External data   Data which is generated outside the organisation by which it is going to be used.

Extrapolation   Estimation of a function value outside two given points.

Extreme point   An intersection of constraints lying within the region of feasibility.

Feasible solution   Values of the variables satisfying every constraint.

Fisher's ideal index   A type of average of the Laspeyres and Paasche indices.

Fixed costs   Production costs incurred when nothing is produced.

Forecast   A prediction based on statistical analysis of a set of data.

Frequency   A count of how many times a value (or series of values) occurs in a set of data.

Frequency distribution   A list of frequencies associated with values of a variable.

Frequency polygon   A special diagram used to illustrate frequency data.

Function   A relationship between variables.

General index of retail prices (RPI)   An index attempting to show economic inflation.

Geometric mean   A special measure used to calculate average proportional change.

Geometric progression   A progression where each successive term is the previous one multiplied by a given constant.

Geometric series   The sum of a geometric progression.

Gradient of a straight line   Amount by which the vertically defined variable increases given a unit increase in the horizontally defined variable.

Graph   Plot of a set of data or of a mathematical function.

Harmonic mean   A special measure used to calculate average rates.

Histogram   A diagram used to illustrate frequency data where the *area* of a column represents frequency.

Hypothesis   A theory or idea used as the basis of a statistical test.

Independent events   Two or more events which have no influence on the occurrence of each other.

Independent variable   The variable in regression which is assumed fixed and is used to predict the dependent variable.

Index of industrial production (IIP)   An index attempting to show changes in the output of production industries.

Index number   A device that attempts to express average changes in economic activity over a period of time.

Intercept of a straight line   Point where the line crosses the vertical axis.

Interest factor   The interest rate expressed as a proportion rather than a percentage.

Interest rate   A percentage of an amount invested earned at the end of each period.

Internal data   Data collected within an organisation for its own purposes.

Internal rate of return   The cost of capital that enables a project to break even.

Interpolation   Estimation of a function value between two given points.

Intersection of sets   The set of all elements that belong to both sets.

Laspeyres index   Gives the relative change in the costs assuming the same quantities as in the base period.

Least squares   A technique used to find 'best fitting' equations in regression.

Left skew   Data has a left skew if there is a long tail of few values to the left of the distribution. It is commonly known as 'negative skew'.

Linear function   A function with no square or product terms.

Linear programming   Mathematical programming where all constraints and objective function are linear expressions.

Lorenz curve   A diagram used to illustrate the equality (or otherwise) of two distributions.

Mathematical programming   Techniques for solving constrained optimisation problems.

Mean   The common shorthand for the arithmetic mean.

Measure of dispersion   A single number used to indicate the spread of figures in a set of data (e.g. standard deviation, quartile deviation, range).

Measure of location   A single number used to indicate the size of figures in a set of data (e.g. mean, median, mode).

Median   An average which is the middle value of a distribution once it is in numerical order.

Mode   The most frequently occurring value in a distribution.

Mortgage   A loan with some large capital possession held as security.

Moving averages   A technique used to evaluate sources of variation in a time series.

Mutually exclusive events   Events which cannot occur together.

Mutually exclusive sets   Sets whose intersection is empty.

Negative skew   Data is negatively skewed if it has a long tail of values to the left-hand end of the distribution.

Net present value   The current value of expenditure or revenues pertaining to future intervals.

Non-negativity conditions   Constraints restricting the variables to positive or zero values.

Normal distribution   A continuous probability distribution used to represent the variation in results obtained for a continuous measurement. It is used widely for most physical measurements which can vary.

Null hypothesis   The theory which is assumed to be true at the start of a statistical test. It is a specific assumption.

Objective function   The feature of a mathematical programming problem that is to be optimised (maximised or minimised).

Ogive   A cumulative frequency curve.

Open-ended interval   An interval used in a frequency distribution which is of the form 'greater than . . .' or of the form 'less than . . .'.

Optimal solution   The feasible solution optimising the objective function.

Original variable   One of the variables in which the problem was described.

Outcome   Each separate or distinct result of a statistical trial.

Paasche index   Gives the relative change in the costs assuming the same quantities as are required now were used in the base period.

Panel   A group of people who agree to keep detailed records of specified aspects of their life.

Parameter   The true value of a population characteristic.

Percentile   The value of a variable which corresponds to a specified percentage in a cumulative frequency distribution. The 84th percentile corresponds to the value of a variable which has 84% of all results below it.

Perpetual annuity   An annuity that continues paying an income indefinitely.

Pictogram   A diagram which uses pictures of the variable being represented to illustrate frequencies.

Pie chart   A diagram which uses segments of a circle to illustrate how a total figure splits into its component parts.

Pilot study   A small survey carried out prior to the main survey. It is used to ensure the proposed survey is appropriate.

Poisson distribution   A discrete probability distribution used to determine the probability of a specified number of 'successes' when 'successes' occur randomly but at a fixed average rate.

Population   The whole group of items or individuals to be investigated.

Positive skew   Data is positively skewed if it has a long tail of values to the right-hand end of the distribution.

Precision   Precision describes the amount of natural or random variation in a set of data.

Price relative   A ratio of current year's price for a unit of commodity divided by the base year's price for that same unit.

Primary data   Data which was collected specifically for the purpose to which it is being put.

Probability   A measure of chance or uncertainty ranging from 0 to 1.

Probability distribution   A list of outcomes with their associated probabilities.

Progression   A string of numbers arranged in a certain order with each number being related to the previous number or numbers by some rule.

Quadratic equation   An equation formed by equating a quadratic function to some constant value.

Quadratic formula   Mathematical formula for solving a quadratic equation.

Quadratic function   Function in which the highest power of the variable is square.

Quartile   The value of a variable corresponding to a specified quarter of a distribution. The first quartile corresponds to the 25% point, the third quartile to the 75% point.

Quartile coefficient of dispersion   A measure of spread based on the median, first and third quartiles.

Quartile deviation   The difference between the first and third quartiles halved.

Questionnaire   A series of questions designed to illicit the required information in a survey or census.

Random sampling   A method of sampling where every member of the population or stratum of a population has an equal chance of being sampled.

Random variation   The natural variation that occurs when a measurement of a variable is repeated.

Range   The difference between the largest and smallest results in a set of data, used as a measure of spread.

Region of feasibility   Set of feasible solutions.

Regression   A means of fitting an equation to a set of data values where two (or more) variables are thought to be related.

Right skew   Data has right skew if there is a long tail of few values to the right of the distribution. It is commonly known as 'positive skew'.

Sample   A group of items or individuals chosen to represent a population.

Sampling frame   A complete list of the members of a population.

Sampling method   The method used to select a sample from a population.

Scatter diagram   Diagram used to illustrate the relationship between two variables.

Seasonal effect   A numerical value for the influence of a seasonal pattern at a time point within that pattern.

Seasonal pattern   Variations in a time series which repeat each year or part of a year.

Secondary data   Data which was not originally collected for the purpose to which it is presently being put.

Series   The sum of the terms of a progression.

Set   A collection of items, together with a rule defining what links the items.

Significance level   The risk taken in a statistical test of rejecting the null hypothesis when it is true.

Simple interest   Constant interest paid on an investment at the end of each period.

Simplex method   Mathematical technique for solving linear programming problems.

Simultaneous equations   Two or more equations with a set of variables that can take the same values in each equation.

Sinking fund   An investment fund into which a constant, annual sum is added to give a lump sum payment at some time in the future.

Skewness   Data is said to be skew if it lacks a symmetrical shape.

Slack variable   A variable used to convert an inequality into an equation.

Spearman rank correlation coefficient   A measure of correlation based on ranking two variables.

Standard deviation   The most commonly used measure of spread.

Standard error   The standard deviation of a statistic calculated from a set of data.

Standardised normal variate   A variable calculated by subtracting the arithmetic mean from the original variable value and then dividing by the standard deviation. This standardised value is required so that the normal probability tables can be used.

Statistical test   A statistical procedure used to choose between alternative hypotheses.

Straight line   Graph of a linear function.

Stratum (pl. strata)   A homogeneous group within a population.

Subset   A set contained entirely within another set.

Surplus variable   A slack variable in a '$\geqslant$' constraint.

Survey   An investigation based on a sample from a population.

Term   A number in a progression.

Test statistic   A value calculated from a set of data and used to determine the result of a statistical test.

Time series   A set of values recorded through time.

Time series plot   A picture of a time series.

Tree diagram   A diagram used to illustrate a set of probabilities.

Trend   The general behaviour of a time series.

Turning point   A maximum or minimum point on a curve.

Union of sets   The set of all elements that belong to either set.

Universal set   The set of all elements that could possibly be considered in the context of the problem.

Variable   Any measurement which can vary from one item or individual to another.

Variable costs   Production costs of making one unit of product, in addition to fixed costs.

Variance (statistical)   The square of the standard deviation.

Venn diagram   A method of illustrating sets.

Z-chart   A time series chart consisting of three graphs, used to chart progress.

Bibliography

In Chapter 2 several Government publications are mentioned. All are published through Her Majesty's Stationery Office (HMSO). Most of them are published directly by the Central Statistical Office (CSO) or in conjunction with the appropriate Government department. Below is a full list of those responsible for publication:

Annual Abstract of Statistics (CSO)
British Business (Department of Trade and Industry)
British Labour Statistics (Department of Employment)
Economic Trends (CSO)
Employment Gazette (Department of Employment)
Financial Trends (HM Treasury)
Guide to Official Statistics (CSO)
Guide to Public Sector Financial Information (HM Treasury and CSO)
Monthly Digest of Statistics (CSO)
Regional Trends (CSO)
Social Trends (CSO)
Statistical News (CSO)
United Kingdom Balance of Payments (HM Treasury)
United Kingdom National Income and Expenditure (HM Treasury)

Useful addresses for further details are as follows:

Her Majesty's Stationery Office Publications Centre
PO Box 276
London SW8 5DT
(Enquiries tel.: 01-211 5656)

Central Statistical Office
Great George Street
London SW1P 3AQ
(Enquiries tel.: 01-270 6363/4)

Index